TEMPERANCE

RECOLLECTIONS.

LABORS, DEFEATS, TRIUMPHS.

AN AUTOBIOGRAPHY.

BY JOHN MARSH, D. D.,

SECRETARY OF THE FIRST THREE NATIONAL TEMPERANCE CONVENTIONS, AND THIRTY YEARS CORRESPONDING SECRETARY AND EDITOR OF THE AMERICAN TEMPERANCE UNION.

QUORUM PARS FUI.

We speak that we do know, and testify that we have seen.—*John.*

NEW YORK:

CHARLES SCRIBNER & CO., 654 BROADWAY.

1866.

JOHN F. TROW & CO.,
PRINTERS, STEREOTYPERS, & ELECTROTYPERS,
50 GREENE STREET, N. Y.

LUCIUS MANLIUS SARGENT,

AUTHOR OF THE TEMPERANCE TALES.

DEAR SIR:—If the wonderful powers given us, sometimes, in a measure, fail, as we draw to the close of our earthly career, it is happy for us that affection does not; but that the attachment of early days—days of joy and hope in spirited and fruitful labor, rather strengthens and makes our setting sun beautiful and blessed. Permit me, in response to the long kindness and support you have afforded me in days and years of anxiety and toil, to lay upon your table a few reminiscences of labors and events in which you have been a prince and a Nestor; keeping us up and pressing us forward by your admirable Temperance Tales; borrowing nothing from fiction, but presenting to the mind and heart the many sad scenes flowing from that most delusive cup, to which our countrymen, both rich and poor, have bowed the knee.

May your last days, my dear Sir, which, in the mysterious providence of our heavenly Father, have been days of sadness, through bereavements by war and disease, yet be days of gladness and comfort, in the assurance of good done by your long labors in the temperance cause; and in the prospect, which you may rightfully indulge, of the reward of those who have turned many to righteousness—shining as the stars forever and ever.

Most affectionately yours,

JOHN MARSH.

BROOKLYN, N. Y., *April* 2, 1866.

CONTENTS.

CHAPTER I.

CHAPTER II.

CHAPTER III.

CHAPTER IV.

CHAPTER V.

CHAPTER VI.

CHAPTER VII.

CHAPTER VIII.

CHAPTER IX.

CHAPTER X.

CHAPTER XI.

CHAPTER XII.

CHAPTER XIII.

CHAPTER XIV.

CHAPTER XV.

CHAPTER XVI.

CHAPTER XVII.

CHAPTER XVIII.

CHAPTER XIX.

CHAPTER XX.

CHAPTER XXI.

CHAPTER XXII.

CHAPTER XXIII.

CHAPTER XXIV.

CHAPTER XXV.

CHAPTER XXVI.

APPENDIX.

PREFACE.

MEMORY is a wonderful power of the mind. By it are brought the events of seventy years, fresh within the passing hour. By it we make a record of events and facts, whose verity few will be disposed to question. But all that it holds, unless recorded, is gone in a moment when death touches the silver cord. As in the extinguishment of a lamp, all is darkness. No man can remember for his brother.

Retired from thirty years of editorial and office labor, the writer has been pressed by friends to commit to the stereotype plate what is upon the brain, of the rise, progress, and agencies of the temperance cause; testifying especially to that of which, in the good providence of God, he has been an eye and ear witness, and also an humble agent. The style of autobiography he has adopted as the most easy and natural, but the rather, as in most cases, official; though with some it may savor of vanity, while he may have been the least of all instrumentalities. To criticism from those who were early actors, he will not be much exposed; as they have nearly all passed away. Few may be interested in so long a story. But all may see in it something of the vast work that has been done to overthrow those drinking usages which have filled the world with sadness; and to suppress that traffic, which an eminent individual, Chancellor Walworth, has denominated "a traffic in the souls and bodies of men." Had he given a full account of all which has been done, and all which has been written on the subject, the world would not contain the books. The incidents mentioned in the pages of contents, are, with him, the most memorable, as well as the leading incidents; especially in our own country. The work is rather a record, than a history to be read through. Some will turn to the early stages of the cause; some to the wonderful Washingtonian movement; some to the Irish reform; some to the Maine law operation. Of the fitness of the writer to make the record, others must judge. His desire has been to present to those who come after him a connected series of the great and small events of days gone by; to excite their gratitude for what God hath wrought; and to strengthen them in all their future labors. What has been done once, can be done again, and inconceivably more. The battle is "God's battle," and must and will be continued by those who desire the coming and kingdom of Him who will redeem the world from iniquity, and wipe away all tears from all eyes.

BROOKLYN, N. Y., *April*, 1866.

TEMPERANCE RECOLLECTIONS.

CHAPTER I.

Birth—Education—Ministry.

I WAS born in Wethersfield, Ct., April 2, 1788. My father, the Rev. John Marsh, D. D., was long pastor of the Congregational Church in that place. His ancestors came from England at an early date and first settled at Hingham, Mass., whence they soon removed to his birth-place, Haverhill, on the banks of the Merrimac. Through successive generations, the Marshes were remarkable for stability and longevity. Twelve children all survived his mother, who counted 92 years. The eldest daughter was married to Rev. Benjamin Tappan, of Manchester, and from them descended Benjamin Tappan, Esq., of Northampton, the father of John, of Boston, and Arthur and Lewis, of New York; also Professor Tappan, of Harvard University, father of Rev. Dr. Tappan, of Augusta, Me.; bringing me into close relationship and friendship with these active and influential men. From a brother of my father, descended Samuel Marsh, Esq., of New York, and Nathaniel Marsh, the devoted and laborious President of the N. Y. & Erie Railroad. After filling the office of tutor for nine years at Harvard University, where he graduated in 1761, my father was called to the pastoral charge of the church at Wethersfield and was there ordained Jan. 4, 1774. He was soon connected by marriage with Ann, daughter of Capt. Ebenezer Grant, of East Windsor. Wethersfield was at that time one of the most important towns of the State, and was distinguished for its intelligent and patriotic population. At the first tidings of blood-shedding at Lexington, in 1775, a company of one hundred volunteers flocked to the field of strife. The news was received on the morning of the Sabbath as the people were assembling for divine service. On consultation it was agreed that the afternoon service should be dispensed with, and that the men volunteering should assemble at 5 P. M. on the green, and march for Boston. Then there was hurry and bustle, and partings and tears. At the appointed hour the company were on the ground, under command of Capt. John Chester, and marched to the river side, where the young pastor commended them to God. They soon crossed, and the night closed upon them on their way to battle. The next day, however, on hearing that all was over, they returned. But they soon found it was otherwise, and they hurried on and were at the battle of Bunker Hill, fighting valiantly for their country. Noble men. If they resisted one tyranny, which was not to be borne, they were unwittingly leaving their children to another which would destroy its thousands and tens of thousands.

In this town, so attractive and filled with enterprising and influential families, General Washington and Count Rochambeau met with their suites, in 1780, to make their military arrangements. The General's headquarters were at the house of Joseph Webb, Esq., still standing. During his stay, my father acted as his chaplain, preached before him on the Sabbath, from the text "Blessed are the poor in spirit" (the sermon is still among his manuscripts, marked "preached before Gen. Washington"), and sat daily on his right at the table. Many interesting anecdotes have I heard him relate of that momentous period.

Great was the hospitality of the New England ministry. No travelling clergyman was ever suffered to see the inside of a public house in Wethersfield. Well do I remember the difficulty of accommodating all the ministers' horses the night before the General Election at Hartford. The drinks dispensed and highly prized were good bottled cider, my mother's currant wine, and spring beer. The drawing of corks afforded great merriment, as he who performed the ceremony was in danger of a smart shower on his new black coat. At freemen's meetings, at associational, ordination, and other clerical gatherings, a rich display of decanters with stronger liquors (usually furnished by some generous parishioners) covered the sideboard and were resorted to by all without any sense of wrong doing; though not in all cases without results which were the subject of much private conversation. In my boyhood, FLIP, a drink made of small beer, a glass of spirits with sugar and nutmeg, made warm by a red hot poker, was a usual drink on the Sabbath, in the winter months, on returning from church. Well do I remember crying in meeting from the cold (there were then no stoves), and holding on to my chair after drinking the FLIP till my head became steady. The town was settled, as were most of the towns in Connecticut, with hard drinkers. Some large families, fathers and sons, had nearly all filled drunkard's graves; and one huge man with a modern unshaven face, a notorious cider drunkard, who often appeared in our back kitchen to beg a mug of cider, was my great terror. In the summer, my business was the supplying of the hay-field with the bottle of New England rum, from which the mowers and others took copious draughts; showing soon how perfectly it unfitted them for continuance in labor. The lessons then taught never faded from memory.

At the age of ten, I was sent to the school of the Rev. Azel Backus, in Bethlem, Litchfield County. About thirty lads were there, gathered by the fame of that noble man from the South as well as the North; many were sons of

1*

rich men, accustomed to every indulgence. On the 4th of July, 1800, great preparations were made in a grove for a patriotic celebration of independence. A generous supply of wines was provided and many a patriotic speech made from youthful tongues loosened by the generous draughts. At nightfall, the prostrate and pitiable condition of more than half the school aroused the wrath of our instructor and guide, and on summoning us to morning prayers, with a brow dark and terrible as a cloud moving onward with roaring thunder and forked lightning, he enacted his Maine law, forever expelling the winecup from his school and all its festivities. Here, in my first witness of social drunkenness, I, being quite the junior, escaped. Not so fortunate was I in the second. I entered Yale in September, 1800, at twelve, having mastered the four Evangelists, six books of Virgil, and four Orations of Cicero; prepared, alas! in the estimation of that day, to grapple with all the hard problems of mathematics, and become in four years profound in philosophy and complete in all elegant literature. A political revolution had occurred in the country. Thomas Jefferson, the democratic candidate, had attained to the Presidency; and party politics raged with a violence since unknown. Every boy was a patriot, ready to fly to arms. The College, with few exceptions, were strongly enlisted, under President Dwight, in behalf of Washington, Adams, and, what were considered constitutional and fundamental principles; and it was resolved, when the fourth of July should return, to have a celebration of independence worthy of the day and worthy of Yale. At the dinner in the College Hall, a barrel of wine was elevated on a table and none were expected to leave the Hall until, amid shouts, and songs, and harangues of all descriptions, the barrel was emptied. The result was Io BACCHE, the triumphs of Bacchus. But for that, I should have escaped a common maxim in days gone by, that there was no man to be found who had not been drunk at least once in his life. The sensation has not been forgotten. As I went out of the Hall I saw the buildings moving round and discharged the contents of my rebellious stomach. The next year was a year of unusual seriousness in College. More than a hundred of the students became hopefully pious, and, for the remainder of our course, intemperance was but little known. President Dwight preached to us his admirable sermon, a part of his course, on the nature, causes, and evils of drunkenness and the means of avoiding it. In this he solemnly warned us against the beginnings of evil, and proclaimed the duty of entire abstinence from spirituous liquors by all who found in themselves any peculiar relish for them. But an universal abandonment to save the country, was not then contemplated.

To the alarming evils of intemperance the public mind was at that period being awakened. Dr. Rush, of Philadelphia, had created a great sensation by his tract on ardent spirits, published in 1804; and Rev. Ebenezer Porter, of Washington, Ct., had roused the ministry and the churches by a sermon, in 1806, on the death of a man in the snow with a bottle of spirits at his side. In a note, he computed that the spirits then consumed in the United States would load 100,000 wagons, which, in complete order, would extend more than 1,000 miles; and, in cost, would annually exceed 600 tons of dollars. Such footholds had the alcoholic demon in the nation. Some gentlemen in Litchfield had entered into an agreement not to furnish laborers with spirits; but no temperance society was known until 1808, when one was formed at Moreau, in the State of New York. 47 persons signed the constitution and no one was allowed to drink ardent spirits under a penalty of 25 cents. In 1813, however, a society of considerable consequence was formed in Massachusetts, through the mutual influence of a Congregational and Presbyterian Alliance, and under the counsels of the Hon. Samuel Dexter, a distinguished lawyer, who had said that he would pay all the taxes of Boston and of the State of Massachusetts if he might have the profit on the traffic in spirituous liquors. This society was called THE MASSACHUSETTS SOCIETY FOR THE SUPPRESSION OF INTEMPERANCE. But it did little but observe an anniversary and have a sermon preached, after which preacher and hearers would repair to tables richly laden with wine, and was therefore without efficacy in rooting out the evil. In Connecticut the ministers of Litchfield South Association were moved by Mr. Porter's sermon, to appoint a committee to inquire and report what remedy could be found for the greatly increasing evil of the day. After considering it for some time, they reported in 1811 that they could find no remedy. Rev. Lyman Beecher, then just settled in Litchfield, moved that the committee be discharged and a new committee be appointed. It was agreed to and he was appointed chairman. Almost immediately they reported that a remedy could be found in the agreement of all good Christian people to use no longer spirituous liquors; but so ludicrous was the idea, on the one hand, and so impracticable, on the other, that it does not seem to have been harbored or commended. The light shone in darkness, but the darkness comprehended it not. But it was a great thought and a noble testimony. Soon after the Consociation of Fairfield Co. resolved to reform their own body. They excluded all spirituous liquors from their meetings, and, in 1812, published an able appeal to the public against the drinking usages of the day. This was the joint work of Rev. Roswell R. Swan, of Norwalk, and Rev. Heman Humphrey, of Fairfield, afterwards President of Amherst College. These and other efforts were not without their influence; and, but for the war with England which commenced in 1812, might have produced even these great results.

Having commenced preaching at twenty-one I met the kind hospitalities of the families of ministers, elders, and deacons wherever I went, and had pressed upon me after service, though not in the least exhausted, the recruiting drink. From Oct., 1814, to April, 1815, I supplied the Wall Street Presbyterian pulpit in New York, vacated by the removal of Dr. Samuel Miller to Princeton Seminary, and here I mingled with some of the first families in the city. Robert Lenox, Esq., Judge Brockholdst Livingston, Mr. Edgar, Dr. John Rogèrs, and others, had me at their tables, where were the choicest wines, and where, not to drink with the lady of the house was to the young minister an impossibility. Frequent invitations from one and another to a glass were given, and no wonder that some of the sacred order were privately and even publicly spoken of as already ruined men. The rumors made me resolve to drink as little as possible consistent with politeness. The same temptations and snares were before me in other cities and towns and in the most pious families. How different now! How mighty the change!

In December, 1818, I took the pastoral charge of the Congregational Church, in Haddam, Ct. Here I had labored for six months in a powerful revival of religion amid a staunch, well informed, but plain people, whose labors were in shipyards, coasting, fishing, quarrying, and farming; labors in which, at that time, ardent spirit was a daily ration at eleven and four, as regularly as food was provided at other hours. In my arduous labors, preaching almost daily and conversing from house to house, I had pressed upon me the best of drinks which the people could afford; but I invariably declined excepting where, in some humble family, it would have caused grief, as not sufficiently good in my estimation. My greatest foe was the hard cider, soon producing, by its oxalic acid, headache. But it was the only drink then upon the dinner-table, and used freely at all times. A pitcher of water, as a part of table furniture, was unknown. No one, not the most delicate females, used it. All drank cider. At my ordination an amusing circumstance occurred, which became an instrument of great sharpness among the ministry. Returning from the services to the public house, on a very cold day in December, the council, composed of some thirty ministers and delegates, were ushered into a large tavern chamber, where was a bright fire on the one side, and, on the other, a table filled with all the materials for warming the stomach and preparing for the repast which would soon be in readiness. Among the ministers present was one who had thrown off the dominion of King Alcohol. This was the Rev. Calvin Chapin, of the parish of Rocky Hill, in the town of Wethersfield; a man in whose heart was the law of kindness, but whose tongue was, when needed, beyond all others, a sharp sword. As the Rev. Mr. K., of Killingworth, a lovely brother, but not able to cope with him, was with twenty others mixing his tumbler of good things—Mr. C., singling him out for an attack, said: "Brother K., what are you going to do with that stuff?" "Stuff," said Mr. K., "It is not stuff; it is good brandy." "Well! what are you going to do with it?" "Do with it? why what do you suppose? Drink it, to be sure." "Well," asked Mr. C., "what are you going to do then?" "Do! why walk about, I suppose." "But suppose," said Mr. C., "you cannot. There has been many a man who, after drinking that, could not walk at all; and I doubt whether, if you drink it, you can walk a crack. I will challenge you to do it." Mr. K., still stirring his liquor, not able amid this storm to drink, and now the object of all present, said: "Well! I believe I shall try it." "You had better not," said Mr. C., "you had better come and throw it in the fire or out of the window. If you want to get warm, take a coal of fire into your mouth, but don't take that and have it said, as it may be, that Rev. Mr. K. went to ordination and could not get home." At length, one of the Fathers, provoked beyond measure by this universal stop put to the drinking custom, said, with a loud voice, "Mr. C., do you let Brother K. alone and let him have his drink; you are a real pest, a genuine blackguard," and here ended the matter. But that was the last ordination in that district of country at which liquor was provided. The Rev. Mr. K. afterwards became one of the most zealous and determined advocates of temperance, and, for his opposition to the rum interest, was driven from his parish.

My pastoral labors, amid a large church and a hundred and fifty newly converted individuals, all looking to me as the means of their spiritual life, were very pleasant. But if my parish was an Eden, there was a serpent there; and as the sons of God came together, Satan also came among them. Haddam, the birth-place of David Brainerd, was yet a rum-cursed community; and if the Spirit of God had borne multitudes captives in Messiah's train, the spirit of the pit had a hold of them to confound and disgrace, if not draw some back to perdition. All the laboring men, as I have remarked, drank ardent spirit in their work; nor was it then, more than it had for a hundred years, been viewed as inconsistent with Christian experience or Christian character. No enquiry was made, as they submitted their hearts to Christ, "Do you yield up this indulgence?" nor, as they came into the church, "Do you pledge yourselves neither to use, buy nor sell?" Two respectable members of the Church, one of them a Deacon, had, for a considerable time, planted themselves on the doctrine of total abstinence, and they would not give strong drink to those they employed, but it was viewed as a singular freak, and they had but little influence. A large distillery in the place was considered a great blessing, and stores kept by church members freely dealt out the poison without reproach or any sense of wrong-doing. But in time past many church members had brought reproach upon the cause of their Master by intemperance; seven eighths of all cases of discipline were for this sin. Some were in the church who were still a vexation, and it was soon manifest that some of the late hopeful subjects of divine grace, were not to be exempted from the effects of the drunkard's drink if they continued to use it. That grace was sufficient for them, but could a man take fire in his bosom and not be burned? could he walk on hot coals and his feet not be burned? The young shepherd was jealous for the lambs of his flock. Some rumors of irregularities from the too free use of spirit in drinking places reaching his ears, he prepared and delivered a sermon of admonition and warning—shewing the amount of liquor drank in the place, (fifty-two hogsheads of New England rum had in that year been sold,) its cost, and consequent waste to the people, the evils of intemperance, the dangers of moderate drinking, especially to young Christians, its hindrance to growth in grace, and its occasion of much improper conversation and conduct. Some of the fathers were angry; suffering women said, "It is all true;" but the whole was the subject of merriment among the young men, and more was drank the next day in the ship-yards and quarries than before; but an impression was made on many of the subjects of the recent revival, and a few resolved that they would carry no more spirit to their field of labor. A conflict was commenced, and a second work of conversion was to be effected. I need not say, it was a laborious and often painful one. It alienated many friends, especially among the older class. It at times interrupted religious effort; but it was a necessary work, removing one of the greatest obstructions to the reception of the Gospel, and the purity and prosperity of Zion. In suceeding revivals, several hard drinkers were awakened; and long was the struggle between giving up the cup or the Gospel salvation. An abandonment of drink was often the point of submission to the Gospel. When it came to be understood that but little credit was given to a religious hope connected with a continuance in moderate drinking, and that none would be received into the church but upon an abandonment of the cup; the victory was gained.

While in this revival labor, I was visited by the Rev. Asahel Nettleton, the distinguished revival preacher, and I saw him often in an adjoining town, the place of his birth. We conversed much on this subject, the destructive influence of spirit-drinking on the soul. He strengthened me in the position I had taken, as he afterwards did many others, in an admirable letter which he published on the subject in the Spirit of the Pilgrims, in 1829. Several strong cases are in my recollection, shewing the power of the drink over good men. A much-loved deacon was greatly tried, believing that a daily use of spirit was essential to check the progress of a disease with which he was afflicted. A hasty young convert refused to take from him the Sacramental Elements at the Lord's table; on inquiry, after communion, for the reason, the convert said he would not take bread from the hands of one who drank brandy. The deacon went home distressed, and said to his wife: "Live or die, I will become an abstainer." In a few weeks he came to me with a bright countenance, saying, that his complaint had left him, and he was satisfied, it was the brandy which had caused it. Another excellent brother was so devoted to revivals, that temperance meetings and temperance sermons were a great annoyance. He almost considered them the work of the adversary to put a stop to revivals. I labored with him much, but it was all in vain. He absented himself from prayer meetings, because he could not unite in prayer for the success of the temperance cause; and from the communion table, for the temperance brethren could not fellowship him. Yet he was a good man; a precious brother in revival seasons. I made him a special visit; I talked, I reasoned, I pleaded; finally I said: "Have you ever made this the subject of prayer? "No," said he, "and I won't." "Then," said I, "Brother, you are wrong; for if there is any subject on which you are unwilling to ask counsel of God, there you are wrong; conscience condemns you, and you feel or fear that God will condemn you." He saw it, and promised he would carry the case to God. The next time I met him, his face shone as did the face of Moses when he came down from the mount. "It is all over," said he, "the moment I was on my knees, I saw you were right and I was wrong; I could not pray that the temperance cause might not prevail." From that time he became one of our best temperance advocates.

In the midst of this conflict I took one of those practical stands which try the hearts of many. I had commenced building a house; my frame was all ready, and a general invitation was given to my parishioners to come to the raising. But it was understood, it was to be a cold water raising. Good refreshments would be provided, but no liquor. This was an unheard-of thing. Raisings were great times for drunkards and hard drinkers. Liquor was free and abundant, and the jugs and demijohns were well emptied; awful scenes for Christian communities. A raising was one of the devil's harvests, and not a few were the distressing accidents then occurring. It was predicted that men enough could not be collected to put up the building. Attachment to the youthful pastor, however, and a sense of shame at staying away for want of the drink, brought out a goodly force. And the frame went up, amid much exhilaration on the part of the abstainers. But several individuals, and among them members of the church, came to see the failure, and seating themselves on a bank near by, looked on, like Shimei, cursing as the timbers went up, and at last, as they saw they would go, retreating in vexation. After this, raisings were effected without liquor, and soon the tables were turned; the rum men being the feeble party.

Besides preaching occasionally on the subject, I prepared and published two tracts which I circulated freely among my people; one, an "Appeal to Professors of Religion on the Use of Ardent Spirits;" and the other, "The Rum-drinking Christian": *The Lord pardon thy servant in this thing. Is it not a little one?* to meet the cases of pious brethren who plead that they drank but little. In my action I had the strong sympathy of neighboring ministers and churches, and on September 8, 1828, a large County meeting was held in my church, and a County Society was organized; Charles Griswold of Lyme, a gentleman of high character, was appointed President. Monthly meetings were established, which the ministers almost without fail attended; and by some one an able address was prepared. Soon we had 600 men in the county pledged to total abstinence from ardent spirits, before it was supposed there were half that number in the whole State. The next autumn the Middlesex Consociation met in my church, and such had been the influence of our County meetings on the ministers and churches that it was unanimously

Resolved, That this Consociation do highly approve of the measures which have been recently adopted for the suppression of Intemperance, and that the success of these measures calls loudly for the gratitude of the churches to God under whose blessing it has been attained.

Resolved, That the Consociation do recommend to the members of the churches in their connexion total abstinence from the common use of ardent spirits and a union with the temperance societies; these societies being the most powerful antidote to the alarming evil of intemperance, which the providence of God has pointed out to his people.

But we were but one of a mighty host which was gathering to the battle. In February, 1826, the American Temperance Society had been organized at Boston. A weekly paper called the National Philanthropist had been established by Wm. Collier. Its motto was, "Temperate drinking the downhill road to intemperance." This was removed to New York and succeeded by the Journal of Humanity, established by the society at Andover, and edited by Rev. Edward W. Hooker. Rev. Justin Edwards, of Andover, and Rev. Nathaniel Hewitt, of Fairfield, Ct., had entered on those great labors which, it was hoped and believed, would result in the overthrow of this kingdom of blood. The principle of total abstinence had been established in the Christian Spectator by the pen of Rev. Joshua Leavitt, of Stratford, Ct. The well-conducted farm, a tract from the pen of Rev. Justin Edwards, describing the farm of S. V. S. Wilder, Esq., of Bolton, conducted on strict temperance principles, had awakened the attention of farmers throughout the country to the uselessness and the injurious effects of ardent spirits in all agricultural pursuits. A series of papers, in the Connecticut Observer, from the caustic pen of Rev. Calvin Chapin, on total abstinence the only infallible antidote, over the signature T. I. A., commencing January, 1826, had confounded and put to silence pleas for moderate drinking; and the Six Sermons of Rev. Lyman Beecher, of Litchfield, in the ensuing summer, on the nature, signs, evils, and remedies of intemperance, with an electrifying address, soon after, by Jonathan Kittredge, of New Hampshire, on the effects of intemperance, had set the country on fire; and everywhere State, county, and town societies were being established with a resolution and vigor which promised and actually secured the greatest results.

The flame spread across the Atlantic, and a fire had been kindled in England, Scotland, and Ireland. The first temperance society in the old world, on the abstinence system, was formed in 1829 by Rev. George Carre, of New Ross, in Ireland. Voluntary abstinence from doing evil, as an essential prerequisite to doing well, had been proclaimed, at Belfast, by the Rev. Mr. Penny, of Rochester, N. Y., and on this as a base, numerous societies sprang up in that year, in Ireland and Scotland, numbering over 14,000 members.

One of the earliest of the State societies was the Connecticut. It was organized at Hartford, May 20, 1829; Rev. Jeremiah Day, D. D., President of Yale College, President; Rev. Calvin Chapin, Chairman of Executive Committee; and myself, Secretary and General Agent. The appointment led me, without leaving my pastoral charge, to visit various parts of the State, attend meetings, make addresses, and institute inquiries relative to the extent and evils of intemperance. In October of that year I was invited to address the Windham County Temperance Society at Pomfret, a distance of forty miles from my residence. I thought it idle to perform such a journey, then difficult to address a meeting, and dismissed it from my thoughts. But on rising from dinner one day, I burst into a laugh. My wife inquired what so amused me. I said, "I am going to Pomfret." "Why!" said she, "I thought you had given it up; pray what has changed your mind?" I replied, "That is the place where Putnam killed the wolf, and I will make a temperance address out of that, PUTNAM AND THE WOLF;—the wolf devouring the sheep, and the people out upon the hunt." I ran up to my study, found in a school book Gen. Humphreys' story of the hunt, and, before I went to bed, which was past midnight, I had finished my address; amused and exhilarated beyond measure at the wonderful adaptedness of the affair to the subject. The next day, a letter was despatched to the secretary of the county society saying, I would be on hand. The 28th, the day of the meeting, was fine. The large Pomfret meeting-house was full. Venerable men, well conversant with the story, sat around the pulpit. The den of the wolf was not far off, and descendants of the hero were near by. Commencing with an account of that marvellous affair, and bringing it to bear upon the present hunt after an enemy among us devouring, not sheep, but men, and having among us his apologists by scores, no small emotion was excited. The old men first looked up and smiled, and then put their heads down between their hands and knees to repress their laughter, while the active combatants in the field felt that they had a new weapon in their hands against the rumseller and the distiller which would hew its way and bring great results. Often, with difficulty, could I keep as composed as became the orator; and when I had finished, and gained the open air, there was a rush upon me for a copy for the press. I replied they might have it if they would go to Hartford and get from an engraver a picture of Putnam dragging the wolf from the den. They did so at once. An enterprising bookseller undertook the publication, and, in a short time, disposed of 150,000 copies. Soon after, the American Tract Society adopted it as one of their permanent tracts, and have scattered abroad thousands on thousands. Such was the result of a happy caption to an address which otherwise would have attracted no special attention.

In 1830 I published my First Report as Secretary of the Connecticut Temperance Society. The anniversary was held May 19, in the Centre Church in New Haven. It was a proud occasion for the friends of the cause. The assembly was large. The Governor and most of the Legislature were present. Prayer was offered by President Day. After the reading of the Report, able addresses were made by the Hon. Timothy Pitkin of Farmington, long a distinguished member of Congress, Daniel Frost, Esq., Agent of the Society, the Hon. Minot Sherman, and the Hon. David Daggett. An advocacy by such gentlemen made a deep impression. Mr. Sherman was one of the most finished speakers of the day. He took a lively interest in the cause, and was ready at all times to speak in its behalf. He put all opponents to shame, and imparted great strength and courage to those who were engaged in its promotion. Judge Daggett bore ample and powerful testimony to the intimate connection between intemperance and crime. He viewed the dram-shop as the "curse of the community," the "outer chamber of hell," and he then, and often, expressed the opinion that there was little hope of much success in the cause, until the sale of ardent spirits was placed on a par with counterfeiting and thieving. In the Report, I was able to present a mass of information relative to the extent and evils of intemperance in the State which, to the uninformed and unreflecting, was truly appalling. In addition to constant importations of rum from the West Indies, there were two large rum-distilleries in the State, and ten gin and whiskey distilleries, doing a great business; with 300 smaller distilleries on the farms, chiefly cider distilleries. Licensed retailers and licensed taverns were in every town. The consumption of spirituous liquors in the State, containing a population of 275,248, was annually about 1,238,616 gallons, which, at 62½ cents a gallon, cost the people $782,-894.95. In several of the farming towns, merchants gave an account of their annual sales of 10,000 gallons and upwards. Among 45,000 families, every twenty-fifth family was engaged and found support, at least in part, in supplying the remainder with intoxicating liquors. As the result of all this terrible enginery, besides the waste of property, the idleness, sabbath-breaking, contention, murders and general demoralization, there were in the State thousands of common drunkards, one in ten of whom went annually to the grave, leaving their places to be at once supplied by a new generation. In nine parishes in the county of Hartford there were reported by the Hartford County Society, from an actual inspection of every adult in those parishes, 594 drunkards; giving 2,005 to the county. Of 172 paupers in Middlesex County, 114 were reduced to beggary by intemperance, and Captain Pillsbury, Warden of the State prison at Wethersfield, a noble temperance man, said to me, on inquiry, "that he might say of his 167 prisoners that the whole were brought there by intemperance." To meet and overthrow this terrific evil, the combination in the State had now become mighty. Eight counties and 174 towns and societies were reported with 22,532 members pledged to total abstinence from the use of and traffic in ardent spirits as a beverage. The county societies were headed by some of the most distinguished men of the State: Hon. Timothy Pitkin of Farmington; Hon. David Daggett of New Haven; Hon. John Cotton Smith of Sharon; Darius Matthewson, Esq., of Windham; William P. Greene of Norwich; Elisha Stearns, Esq., of Tolland; Charles Griswold, Esq., of Lyme; His Excellency, Gideon Tomlinson of Fairfield, Governor of the State. These gentlemen all took a pride and pleasure in attending the county meetings and advancing the cause. The medical faculty throughout the State were, as a body, deeply interested, and at their State Convention in 1828 they passed a series of strong resolutions in its favor. They especially declared that it was the duty of all physicians to abstain from the use of ardent spirits in their attendance upon the sick; as such use rendered the system more susceptible of contagion and other causes of disease.

They also recommended entire abstinence to nurses and all attendants. But with no individual did I meet in the State more clear in his views, and more decided and influential in his practice than Mr. James Brewster of New Haven, the head of a large mechanical establishment. More tools he assured me were destroyed and more work spoiled through ardent spirits than from any other cause. He made a thorough cleansing of his own establishment, and his influence was great in inducing other mechanics throughout the State to banish the poison from their works. He still lives; a great ornament and blessing to his race.

Amid such conflicts and successes was it my happiness, while in the ministry, to do something for the introduction and advance of the principle of entire abstinence in my native State.

CHAPTER II.

Taking a three months' Temperance Agency—Labors in Baltimore and Washington—Gathering of First Congressional Temperance Meeting—Acquaintance with Judge Cranch, Dr. Sewall, and others—Appointed Permanent Agent of American Temperance Society—Dismission from Pastoral Charge—Attendance on First National Temperance Convention at Philadelphia—Made Secretary—Labors in Connecticut and Massachusetts—Removal to Philadelphia—Three years' labor in connection with Pennsylvania State Society.

"As the lightning shineth out of the East unto the West, so also shall the coming of the Son of Man be;" and so was the rapid extension of the temperance reformation. In May, 1831, there were reported nineteen State societies, embodying 3,000 local societies, with more than 300,000 members, pledged to entire abstinence from the manufacture, sale, and use of ardent spirits as a beverage. Maine, Alabama, Louisiana, Illinois and Missouri were the only States in which a State society had not been organized. Some of the State societies were very large and efficient, especially the Society of the State of New York; and it was the opinion of the Chairman of the Executive Committee of that society that there had been saved to the State in that year, in the diminished use of ardent spirits, at least $6,250,000, and that there was everywhere manifest both an improved state of morals and fresh vigor in every department of human industry: 3,000 lost drunkards in the country had, it was supposed, been reclaimed, and more than 10,000 men, on the brink of ruin, had been kept back from falling and once more had gained firm footing;

while more than a million had already resolved not to enter the drunkard's path or become liable, in any degree, to the drunkard's end. More than a thousand distilleries had been stopped, and serious conscientious venders, who had been unwittingly engaged in dispensing for gain the delusive and destructive poison, had, without number, abandoned their business. The press had become very prolific in spirited and stirring appeals and addresses. Besides the publications already noted, the community had been favored in 1827 with two "Discourses on Intemperance" by Rev. John Palfrey of Boston, and "Effects of Spirituous Liquors on Society," by S. Emlen, M. D., of Philadelphia. In an address before the Medical Convention of New Hampshire, by Reuben Mussey, M. D., Dr. Mussey developed the "True Nature of Alcohol," and showed that it was neither needful nor useful in all the labors of life. An address before the Canterbury Society in Connecticut, by Daniel Frost, Esq., a lawyer, who had entered the field as a temperance lecturer, attracted much attention from his own sad personal experience. In 1828 twelve "Essays on Intemperance" were presented, by Albert Barnes, then a young minister in Morristown, N. J.; but, though able, their circulation was very limited; also, "Intemperance, a Just Cause of Alarm," by Rev. W. Sprague of West Springfield, Mass. A masterly "Parallel between Intemperance and the Slave Trade," by Heman Humphrey, D. D.; "An Appeal to the People of Lower Canada," by Joseph Christmas; and "An Address to Manufacturers and Venders of Strong Drink," by Jonathan Kittredge, appeared in the same year. But the most effective publication of the time was, "AN APPEAL TO THE INTEMPERATE," by Samuel Nott of Galway, N. Y. It was a small, but thoroughly practical common sense view of the subject; showing that the temperate were the guilty cause of all the intemperance in the land. It had a very wide circulation. The First Report of the American Temperance Society for 1827, prepared by Rev. Dr. Hewitt, was extensively circulated. And in 1829 appeared "Beman's Song of the Drunkard;" "Sweetzer's Dissertation;" "Putnam and the Wolf;" and "Professor Hitchcock's Argument against the Manufacture of Ardent Spirits." These and other publications, too numerous to mention, had great influence on the public mind.

At this time, 1831, Dr. Hewitt had not only aroused the attention of his countrymen, but had electrified England, Scotland and Ireland by the power of his eloquence; while Dr. Justin Edwards of Andover, Mass., fastened conviction of truth and responsibility upon the minds of men as it had never been before; and in a visit to the city of Washington, in the winter and spring of that year, he addressed the citizens of the District and also both houses of Congress, making a deep impression upon them and upon the several Heads of Departments. On leaving that city to return home, earnest requests were made for some similar aid another season; and on application through him from the Baltimore Temperance Society, I was induced to leave my pulpit in the hands of another for the space of three months, and do what was in my power in aid of the cause both there and in the capital of the nation. I left my home in the month of November, and immediately on my arrival at Baltimore commenced my work. It was an inviting field of labor. A large Committee of the Baltimore Society were ready to coöperate with me. The first pulpits of the city were opened to me, and I preached morning and evening on the sabbath; addressed ward meetings in the week; and schools, almshouses and prisons as time would admit; and during a National Political Convention held an immense public meeting. For this I had the promised aid of the Hon. John Sargent, one of the first lawyers of Philadephia, and the Hon. William Wirt, the eloquent attorney-general of the United States. Mr. Wirt entered into the subject with great ardor and zeal, but alas! was kept from the meeting by the sudden illness of his daughter; yet, while in her sick room, he wrote me the following letter of apology, which I read in the meeting, and which may be read with profit while the world lasts:

BALTIMORE, *November* 28, 1831.

REV. MR. MARSH,

DEAR SIR:—I have been for more than forty years a close observer of life and manners in various parts of the United States, and I know not the evil that will bear a moment's comparison with intemperance. It is no exaggeration to say, as has often been said, that this single cause has produced more vice, crime, poverty, and wretchedness in every form, domestic and social, than all the other ills that scourge us combined. In truth, it is scarcely possible to meet with misery in any shape, in this country, which will not be found on examination to have proceeded, directly or indirectly, from the excessive use of ardent spirits. Want is one of its immediate consequences. The sad spectacle of starving and destitute families, and of ignorant, half naked, vicious children, ought never to be presented in a country like this, where the demand for labor is constant, the field unlimited, the sources of supply inexhaustible, and where there are none to make us afraid; and it never would be presented, or very rarely indeed, were it not for the desolation brought upon families by the general use of this deadly poison. It paralyzes the arm, the brain, the heart. All the best affections, all the energies of the mind, wither under its influence. The man becomes a maniac, and is locked up in a hospital, or imbrues his hands in the blood of his wife and children, and is sent to the gallows or doomed to the penitentiary; or, if he escapes these consequences, he becomes a walking pestilence on the earth, miserable in himself, and loathsome to all who behold him. How often do we see, too, whole families contaminated by the vicious example of the parent; husbands, wives, daughters, and sons, all drunkards and furies: sometimes wives murdering their husbands; at others, husbands their wives; and worst of all, if worse can be in such a group of horrors, children murdering their parents. But below this grade of crime, how much is there of unseen and untold misery, throughout our otherwise happy land, proceeding from this fatal cause alone. I am persuaded that if we could have a statistical survey and report of the affairs of unhappy families and individuals, with the causes of their misery annexed, we should find nine cases out of ten, if not a still greater proportion, resulting from the use of ardent spirits alone. With this conviction, which seems to have become universal among reflecting men, the apathy shown to the continuance of the evil can only be ascribed to the circumstance that the mischief, though verbally admitted, is not seen and felt in all its enormity. If some fatal plague, of a contagious character, were imported into our country, and had commenced its ravages in our cities, we should see the most prompt and vigorous measures at once adopted to repress and extinguish it: but what are the most fearful plagues that ever carried death and havoc in their train through the eastern countries, compared with this? They are only occasional; this is perennial. They are confined by climate or place; this malady is of all climates, and all times and places. They kill the body at once; this consumes both body and soul by a lingering and dreadful death, involving the dearest connections in the vortex of ruin. What parent, however exemplary himself, can ever feel that his son is safe while the living fountain of poison is within his reach? God grant that it may soon become a fountain sealed, in our country at least. What a relief, what a delightful relief would it be to turn from the awful and horrid past, to the pure, peaceful, and happy future! to see the springs of life, and feeling, and intelligence renewed on every hand; health, industry, and prosperity glowing around us; the altars of domestic peace and love rekindled in every family; and the religion of the Saviour presented with a fair field for its celestial action.

The progress already made by our temperance societies, in advancing this golden age, proves them to be of a divine origin. May the Almighty crown his own work with full and speedy success. I remain, dear sir, respectfully and truly yours,

WILLIAM WIRT.

By request of citizens of Washington my labors were divided between Baltimore and the capital, where I preached both in the Presbyterian and Methodist churches, and at once, in connection with the Rev. Dr. Post, Dr. Sewall and others, entered on the gathering of a Congressional temperance meeting which should make a powerful impression on the nation. Having procured the use of the Hall of the House of Representatives, our great business was to obtain speakers who would enter heartily into the work, command respect, and secure an audience. Of one we were sure from the first; indeed he was a tower of strength to us—the Hon. Theodore Frelinghuysen, U. S. Senator from New Jersey; but he was doubtful whether another one, unless it was Mr. Grundy, Senator from Tennessee, who had recently talked loudly against wine drinking, would open his lips. But who would preside, to give character to the meeting? We called upon Mr. Adams, the late President, and stated our object. He treated us kindly, and promised attendance, but nothing more. We next called upon Gen. Cass, Secretary of War, who we knew had never been known, in all his arduous Western campaign, to taste of ardent spirit. He cordially received us, entered warmly into our object, and agreed to preside. Success was now certain. We next wended our way to the house of the Tennessee delegation. There we found the two senators and three or four representatives all decided temperance men; they had entirely discarded ardent spirit from their table, for the cause had made much progress in their own State. The Hon. Felix Grundy, U. S. Senator, said he would speak; but, if he did, he should be an ultra, for he should go against wine; he had no idea of calling upon the laboring population to give up their ardent spirit and leave the more refined and wealthy to drink their wine, when he knew it was equally a source of drunkenness;—and he did it faithfully. To the Hon. Isaac C. Bates, of Massachusetts, a gentleman of great purity of character and eloquence of diction, and whom I had the happiness to know, we next successfully applied; and, as one from the South and the opposite side in politics was desirable, the Hon. James M. Wayne, member of the House from Georgia, since Judge of the Supreme Court, was commended to us. He assured us that our principles met his approbation, especially in relation to the army and the navy, and he would speak on that point. We now seemed to have a full corps. But there was one who, of all others, was the great favorite in Washington, and, if we could secure his name, we should not want for an audience; that was the Hon. Daniel Webster, U. S. Senator from Massachusetts. Having once preached in Portsmouth, N. H., where he attended worship, I had no difficulty in presenting my petition. But not the least encouragement would he give me, because of his engagements. I left with him, however, a resolution to offer, and had liberty to call again. On entering his room the next day I found him in a pleasant mood. He handed back my resolution, saying, Ministers never know how to make resolutions, they use too many superlatives—lawyers are more careful and precise; there, take that, handing me one he had written, and saying, If you want this you shall have it; it shall be my speech—long enough—and it will be all I can make.

The meeting was now announced, and six hundred cards of invitation were sent out, having upon them the names of the presiding officer and the expected speakers. The evening was fine, and the splendid Hall was perfectly filled with the élite of Washington. To make it entirely Congressional, Walter Lowry, Esq., Secretary of the Senate, was made Secretary of the meeting, and the meeting was opened with prayer by Dr. Post, Chaplain of the House, and closed by Dr. Durbin, Chaplain of the Senate. Mr. Grundy made the opening speech, after I had briefly stated the object of the meeting, and was followed by Messrs. Frelinghuysen, Bates, and Wayne. Mr. Webster, I feared, had failed me, as he was nowhere to be seen; but when his name was called, he rose in the back part of the Hall, where he had been the entire evening, and coming forward a little, standing upon a seat, he read with great distinctness and force his resolution, with a few appropriate remarks. All the speeches were worthy of the subject and of the speakers. Some were truly eloquent. Mr. Grundy was sportive upon wine drinkers, and put the audience in fine humor. Mr. Frelinghuysen was in sober earnest, tender, and subduing. He had seen too many promising men, and even members of Congress, fall before the destroyer, not to have much feeling as he spoke. Mr. Bates was very finished and eloquent. Mr. Adams sat near him, and was much moved. He turned to him at the close, and, wiping a tear from his eye, said: "Mr. Bates, I thank you for that figure of Laocoon—father and sons wrapped together in the enormous folds of the serpent—it is one of the most striking and truthful I have ever heard." I remained in my mission until I had collected the speeches and proceedings in pamphlet form, and had them circulated, through the assistance of members of Congress, over the land.

While in Washington I made the aquaintance of Judge Cranch, of the United States District Court, who was very kind to me and of essential service. He had turned his attention much to the subject in which I was engaged, and had given the result of his investigations in an address to the citizens of Washington. Judging from the quantity of ardent spirits actually consumed in the city of Washington, he estimated that six gallons was the average annual consumption by each person in the United States; and as we had a population of twelve millions, the consumption would be 72,000,000 gallons of ardent spirits; which at 66½ cents a gallon, would be forty-eight million dollars. He estimated that there were 375,000 drunkards in the country, and that three-fourths of the crime and pauperism of the nation might be traced to intemperance. The entire liquor bill for the country he made to be annually 94,425,000 dollars. Such an annuity would in twenty years, with simple interest only, at six per cent. per annum upon each year's annuity, from the time it became payable to the end of the twenty years, amount to 3,064,800,000 dollars. The valuation of all the houses, land, and slaves in the United States was 2,519,009,222 dollars; so that the amount annually lost to the country by the use of ardent spirits, would be more than sufficient to buy up all the houses, land and slaves in the United States once in every twenty years. Such presentations from so accurate and distinguished a gentleman, could do no otherwise than excite alarm throughout the community. I became also intimately associated with Dr. Thomas Sewall, who was then giving much attention to the subject of temperance in his high profession, and with Dr. Harvey Lindsley, author of "A Prize Essay on Alcoholic Stimulants, and Substitutes for, in the Practice of Medicine," who from that day gave me ever after a delightful home in his dwelling.

The American Temperance Society at Boston were now finding a vast work upon their hands, and the need of more laborers in the field; and they resolved, if the means could be found, to sustain an agent in each of the great points of influence in the United States—Philadelphia, Cincinnati, St. Louis, Charleston and New Orleans—who in coöperation with their Committee and Corresponding Secretary at Boston should aid in the diffusion of information and in giving impulse to the work. In a letter from the Secretary, Rev. Justin Edwards, D. D., dated January 21, 1833, I was invited to leave my pastoral charge with a view of removing to Philadelphia, and occupying that post; certain gentlemen there having guaranteed my support. The tie which bound me to my people was strong. I had been with them fourteen years, in as perhaps arduous labor as was the allotment and privilege of any of my brethren; for there was, from the extent and roughness of the place, no harder field. But it was a fruitful one. Three powerful revivals had created a large and flourishing church. Attachments between pastor and people were strong. Not with an individual had I any conflict, excepting on the temperance question, and here the battle was nearly over and the victory won. Another, it was supposed, might enter into my field, while there seemed to be a door of usefulness opened before me which it might be duty to enter. "If," said Dr. Edwards in his letter, "you think it to be the will of God that you should accept the appointment, I should rejoice to have you do so, but not without; because without such a conviction it would not be comfortable to endure the privation, and labor, and trials to which it will call you. These, as you know, must be great; and nothing else will sustain you and carry you forward perseveringly but the conviction that you are probably accomplishing more for the final good of men than you possibly can in any other way."

With these monitions before me, and having consulted my fathers and brethren, and asked counsel of HIM who in wisdom and kindness directs our steps, I requested a dissolution of the bonds which held me to my people. It was granted me on the 1st of April, 1833; the more readily and willingly (an unusual case), by my best friends, because they had become interested, most deeply, in the temperance cause, for which they professed a willingness even to sacrifice their own minister; while to me it was a satisfaction that those who had been most disaffected at my course, most opposed my release.

To come to a sudden stand-still in all the duties of a large parish; to dismiss at once all responsibility, look at mine own and find they were not mine, but another's; to seek another pulpit and leave mine to a stranger, was a shock for which I was not fully prepared; and I could rise above it only by breaking away from all, and engaging resolutely in my new work.

On May 24, 1833, the first National Temperance Convention was held at Philadelphia, in the Hall of Independence. Four hundred delegates were in attendance from twenty-one States. I attended from Connecticut, and was appointed one of the Secretaries. The meeting was probably the largest that had ever been assembled, for a moral purpose, in this or any other country. Chancellor Walworth of New York, then in the prime and vigor of life, and possessed of unequalled powers as a presiding officer, was made President, and Rev. Justin Edwards, D. D., of Massachusetts, chairman of the business Committee. Dr. Edwards had been more conversant with the temperance reform, its necessity and wants, than any other man, and stood ready with a series of resolutions which were calculated to secure approbation, and give a great extension to the temperance principle. Other men of distinction: Robert Vaux of Pennsylvania; John Tappan of Massachusetts; Timothy Pitkin of Connecticut; Peter D. Vroom of New Jersey; Joseph Lumpkin of Georgia; Gerrit Smith, Hugh Maxwell, Edward C. Delavan of New York; D. W. Lathrop of Ohio; Rev. Dr. Hewitt of Connecticut, and a very large body of clergy of various denominations, were present, and took part in the proceedings. Unfortunately the Hall of Independence was not sufficiently large, and the Convention was adjourned to the Arch Street Presbyterian Church, depriving the meeting of much national enthusiasm, and exciting in the minds of some, especially of Friends, a sectarian prejudice. Numerous general resolutions were discussed and adopted with great unanimity; but a resolution declaring the traffic in ardent spirits to be morally wrong, caused great conflict, it being considered as an impeachment of pious dealers of former days. It was, however, adopted by an almost unanimous vote.

A public meeting of great power was held at the Musical Fund Hall, which was addressed by G. S. Hillard of Massachusetts; Thomas P. Hunt of North Carolina; Thomas S. Stockton of Maryland; and Nathaniel Hewitt of Connecticut. Chancellor Walworth also made an address on female influence. Stephen Van Rensellaer, Esq., of Albany, offered to defray the expense of distributing 100,000 copies of the proceedings of the Convention, and did so. The reformation, by this Convention and its proceedings, was now placed upon high ground, and nothing seemed to be wanting but "a bold, manly and steady perseverance to eradicate from the land the manufacture, sale and use of ardent spirits." No other drink was then the object of attack. The sale of none other was considered morally wrong. The harmony prevailing was an assurance of success.

During the meeting of the Convention a large Committee was appointed to organize a "General Temperance Union." The Committee reported, that the officers of the American Temperance Society, and the officers and delegates from the State Societies should form this Union. Accordingly a meeting of all such was convened. Dr. S. Agnew, of Pennsylvania, was called to the chair, and Rev. John Marsh and I. S. Loyd were appointed Secretaries.

On motion, Justin Edwards, Edward C. Delavan, N. S. N. Beman, Thomas Brainard, and G. B. Perry, were appointed a Committee to report officers and prepare business for the meeting. The Committee, after having retired, reported the following members as officers for the present meeting of the Union: Stephen Van Rensselaer, of New York, President. Samuel Agnew, of Pennsylvania; William Jay, of New York; G. B. Perry, of Massachusetts; Richard Boylston, of New Hampshire; Cyrus Yale, of Connecticut; Vice-Presidents. John Marsh, of Pennsylvania; Isaac S. Loyd, of Pennsylvania; Harrison Gray, of Massachusetts; Thomas Brainard, of Ohio; Secretaries.

The Committee further reported a series of resolutions, which were adopted, as follows:

1. *Resolved*, That the officers of the American Temperance Society, and of each of the State Temperance Societies, in their associated capacity, be denominated, The United States Temperance Union.

2. *Resolved*, That the object of this Union shall be, by the diffusion

of information, and the exertion of kind moral influence, to promote the cause of Temperance throughout the United States.

3. *Resolved*, That Isaac S. Loyd, Matthew Newkirk, and Isaac Collins, of Pennsylvania, John Tappan, of Massachusetts, Edward C. Delavan, and Samuel Ward, of New York, and Christian Keener, of Maryland, be a Committee to carry into effect, by all suitable means, the objects of this Union; and that they continue in office till others are appointed.

4. *Resolved*, That the above-mentioned Committee call another meeting of this Union at such time and place as they may judge proper.

5. *Resolved*, That the Corresponding Secretaries of all State Societies be, ex officio, members of this Committee.

The organization thus created consisted of the officers of the American Temperance Society at Boston, twenty-three State Societies, and more than seven thousand associations in counties and smaller districts of the country. Its object was, by the diffusion of information and the exertion of a kind moral influence, to extend the principles and blessings of temperance throughout the world. But though thus established, and with every promise of a blessing, for want of readiness and coöperation, its wheels were not set in motion for more than three years, when its name was changed to AMERICAN TEMPERANCE UNION.

On the breaking up of the Convention I returned to Connecticut and performed some service in that State and in Massachusetts, lecturing and collecting funds for the American Temperance Society. In October, I removed with my family to Philadelphia, where, for three years, I labored in connection with the Pennsylvania State Society. That Society was organized in February, 1829, and had for its President Robert Vaux, Esq., a distinguished citizen, and was sustained by several liberal-minded gentlemen. Early, the doctrine of total abstinence from ardent spirit had been promulgated and practised in Pennsylvania, especially among the followers of William Penn. The tract of Dr. Rush on the effects of ardent spirits upon the human body and mind, published in 1804, had in itself done a great work; and the personal influence of that distinguished man had been great among medical men and in the higher classes of society. In 1827, Dr. Hewitt addressed the General Assembly in Philadelphia, and, as a result, the Assembly adopted numerous spirited resolutions, and recommended to the Presbyteries and congregations under their care to coöperate with the American Society in extending the principles of temperance throughout the country. "Intemperance," they said, "that giant vice, marches through the length and breadth of the land and carries destruction in its train. Its name is Apollyon. It destroys health, wealth, reputation, domestic happiness, conscience, the soul." Though the Quaker city, and though a drunken Quaker was perhaps seldom seen, yet the city of Philadelphia had long been a great sufferer from this evil. The number of paupers received into her Alms House from 1823 to 1826 was 18,825, costing the city $662,940. A great proportion of these wretched men, women, and children owed their poverty and misery, it was declared, to spirituous liquors. So impressed were the College of Physicians and Surgeons with the communications and statements of Dr. Hewitt, that they adopted a resolution to be presented to him, of concurrence with his views, and appointed a Committee to investigate the subject of intemperance in the city; so that Pennsylvania, once the seat of the whiskey rebellion, and still abounding in distilleries, was a field well prepared for temperance action.

At once my mission was inaugurated by a very large meeting in the Locust Street Hall, which was addressed by myself and several gentlemen. An office and press were furnished; pulpits were opened; temperance meetings were frequent; a weekly meeting of an efficient committee opened new doors for action and influence. A paper was established, called the Pennsylvania Temperance Recorder, and, a still smaller, the Monitor; the printing of tracts was commenced, and an Annual Almanac. All of these were to be translated into German and scattered through the German counties. In the winter I went with others to Harrisburg,* and attended Legislative temperance meetings, and in the summer I went twice through the State, lecturing and scattering documents in the principal towns and villages. In our third year the Society printed and distributed 215,000 Temperance Recorders in English; 40,000, in German, 76,000 Monitors and 30,000 Almanacs, in English and German. In some of the German counties much interest was felt in the cause; and, throughout the State, the total abstinence principle prevailed among professed temperance men. In my work I was sustained not only by the committee at home, but by several excellent men throughout the State, and by numerous ministers and churches, whom I ever shall hold in grateful remembrance. Some of those churches attributed powerful revivals of religion to the adoption of the temperance principle.

During 1833, the first Congressional Temperance Society was organized at Washington, and the first of those simultaneous temperance meetings, on the last Tuesday of February, which were continued for many years, was held. The public mind was much excited and the power of reform greatly enhanced by many able issues from the press: as MY MOTHER'S GOLD RING, and other tales,

* During a visit at Harrisburg, I called on the Governor and invited him to sign our pledge. He said he had done it long since; not because he thought himself in any danger, but to save a friend: "The head of one of the best families was evidently becoming intemperate to the great distress of all his household. I saw their consternation and grief. I resolved to speak to him on the subject; did so, and urged him to sign the pledge. He suddenly turned upon me, saying, Governor, I will if you will. It is a bargain, said I, and we went immediately to the office of the Secretary and both signed, and I know not that he ever touched a drop of liquor afterwards. Nothing else would have induced me to sign, but I think of it as one of the best acts of my life."

from the pen of Lucius M. Sargent, Esq., of Boston; THE INTEMPERATE, a tale by Mrs. L. H. Sigourney, of Hartford; BURNING OF THE EPHESIAN BOOKS, a discourse by Rev. John Pierpont, of Boston; and an Address by T. S. Grimke, of South Carolina. In the State of New York a deep impression was made through an examination by Mr. Samuel Chipman of all the poor-houses and jails of the State, to ascertain the connection between intemperance, pauperism, and crime. The expense was borne by Aristarchus Champion, Esq., of Rochester. The results of the examination were of a most astounding character. Though somewhat behind the Eastern States in its date, the New York State Society was soon in advance in action. Edward C. Delavan, a young and enterprising merchant of Albany, having retired early from business, with a fortune at his command, was induced, in connection with John T. Norton and other spirited gentlemen, to throw his whole soul into the enterprise and give it all his power. In 1829–30 he became Chairman of the Executive Committee, and, in less than three years, flooded the State with millions of publications. The Temperance Recorder was placed in almost every family, and 260,000 of the Ox discourse were distributed in a single month. Temperance societies were organized in every town and village, and more than 450,000 persons were enrolled as pledged members.

The traffic was affected in every quarter, and so hard was the pressure upon the Albany brewers that, in 1835, they prosecuted Mr. Delavan for a libel, in eight suits of $40,000 each, laying damages at $300,000, for saying that, in malting, they used filthy water; but all in vain. Mr. D. came off victorious. In New England, a distiller had been stirred to much wrath by a Dream, by Rev. Geo. B. Cheever, a young clergyman in Salem, entitled, Deac. Amos Giles' Distillery, and published in the Salem Landmark. Mr. Cheever was prosecuted for a libel, condemned by the jury, and imprisoned for a few days; but distillation received a blow from which it never recovered. This was followed by Deacon Jones' Brewery, or the Distiller turned Brewer, from the same pen. Here demons were represented as dancing round the boiling caldron, and casting in the most noxious and poisonous drugs:

> Round about the caldron go,
> In the poisoned entrails throw.
> Drugs that in the coldest veins
> Shoot incessant fiery pains;
> Herbs that, brought from hell's black door,
> Do its business slow and sure.

All in chorus:

> Double, double, toil and trouble,
> Fire burn and caldron bubble.

Alarmed at the rapid spread of truth and the power of reformatory principles, Bishop Hopkins, of Vermont, published a book entitled, THE TRIUMPH OF TEMPERANCE THE TRIUMPH OF INFIDELITY; charging temperance with assuming to do what Christianity could not do, and setting Christianity aside as useless; but the work only provoked the smile and pity of all good men. The temperance cause was an emanation from the Gospel, and removed the greatest obstructions to its spread and reception. Others contemned the temperance cause as utterly unable to hold its reformed men, and therefore valueless. Dr. Edwards had said, in his Fifth Report, 1832, that 4,500 drunkards had been reformed and had ceased to use intoxicating drinks. Some were well known to hold out and become blessings and comforts to their families; but many had gone back like "the sow that was washed to her wallowing in the mire," and it was found that in most cases they had done so without breaking their pledge, having become intoxicated on other than distilled liquors. This led to much investigation. Gerrit Smith, Esq., of Peterboro', N. Y., gave a report of numerous reformed drunkards, who had gone back on cider. Others reported relapses on wine. Others on beer. The basis of all these drinks was found to be Alcohol, generated in fermentation and not in distillation; and hence the conclusion was, that if men would have the reform progress, and our children saved, the pledge must embrace all intoxicating drinks. Not only was it impossible for reformed drunkards to stand in the use of fermented drinks, though they abstained from all distilled; but sound and stable-minded temperance men were becoming satisfied that they were far better without them than with them. A circular of inquiry on this subject, addressed to a large number of intelligent gentlemen, brought replies of a most decided character, placing wine, cider and malt liquors under the ban as deleterious articles to the human constitution. No testimony was stronger or more influential than that of Professor Hitchcock, of Amherst College. Said he: "I have watched the reformation of some dozens of inebriates, and have been compelled to witness the relapse of many who had run well for a time. And I say, without any fear of contradiction, that the greatest obstacle to the reformation of drunkards is the habitual use of wine, beer, cider and cordials by the respectable members of community; as in very many, I believe in most, cases, intemperate habits are formed, the love of alcoholic drinks induced, by the habitual use of these lighter beverages. I rejoice to say that a very great majority of the several hundreds of clergymen of my acquaintance, are decided friends of the temperance cause, and both by preaching and practice inculcate total abstinence from all that can intoxicate as a beverage."

CHAPTER III.

Second National Convention at Saratoga Springs, 1836—Appointed first Secretary—Adoption of Total Abstinence from all Intoxicating Drinks —Organization of American Temperance Union—Gen. Cocke, of Virginia, President—Located at Philadelphia—Appointed Corresponding Secretary and Editor—Mr. Delavan's Gift of Ten Thousand Dollars —First Issue of the Journal—Second Visit to Washington—Reorganization of the Congressional Temperance Society—Great Progress —Issues of the Press.

So great was the demand, in all the States, for taking high ground, that a second NATIONAL CONVENTION was called, to be held at Saratoga Springs, in the summer of 1836. Many were strongly opposed, doubting the wisdom of including fermented drinks in the pledge; some believing beer essential and useful to our laboring foreign population, and some dreading all conflict with the Bible on the use of wine at weddings and the sacramental table. But a very large gathering was witnessed from the States and from Canada. Chancellor Walworth was again appointed President. I was made first Secretary of the Convention. The great point, the introduction of the pledge of total abstinence from all intoxicating liquors, was at once reached by a resolution to that effect by the business committee, of which Dr. Edwards was chairman. It was sustained by Dr. Lyman Beecher, and others, and unanimously adopted. A subsequent resolution, giving the reasons why all men should unite in total abstinence from all intoxicating liquors, fermented as well as distilled, as of hurtful and deleterious tendency, drew out severe conflicts; Professor Potter, Dr. Reese, and others, denying the correctness of the classification, and believing that vinous and malt liquors might be harmlessly used; but as their use might lead to evil results with some, they were willing to adopt, from benevolent motives, the total abstinence principle. On motion of Dr. Reese a resolution of total abstinence, without assigning any reason therefor, was substituted for that of the business committee and unanimously adopted, though that of the business committee was strongly sustained by Dr. Beman, of Troy, Geo. N. Briggs, Esq., of Mass., and a large majority of the Convention. A spirit of compromise prevailed and the Convention adjourned. Previous to adjournment, however, the American Temperance Union agreed upon at Philadelphia, in 1833, was reorganized and set in motion by the appointment of John H. Cocke, of Virginia, President, with eight Vice-Presidents; an Executive Committee, consisting of Edward C. Delavan, of Albany, Isaac S. Loyd and Isaac Collins, of Philadelphia, John W. Leavitt, of New York, John Tappan, of Boston, Christian Keener, of Baltimore, and John T. Norton, of Connecticut; John Marsh, of Pennsylvania, and Dr. L. A. Smith, of New Jersey, Secretaries; Robert Earp, of Philadelphia, Treasurer, and Thomas Fleming, Auditor.

In the month of October the Committee met in the city of New York, and resolved on Philadelphia as the seat of their operations, and on the establishment there of a national press. A committee of three were appointed to procure a suitable Editor. To this office, and that of Corresponding Secretary, I was invited, and preparations were at once made to issue a monthly publication of sixteen quarto pages, to be called "THE JOURNAL OF THE AMERICAN TEMPERANCE UNION." Mr. Delavan designed removing to Philadelphia, and taking charge of the whole concern; but being prevented from so doing, he generously placed at the disposal of the Committee the sum of TEN THOUSAND DOLLARS.

A new and wide field of labor was now opened before me; though I had found the one I had occupied in Pennsylvania sufficient to task all my powers.

On the fifteenth of January, 1837, the first number of the JOURNAL OF THE AMERICAN TEMPERANCE UNION was issued. Fifty thousand copies were printed, and gratuitously scattered. It commenced with an Address of the Executive Committee to the Friends of Total Abstinance in the Western Hemisphere. It assumed that Alcohol is the same in fermented as in distilled liquors, an intoxicating agent, never useful but always hurtful to men in health, injuring the mind and the body, and to be discarded by all classes as a common beverage. Appeals were made to the President of the United States, to Governors, Legislators, Magistrates, Farmers; to Parents, to Young Men, to Women, to Teachers, and to Ministers. A Circular was added to the Proprietors and Superintendents of Manufacturing Establishments in the United States and the British Provinces, asking for facts relating to the use and disuse of spirituous liquors in their establishments, with several answers which had been received.

My personal business in the office was regular and pressing; but it was thought advisable by the Committee that I should go to Washington, and aid in reorganizing the Congressional Temperance Society, which was formed in 1833, but had fallen somewhat into decay. At a meeting held in the Capitol, February 24, in the absence of Hon. Lewis Cass, President, the Hon. Felix Grundy took the chair, and I was requested to act as Secretary. A series of resolutions prepared were offered by the Hon. George N. Briggs of Massachusetts, and unanimously adopted; and, on nomination by a committee of three, officers were appointed for the year ensuing. Hon. Felix

Grundy, Senator from Tennessee, President; Hon. G. N. Briggs from Massachusetts, Chairman of the Executive Committee; and L. H. Machin, Chief Clerk of the Senate, Secretary. While at Washington I learned many important facts in relation to our cause. A distinguished medical gentleman, much in attendance upon members, assured me he had known no Congress so temperate as that. A Senator informed me that public sentiment was in advance of the action of temperance societies, and that the general demand was for the thorough total abstinence pledge.

Stationed at the fountain head of temperance action, and called to make record and report of all new and aggressive movements, it was with deep interest that intelligence was daily welcomed. Nothing had occurred to give greater satisfaction than the eighth anniversary of the New York State Temperance Society, which was held at Albany on the 16th of February, 1837. 95 delegates were present from 24 counties, men of high character, much intelligence and zeal. The Annual Report by Elisha Taylor, Esq., was exceedingly flattering. The whole number of publications issued to the 1st of February, 1836, was 12,626,210. The whole expenditure of the Society had been $130,408, 41. The distilleries in the State had decreased from 1149 to 337. More than three thousand drunkards had been reformed in the eight hundred towns of the State, and more than one hundred towns had stopped the sale of liquor. More than forty thousand of the population of New York city had signed the ardent spirit pledge. Out of more than four hundred clergymen in the State, who had been called on by the Secretary, all but nine had signed the total abstinence pledge; and the greater part of the physicians were avowed total abstainers. Chancellor Walworth was reëlected President, and the society adopted the total abstinence pledge. From

Virginia favorable reports were received. One of the oldest State Societies, this had been very active, and though not ready at the annual meeting, February 28, to adopt the thorough total abstinence pledge, more than twenty local societies had reported favorable to it.

In Maine the old Temperance Society declined changing its base, and a new organization sprang into existence, called "The Maine Temperance Union" on the new principle. In Ohio more than 93,500 copies of a State Temperance paper had been circulated in the year. In Michigan a State Society had been formed. Its first anniversary was held on the 1st of February. Most of the Society, with but little opposition, had adopted the principle of abstinence from all intoxicating liquors as a beverage. Exceedingly interesting intelligence, with which we were enabled to enrich our Journals, was received from the Rev. Robert Baird, who had visited the North of Europe, and caused the Permanent Temperance Documents to be translated into the French, German, Dutch and Swedish languages, and twelve thousand volumes to be circulated, making everywhere a great impression.

The period which intervened between 1833 and 1837 was one rich in temperance literature. Besides the very able Reports of the American Temperance Society by Dr. Edwards, discussing great principles, there was a continuous flow of Sargent's Temperance Tales; able addresses, by Hon. Mark Doolittle, Alvan Stewart, Dr. E. W. Channing; "The Immorality of the Traffic," by Albert Barnes, and of "The Use of Ardent Spirits," by Robert R. Breckenbridge; "Medical Prize Essays," by Dr. Reuben Muzzey, and Dr. Harvey Lindsley, showing that ardent spirits could safely be dispensed with in the Materia Medica; "Debates of Conscience with a Distiller," by Heman Humphrey, D. D.; "Prize Essay on Sacramental Wines," by Calvin Chapin, D. D. "Sermons," by Bishop

Meade, of Virginia; Rev. E. N. Kirk, of Albany; Rev. Mark Tucker, of Troy; and "Harvey Boys," by American Sunday School Union. With these and other works, I was able to make myself conversant, which gave me and my fellow laborers good ground to believe that our principles were coincident with the word of God, and the developments of human science, and must ultimately gain a signal triumph.

CHAPTER IV.

First Anniversary of the American Temperance Union—Action of the Chancellor of the Exchequer—Speech of Alvan Stewart—Object and Influence of the Journal—Opening of Marlboro' Temperance Hotel, Boston—Buckingham Festival, Philadelphia—Visit with Mr. Buckingham at Washington—Congressional Temperance Meeting—Mr. Delavan's Present to Queen Victoria—Address to the French Court—Second Anniversary at Philadelphia—President Nott's Address—Prohibition taken in Hand—Rev. T. P. Hunt's Exposure of Frauds in the Liquor Traffic—Terrible Disasters on Western Waters—Circular to Marine Insurance Offices—Circular to Emigrants—Liberal Contributions—Removal to New York—Mr. Delavan's Charge on Leaving for Europe—Third Anniversary at Boston—Good Progress.

On the 9th of May, 1837, the first anniversary of the American Temperance Union was held at the Chatham Chapel in the city of New York. Though the seat of its operation was Philadelphia, it was thought best by the Committee to make its first public demonstration amid the other national anniversaries. In the absence of General Cocke of Virginia, the chair was taken by E. C. Delavan, Esq., of Albany, Chairman of the Executive Committee, and prayer was offered by Rev. Mr. Curtis, of the Baptist denomination in Maine. My first Annual Report was necessarily short, being confined much to our own organization and six months' labor, and yet taking a brief view of the advance in principle, in the adoption of the total abstinence pledge from all that intoxicates; of the action of the Massachusetts Legislature on the license system, and of good progress of temperance in foreign countries. The meeting was ably addressed by Elisha Taylor,

Esq., of Albany; Rev. Thomas Brainard, of Philadelphia; Alvan Stewart, Esq., of Utica; and Rev. Thomas P. Hunt, of North Carolina. What gave a peculiar zest to the meeting, was a letter from Mr. Buckingham, announcing that the Chancellor of the Exchequer had granted permission to an entrance, free of duty, to a very large amount, four millions, of a small pamphlet, which the friends of temperance in America were about addressing to the people of Great Britain, a copy to be placed, if possible, in every family. Mr. Stewart said, "In this there was a moral sublimity which the world has seldom witnessed. But a few years ago, these two nations were at war, sending into each other's borders arrows, fire-brands and death; now, breathing toward each other a spirit of good will, and interchanging, without money or price, the means of reform and blessedness to mankind." To our Annual Report were appended, Hon. Theodore Frelinghuysen's speech before the New Jersey State Temperance Society, on the adoption of the total abstinence pledge; statistics on the consumption of wine in the United States, from John Tappan, Esq., of Boston; and the annual cost of intoxicating drinks in the United States, from the Report of the New York Total Abstinence Society.

While there were more than twenty local temperance papers in the country, the Committee designed making the Journal a feeder to them all, and not merely to them, but to all the religious and political papers of the nation; for could the twelve hundred newspapers published, with an average circulation of eight hundred each, all receive into their columns a small portion of the matter furnished, it would be the publication and dissemination of an amount equal, monthly, to nine hundred and sixty thousand copies of the Journal. If the issue of the Circular proposing this did not entirely effect the object, it was not in vain. Many gratifying responses were received. A subscription of about ten thousand copies was made to the Journal; a gratuity of one number of twenty thousand had been sent out; one to every minister of the Gospel, one to every postmaster, one, monthly, to every member of Congress, and many to foreign countries and missionary stations.

In a most exhilarating scene I became a participant in the opening of the Marlboro' Hotel at Boston, on the 4th of July, as a Temperance Hotel. About two hundred gentlemen sat down to dinner, where, for a new thing under the sun, no intoxicating drink was to be seen. Animated speeches were made, by Hon. Messrs. Rich and Fletcher, members of Congress; Rev. Dr. Pierce, Deac. Moses Grant, Mr. John Tappan and others; and a beautiful poem eulogizing, from scripture history, "Cold Water," was brought out by my friend and classmate Rev. John Pierpont;

> "In Eden's green retreats,
> A water brook * * *
> Was Adam's drink,
> And also Eve's, &c."

And in another, and still greater and more magnificent scene, was I during that year not only a participant, but one of the principal agents: a festival given, February 22, 1838, in the Arch Street Theatre, Philadelphia, to the Hon. James Silk Buckingham of England. Such had been his services for temperance in the British Parliament, that we thought it due to him; and we honored him with an assemblage of two thousand people, and an entertainment of the richest character. It was a work of great labor, but of most happy influences. Afterward Mr. Delavan and myself accompanied him to Baltimore, where a large meeting was held at the Eutaw Methodist Church, and addresses were made by the Rev. Robert J. Breckenbridge, Mr. Delavan and Mr. Buckingham. We next proceeded to Washington, and attended the meeting of the Congressional Society. The Hall was filled with Congressmen and citizens; the Hon. Felix Grundy presiding. In lieu of a Report, I was called upon to give a brief view of the state of the cause in this and in foreign countries, and to offer a resolution of gratitude for success. Resolutions and speeches followed from Hon. John Read, of Massachusetts; Hon. J. C. Noyes, of Maine; Hon. Mr. Randolph, of New Jersey; Hon. Mr. Briggs, of Massachusetts; and Hon. Mr. Buckingham, who occupied an hour and a half, greatly to the delight and edification of his large audience. With foreign countries our intimacies were becoming great. Mr. Delavan had sent to Queen Victoria a beautiful copy of Mr. Sargent's Temperance Tales, and received a grateful response; the meetings of foreign temperance societies and able speeches had drawn us out towards them; and the inquiries of Count Molé, relative to our organization, had led our Committee to send a lengthy communication to the French Court.

Our second Anniversary was held, May, 1838, in the Central Presbyterian Church in Philadelphia, Matthew Newkirk, Esq., a wealthy merchant, in the chair. The meeting was deeply interested in a most eloquent address by President Nott of Union College, giving us, in his peculiarly impressive style, the best passages of his lectures, with which he has since favored the world. Few were the dry eyes and unmoved hearts in that large assembly. In this, my second Annual Report, I was able to present a great variety of advances, as the past was a year of much action. But the most important item was the great subject which was now treading upon the heels of total abstinence, the prohibition of the traffic, or shutting off of temptation from the community. Dr. Edwards, in 1833, in his sixth Annual Report, had most fully and clearly demonstrated, that all laws, authorizing the traffic in ardent spirits, were morally wrong; that this traffic should never be licensed; on the contrary, the people should be defended against the evil it causes. Yet, though conviction of the truth of his position had settled down upon the minds of many of the first men of the country, both legislatures and the people were slow to move; but in 1837–8 there were sensations throughout the country, which could not be suppressed. A committee of the Legislature of Maine took the highest ground which ever had been taken, *viz.:* That the law giving the right to sell ardent spirits should be repealed, and a law prohibitory, except for the arts and medical use, be passed; for the reasons for such a law were as numerous as the evils of intemperance. The entire principle was here advanced which afterwards prevailed, in 1851. Massachusetts followed in a Convention of four hundred delegates at Boston, February 21, 1838, with the same positions. And to the Ohio Legislature was presented from Portage County, in the same month, a memorial unsurpassed, before or since, in eloquence and power. A Committee of the Connecticut Legislature, in May, fell into line, adducing numerous facts most touching to the public heart.

These various documents, woven into the Annual Report, with some consequent Legislative action, formed one of the strongest fortresses for temperance. They can never be set aside. The character of the traffic was at the same time being so developed, as to become the object of public indignation and alarm. No one pursued it with more power and skill than my warm personal friend, the Rev. Thomas P. Hunt, who had spoken with much effect at the Philadelphia National Convention, and who, for years after, stood at the very head of effective temperance lecturers, full of argument and of amusing but striking anecdote. To sustain himself in his declarations relating to frauds in the liquor trade, which were incredible to many and pronounced slanderous by the dealers, he sent to London, and obtained the brewers' guides, distillers' and wine-makers' receipt books, from which he spread abroad the secrets of the infernal machinery of drunkard making. His productions were placed in the Journal, and in the appendix to the Report, producing a deep sensation. The action of most of the great religious denominations, in favor of the total abstinence pledge, was recorded, and more intelligence from foreign countries than had before been collected. By this anniversary, in connection with the Congressional temperance meeting, we were much encouraged, and seemed to be in favor with the people. In a few weeks, terrible disasters, by the burning of steamboats, the Ben Sherrod, Moselle and others, on the Western waters through rum, led the Committee to issue a Circular to the Marine Insurance Offices, calling upon them to make an abatement of ten per cent. in favor of all boats conducted without intoxicating liquors. A large number complied with the request. $500 were put into the hands of the Committee to aid in this object, by General Cocke, President of the Union, and $400 by other gentlemen.

Another document of great importance was issued, viz.: "An Address to Emigrants leaving their native countries for America." Of this short, kind, but pointed tract, a large number were printed, and sent over to be put into their hands as they should leave their own shores, and be well considered on their passage. Five hundred dollars were contributed by Gerrit Smith, Esq., to expedite this matter.

In the course of this year, a change of locality, in some respects painful, in others pleasant, was effected for our seat of operations. The residence of Mr. Delavan, chairman of the Committee, at Albany, and the connection of

New York with Europe, and, indeed, with New England and the opening West, had led the Committee in October to remove their office to New York. Our first Journal in that city was printed in October, 1838. My attachment to Philadelphia, where I had resided and labored in the cause, in connection with such men as Rev. Albert Barnes, Rev. Thomas Brainerd, Rev. Dr. Tyng, M. Newkirk, I. S. Loyd, Thomas and Robert Earp, Dr. Gebhard and others, since 1833, was very great; and I was, perhaps, sacrificing too much acquired influence for an experiment in a new city, especially as we did not come for local labor. New York was already in better hands than our own. An immense temperance work had been done here by a well-organized and efficient City Society, established in 1829, and ably conducted, first under the Secretaryship of Rev. Joshua Leavitt, and afterwards of Robert M. Hartley, Esq. An immense mass of publications had been scattered here; auxiliary societies had been formed in every ward. Ministers and churches had been enlisted, and thousands had signed the temperance pledge. The men of the sea had been gathered in, and happy changes were effected along the docks and on shipboard. With so important and efficient an organization I desired coöperation. But I early found there was a lack of harmony. Few of the members of the City Society had adopted the total abstinence pledge, while all were still admitted to full standing, who signed the old pledge of abstinence simply from ardent spirits. Such a course had been remonstrated against in the Journal, and hence it met with but little favor. The New York Young Men's Total Abstinence Association had long been correct, both in principle and practice, and gave us cordially the hand of fellowship. Without any unhappy controversy or division, however, the principle established by the National Convention of 1836, gradually predominated; and, in the course of time, the old pledge fell into disuse. Here, in this great emporium of wealth and trade, we felt that our field was the world.

While thus locating in New York, Mr. Delavan was just leaving us for Europe, to attend to some private business; but designing to make accurate and extensive researches into the cause there, and to impart all the information in his power, relative to the cause here. He designed making the Journal the medium of his communications; and did so, for near a year, to the great gratification of the public. To me he gave a solemn charge of fidelity, especially in relation to the prohibition of the traffic, which was beginning to agitate the public mind. "Throw out your light," he said, "my dear Sir; teach the people to feel that they are the law-makers. Show all the friends of temperance the folly of sending drinking men to our legislative halls, and then sending them petitions to save the community from the ruinous effects of their own practice."

Our third anniversary was held at Boston, in the Winter Street Church, in the last week of May, 1839. Boston was the mother of temperance, and needed no contributions from abroad; but her children felt it a privilege to gather at the old family seat, and show what was their number and growth, and what they in future expected to accomplish. The following letter was addressed to me by our excellent President:

SARATOGA SPRINGS, *May* 22, 1839.

DEAR SIR: It would give me great pleasure to be able to attend the meeting of the American Temperance Union at Boston for several reasons; but my official engagements are such as to render it absolutely impossible I trust, however, that as many of our friends from this State as possible, will try to give their attendance at the meeting, as I think it is due to our friends in Massachusetts, who have exerted themselves so nobly and effectually in the great cause of benevolence in which we are engaged. And

I hope the time will speedily come, when the State of New York will not be behind any of her sisters in drying up the sources of intemperance, and thereby preventing its numberless attendant evils.

Yours with esteem,

R. H. WALWORTH.

REV. J. MARSH, *Secretary*.

The Report which I was able to make congratulated the friends of the cause on the almost universal adoption of the total abstinence principle. Twenty-four State societies were in full and vigorous action. New ones had been formed in South Carolina, Missouri, and Wisconsin Territory. A great decrease was visible in the manufacture and sale of liquor. The New York Society had reported 1,188 auxiliaries, 2,000 ministers, and 100,000 members on the comprehensive pledge, which pledge was ably sustained by fifteen periodicals, besides our Journal. Seven hundred ministers of Wales, and 150,000 of her people had signed the total abstinence pledge. The Permanent Temperance Documents had been translated into Persian. The rapid spread of our principles, and the thrilling reports coming from all quarters, drew out from one of our speakers the sublime description of the thunder storm among the Alps.

"From peak to peak the rattling crags among,
Leaps the live thunder—not from one lone cloud,
But every mountain now hath found a tongue;
And Jura answers from her misty shroud—
Back to the joyous Alps that call to her aloud."

CHAPTER V.

Fourth of July in Boston—Fifteen Gallon Law of Massachusetts—Youth's Temperance Advocate established—Mr. Delavan's correspondence in Europe—London procession—Dr. Baird's letter from Russia—India—Sandwich Islands—Bacchus and Anti-Bacchus—Character of Scripture wines.

THE Fourth of July, the glorious day of American Independence, began early to attract attention from the friends of temperance. This had long been the great harvest season for the rum power. All men felt that they must, on that day, be joyful as joyful could be; and that, to increase the glorification, it was right and proper to use stimulants to almost any excess. On that day more men went home in a state of intoxication, more hearts were broken, and more children and youth commenced the downward path to the drunkard's end, than on any other. But less and less interest was beginning to be felt in that occasion; and as hostility to Britain had passed away, and there was nothing in the minds of men to kindle enthusiasm or cause the day as a holiday to be profitably spent, the temperance men began to claim the day as their own, as an Independence day from King Alcohol, who had long triumphed and slain his thousands. The Declaration of Independence from King George was made to read in almost the same words as a Declaration of Independence from King Alcohol; large assemblies of men and women gathered; processions were formed in cities and villages with banners, and badges, and bands of music, moving to some church or grove, where a temperance oration was delivered, to be succeeded by some refreshments from tables under the shades of the forest. Large bands of children, called the Cold Water Army, also improved the day for pic-nics and pleasant gatherings, and securing a noble host who should withstand the foe when father and mother were no more.

In many of these gatherings it was my happiness to mingle; but in none to be compared with the temperance celebration in Boston of this year, 1839. Our own city of New York had not then begun to taste of liberty from the liquor-god. Booths filled the Park, and riot and confusion was in every quarter. But Boston friends had met the enemy and the city was theirs; and as the struggle had been great in the previous winter to maintain the law, the entire company of temperance men gave up all business on this occasion and came to the banquet. Fourteen hundred men of noble bearing marched the streets with badge and banner; and at 3 P. M. entered, in great order, Fanueil Hall, the old cradle of American liberty, where were spread numerous tables, decorated with flowers, and loaded with substantial viands, fruits and delicacies. Edward C. Brooks, Esq., a gentleman of high character, presided, supported by some of the first citizens of Boston: Samuel Dorr, Esq., Dr. John C. Warren, James Savage, John C. Gray, Moses Mellen, Henry Edwards, &c. The highly respectable Dr. Jenks, of Boston, and Rev. Dr. Pierce, of Brookline, acted as chaplains. And when the refreshments were used up, the chairman made an address, in which he assured the company that they could well dispense with alcoholic drinks when they were brought to contemplate the privations and sufferings of those who fought and gained our Independence; when we needed no stimulus other than the occasion afforded to warm our hearts with gratitude; and when it would be most disgraceful to mar this holy day with bacchanalian orgies. Numerous toasts were then given, not to be drunk with wine, but responded to by speeches and songs, as: 1. "The day we celebrate;" 2. "Old Faneuil Hall, the cradle of Liberty, to be guarded by the genius of Temperance;" 3. "The memory of George Washington," (received standing;) 4. "Temperance;—The common cause of all good men, confined to no party, sect, profession or country; for each and all it has been a duty and a blessing."

To me, as Secretary of the American Temperance Union, it was assigned to sustain this sentiment; and I could only say that we were this day a spectacle to thousands and tens of thousands, for it was as natural for the people, in all parts of the Union, to cast their eyes toward Boston when they desired or expected any good thing, as for the Persian to look at the rising sun for needed blessings. Boston led in the great struggle which gained our Independence, and Boston would go before us in the great conflict in which we were now engaged. The speaker had entered the vestibule of the temple, not to join in battle, for the seventeenth of June with the glories of Bunker Hill were passed; we had fought our great fight and now were for establishing by our cause the moral independence of our country. After dwelling on the value of the temperance reformation to the agricultural, commercial, political and religious interests of the country, I gave way to others, first rejoicing to behold in that assembly the venerable William Pierce, who, in 1773, had assisted in throwing the tea into Boston harbor, and who had now come forward a second time, in his advanced age, to assist in saving his country. (Great cheering, as the venerable teetotaler rose and bowed to the assembly.)

An ode, by Rev. John Pierpont, was then sung.

Let the trump of fame
  Now to their memory swell,

Who, in Freedom's name,
 Fought and bravely fell, &c.

On the heroes moved,
 With death on every side,
For the land they loved,
 They died, they died,

Come pledge the Temperance cause, &c.

Other sentiments followed, and spirited speeches were made, first by Samuel Hoar, Esq., of Concord, a member of Congress, and next by Hon. Josiah Quincy, President of Harvard University. He had asked his friend James Savage if it was consistent for him to come to the meeting, as he had not signed the pledge. He was told it was, And so, said he, HERE I AM. (*Great cheering.*) He took a view of the state of things as they existed thirty years before, compared it with the condition at the present time, and declared the wonderful change effected by the temperance reformation greater in some important points than had been produced by the American revolution. He would say to the temperance men in the language of the times: "GO AHEAD; FEAR NOTHING." For the Judiciary, James T. Austin, Esq., Attorney-General of the Commonwealth, spoke with great strength. Robert Rantoul, Esq., of Beverly, one of the chief politicians and practical reformers, offered a series of strong resolutions. JONATHAN'S INDEPENDENCE, a new poem by Rev. Mr. Pierpont, was then sung by Mr. Colburn, to the tune of Yankee Doodle, amid great éclat.

Says Jonathan, says he, To-day
 I will be independent,
And so my grog I'll throw away,
 And that shall be the end on't.
Clear the house, the tarnal stuff,
 Sha'n't be here so handy,

Wife has given the winds her snuff,
So now here goes my brandy.

CHORUS—Clear the house, &c.

* * * * *

And now, says Jonathan, towards Rum
I'm desperate unforgiving,
The tyrant never more shall come
Into the home I live in.
Kindred spirits, too, shall in-
To utter darkness go forth,
Whiskey, Toddy, Julep, Gin,
Brandy, Beer, and so forth.

CHORUS—Kindred spirits, &c.

While this cold water fills my cup,
Duns dare not assail me,
Sheriffs shall not lock me up,
Nor my neighbor bail me.
Lawyers will I never let
Choose me as defendant,
Till to death I pay my debt,
I will be independent.

CHORUS—Lawyers, &c.

The Rev. Mr. Rogers, of Winter St. Church, spoke for the Clergy, and the Hon. Samuel J. Armstrong, once a practical printer, and afterwards acting-Governor of the State, spoke for the Mechanics of Boston, distinguished for their enlightened devotion to the cause of education and good morals. Eleven years before, he said, the Mayor of Boston, Mr. Quincy, came near losing his life for attempting to enforce the law against the grogshops; now behold fourteen hundred stalwart men in Faneuil Hall at a temperance dinner! A national ode was next sung by the choir.

Our country's banners play,
On this her native day,
With every breeze, &c.

Here at her altar swear,
Your country's ark to tear
From despot's hand;
'Midst drunkards' hosts to brave,
Your holy birth-right save,
Roll back that hellish wave
Which sweeps the land.

Dr. L. Pierson, of Salem, spoke for the Medical Profession. Dr. P. alluded to the struggles the Medical men had to make against the demon. The cup had been offered to the physician every visit he made, but his friends would now as soon think of offering him any other drug.

The venerable Pierce, in his 96th year, was toasted; also the Rev. John Pierpont, author of the odes for the occasion. Rev. Robert Baird gave some account of his mission in the North of Europe. No evidence was wanting, that a sufficient jollification could be had, without the maddening influence of wine. All retired at seven, feeling that it was a day of great glory for the temperance cause in Boston.

Our Boston friends we found in a state of great excitement, through a strong effort on the part of the liquor dealers, to have the fifteen gallon law repealed. This law was enacted by the Legislature of 1838, and went into operation, 14th April, 1839. It forbade the sale of any spirituous or mixed liquors in less quantities than fifteen gallons. Great efforts had been made for its repeal. 17,000 persons, at one time, petitioned for it, and 32,000 males and 42,000 females remonstrated against it. An able and eloquent argument was made in its favor by Hon. Peleg Sprague. By two successive Legislatures it was sustained; but by others, under a new political Governor, chosen by one vote, it was repealed. The repeal produced great excitement among the friends of temperance, inasmuch as it re-established the old license system; and on the 12th of February, a Convention of 1481 gentlemen assembled in Boston, to know what they should do. The conclusion was: that they would continue to operate by light and love, through sound argument and kind persuasion, on the people, *the people*, till they demand and secure to themselves protection from the great evil.

In 1839 I established the "Youth's Temperance Advocate," that the children and youth of the country might early be rescued from the temptations to which they were exposed, and brought under the influence of our reform. On proposing it to Mr. Frelinghuysen, he wrote me the following note:

New York University, *October* 29, 1839.

Dear Sir:—I have examined your proposal for publishing monthly from the office of the American Temperance Union, a small temperance paper, adapted to the vast body of children and youth throughout our country, and am happy to give it my full and hearty approbation. Could such a paper be distributed monthly, by the friends of temperance, in all our Sunday-schools it could not fail of exerting an influence unspeakably important, not only over the minds of children and youth, but even of parents and relatives, in whose path it might thus providentially be scattered. That success, more and more abundant, may attend you and others in the great work of rescuing our land from intemperance, is the wish of your sincere friend,

Theodore Frelinghuysen.

Of the first number we printed and scattered, chiefly through Sunday-schools, 20,000. It soon became a favorite, and obtained large circulation, and has never missed a number in its regular issue to the close of the year 1865.

During the latter part of 1838, and the former of 1839, my mind and heart were much engaged in the correspondence of Mr. Delavan, the chairman of our Committee.

This true reformer had gone to England and France, to make observations on the state of those countries, and aid, if possible, in extending the temperance reformation. On his passage out, he induced his fellow passengers in the Great Western, to memorialize the directors to remove all intoxicating liquors from the table to a bar; and on his arrival in London, he made provision for circulating a thousand copies of our last Annual Report, and two thousand Permanent Documents, among the influential classes; also for placing our address to Emigrants in the hands of all who should come to America. He was at once recognized and welcomed by the friends of temperance, and he sent home frequent letters of the deepest interest, which it was my province to give to the public, through the Journal. He was in London during the great controversy, relating to the short and long pledge, and mingled freely with men belonging both to the new and old societies—one pledge was of personal abstinence, but did not promise not to give to others; the other pledged not to drink, and not to give or offer to others, except for medicinal or sacramental purposes. In France he had an interview with Louis Philippe, then on the throne, who assured him that the drunkenness of France was on wine. Of thirty-four millions of people, he found fourteen millions engaged in making or vending intoxicating drinks; and he endeavored to show them how much better it would be for France, if her soil and people were devoted to stock and grain. He agreed with Dr. Hewitt, that if there was little actual drunkenness visible, the people were burnt up with wine, as were the people of New England formerly, with cider and cider brandy. At Rome he became intimate with Judge Acton, one of the most able jurists, who assured him that nearly all the crime of Italy, was from intoxication on wine. In the spring he attended the great anniversaries in England and Scotland; and when he left

England, in June, 1839, it was with the strong conviction that the principle of entire abstinence was to spread in Europe, until its healthful influence would be felt and acknowledged by all classes. The following is the account which he gave me of the great procession, which he had the happiness to witness in London:

May 26, 1839.

MY DEAR SIR:—The 20th of May was a day that will not long be forgotten. Eight thousand total abstinence men this day marched through the streets of London. The grand procession was most imposing. For miles and miles, as the procession moved onward, a dense mass of human beings filled the streets, and side-walks, and doors, and windows, and it appeared that London had poured forth its whole population to witness so singular a spectacle. The orderly demeanor of the members of the society, their numbers, the immense length of the procession, between two and three miles, the beautiful and appropriate banners, bearing inscriptions "Total Abstinence," "Try our Principles," "Down with the Tyrants," "Come with us and we will do thee good," the one hundred and sixty carriages filled with well-dressed females, every female and every member bearing a rosette, composed of white and blue satin ribbons, and the majority wearing the temperance medal, was deeply affecting; and though it drew forth the jeers of the liquor dealers and their customers, I could not but notice the degree of thoughtfulness and expression of approbation on the countenances of all well-dressed and respectable spectators. I trust a blow has been struck in London by the total abstinence society that will tell favorably on millions yet unborn.

From the Rev. Robert Baird, who for the third and fourth time was in Europe, circulating his Temperance history, and making a great impression in Sweden and Russia, Denmark and Norway, I had frequent letters. In his third visit, in 1840, he travelled 6,500 miles, and had frequent interviews with all the crowned heads. In the following letter he described his interview with the Emperor of Russia:

ST. PETERSBURG, *October* 17, 1840.

To the Corresponding Secretary American Temperance Union:

MY DEAR BROTHER:—I wrote you fully from Stockholm in relation to the efforts which I had made in behalf of the temperance cause on the present journey, until that date. The next day after, I left that city for Russia. I have now spent six weeks in this city and in Moscow. On a former visit, made three years ago, I made arrangements to have my history of the temperance societies translated and published in the Russ language. It was undertaken by Dr. Haus of Moscow, and $400 were sent for its accomplishment. Upon my arrival I found it was delayed, and it was necessary for me to go to Moscow. [Here he met Prince Galitzin and other distinguished men, who were anxious that he should see the Emperor on the subject.] The result was that I was invited by His Majesty to attend the service of His Majesty in the palace at Tsarskoe Telo last Sabbath morning. I repaired thither, and was presented, after service, to the Emperor, the Empress, and the Grand Duchesses, their daughters. The Emperor, in a long interview, in which I was allowed to present the subject fully to him alone, received me in the kindest manner, and acceded at once to the proposal to have the history of the temperance societies published in the Russ. He even went farther, and expressed a desire that it should be translated into the Finnish language, and published and scattered as far as that language is spoken. At dinner His Majesty again alluded to the subject, as did the Empress and the Grand Duke. I cannot tell you how much delighted I was with the expressions which the ruler of this great empire made to me, in response to this great subject. Twenty-five million dollars are the revenue derived from whiskey; a fact which shows the fearful extent to which it is used. But we may now hope its ravages may be stopped.

Yours, truly,

ROBERT BAIRD.

In 1839, the attention of temperance men in England and Scotland was arrested by two works developing, what their authors supposed to be, the true character of the wines spoken of in scripture—Bacchus, by Dr. Grindrod, and Anti-Bacchus, by Rev. Benjamin Parsons. They contended that the wines commended as a blessing, used at the Passover and at the marriage at Cana, were not intoxicating; differing entirely in this respect from the wines which were condemned and forbidden as a mocker. The distinction was not a novel one in America. In 1830, Professor Stuart, of Andover, in a prize essay, examined the question whether it was consistent with a professor of religion to use distilled liquors or traffic in them, or to use wine. The use of distilled liquors he condemned, but of wines he allowed, provided there was no excess; as the natural wines of the East, though slightly intoxicating, were used by holy men of old. Professor McLean, of Princeton, contested his first position and vindicated the use of strong drink, as well as wine, on Bible principles, provided there was no excess. While the controversy was running high, the Rev. George Duffield, now Dr. Duffield, of Detroit, in 1835, thought he could relieve Professor Stuart from the embarrassing position in which he was placed, by showing that there were two kinds of wine spoken of in scripture, one under the term Yayin, the other under the term Tirosh; the former, fermented and alcoholic, a mocker, the "poison of asps;" the latter, the juice of the grape, unfermented and harmless;—a wine that was preserved by the Romans, and might be by us. Professor Stuart acknowledged great indebtedness to Mr. Duffield, but his positions also were severely contested.

These works from England came in support of Mr. Duffield's views. Mr. Parsons, author of Anti-Bacchus, had engaged in a most laborious search into the character of ancient wines, to ascertain if those whose use was permitted or commended in the Bible, were of an intoxicating character. The result of his inquiries confirmed the temperance community, generally, in the belief that total abstinence from all intoxicating beverages was in accordance with the letter and spirit of the word of God.

So interested did the community become in these works, that I ventured to publish, though not a professed publisher, an edition of a thousand copies of Anti-Bacchus, which I thought most immediately useful; with an introduction, showing how seriously we were obstructed in our progress by the belief that God had pronounced wine a blessing, and that the Divine Saviour both drank intoxicating wine and made it by miracle to replenish vessels which once had been filled; and what a relief it would be to us if the points presented could be established. Among 2,270 clergymen of the State of New York, nineteen hundred had signed the total abstinence pledge, resolved to dispense with the use of all wine as a beverage, and were pleased with the new theory. Such as refused did so generally, they said, in deference to Scripture representation and the Saviour's example. But the warmest advocates of the new theory, while gratified with this vindication of Scripture and total abstinence, felt and acknowledged the difficulty of procuring the good wine, the unfermented wine for use; and not needing or caring for it, considering water as the best and only needful drink for man, were indifferent to the matter, excepting for sacramental purposes, where they were very anxious and strenuous. The Rev. Calvin Chapin, D. D., believing that none other than alcoholic wines could here be procured, and opposed to their use in the sacrament, even though the infusion of alcohol might be very small, supported in a prize essay the use of water at the sacrament as most appropriate to this cleansing ordinance.

During the year 1839 my attention was specially called to the subject of Asylums for Inebriates (now so well understood) by having a series of essays upon them by Dr. S. B. Woodward, Superintendent of the Insane Hospital at Worcester, put into my hands. Dr. Woodward had for many years been at my father's home a family physician, and in him I had great confidence. He was of opinion that if there were thirty thousand drunkards in a district of country, one half would be susceptible of cure in such asylums, and he was satisfied that wealthy families (and they were numerous) who were cursed with drunken inmates, would spare no expense in procuring the aids of such institutions. He felt most deeply, he often assured me, because fathers and wives of these wretched men would come to his hospital and entreat him to take their ruined ones; but it would be impossible, as they were not accounted insane; and he was compelled to turn them off with grief. Surprising it has been that more attention has not been paid to the subject, though grateful we are that such institutions as the Washingtonian Home at Boston, and the Binghamton Asylum in New York are now in successful operation. But it led us to ask then, and it leads us to ask now, Why must we have drunkards among us? Because and only because men for money will traffic in intoxicating drinks. It led me then, in my third report, and it leads me still warmly to remonstrate with my fellow citizens engaged in this horrid business, and to say:

"Men and brethren! we approach you earnestly as friends, not as enemies; we come not to wound, not to vilify, but to touch a chord in your hearts which we know must vibrate to the woes and sufferings of a bleeding community. 'Oh, if you can cure him, we shall owe you an eternal debt of gratitude'—this was the language of a distressed father bringing his son to the door of a lunatic asylum. But the door was closed upon him. He could not be admitted. He was not a lunatic, only a drunkard. And what brought all this misery upon that family? The business in which you are engaged, and engaged to pour luxury into the lap of your own family. Father after father and wife after wife come up from all parts of the land, and cry: Oh, what a curse! Is there no deliverance? We feel that there must be, there is in the arm of the law, but why must we be driven thither? Are you not men? Have you not the feelings of men? Have you not the responsibilities of men? Can you, will you, because no arm holds you back, set fire to your neighbor's dwelling, smite him on the head and deprive him of his reason? Will you compel us to rouse the State or the nation to say, you shall cease from this traffic? Should not the sight of a single family, scourged, withered, blasted, cause you to roll every hogshead forth and pour its contents into the streets, and to vow before high heaven that you will no longer be concerned in such guilt? The eyes of the nation are upon you. Through the length and breadth of the land, thousands wait to see what you will do. The wife of the drunken sot; the father of the drunken son; the parents of little flocks yet uncontaminated, all over the world, are waiting to see what you will do. We know that sooner or later you will yield. But will you do it only when compelled by an indignant community weeping over its thirty thousand slain?"

CHAPTER VI.

Wonderful Events in Ireland—Letter from Richard Allen—Father Mathew and his Operations—Six Millions take the Pledge—Dr. Brownlee's Conjecture—Reformed Drunkards in Baltimore—Great Work in New York—Attendance upon it—Third National Convention, 1841—Harvest Gathered—John H. W. Hawkins' Character and Labors—Hannah Hawkins—Christian Keener.

THE cause was now just bursting out in Ireland with a power never before known. The first intimation we had of it in America was in a letter received at our office from Richard Allen, Corresponding Secretary of the Irish Temperance Union, dated Dublin, November 19, 1839. Its contents surpassed all belief; but soon we learned that far more than was first told was true. Rev. Theobald Mathew, a young priest of Cork, under the influence of William Martin, a FRIEND, had formed among his people, working on a new church, a total abstinence society. Almost as by magic, thousands on thousands, of Cork and the neighboring towns and cities, pressed upon the reverend Father to take from him the pledge. In few places less than 10,000; in some 50 and 100,000; by the first of March more than four millions, with eight prelates and seven hundred Catholic clergy.

In Maryboro, in three days, 65,000.
Ahascragh, 90,000.
Killaloe, 15,000.
Athlone, 100,000.
Dublin, 72,000.

Limerick, 10,000.
Thurles, 65,000.
Templemore, 70,000.
Ballyshannon, 60,000.
Enniscorthy, 15,000.

Castlerea, 65,000.
Kells, 100,000.
Tipperary, 60,000.
Carlow, 100,000.
Maryborough, 100,000.

In a letter to me dated, April 10, 1841, said Mr. Allen:

"The battle is gained, the victory won! The great mass of the people in Leinster, Munster and Connaught are teetotalers; our jails are comparatively empty; a drunken man is a rarity. Ireland needs but few soldiers to keep her in order. Distilleries have sunk in value from 50 to 70 per cent., and the duty on spirits has fallen off in a year £354,000; while a great increase is reported on tea, and other conveniences and comforts of life."

The flame spread to America, and in many of our cities, from five to ten thousand of the sons of Erin took the pledge.

In New York, 10,000.
Brooklyn, 3,000.
Philadelphia, 6,000.
Albany, 3,200.
Boston, 6,000.
Washington, 400.
Providence, 1,000.
Louisville, 2,000.
Detroit, 1,000.
Montreal, 6,900.
Baltimore, 3,000.

The words of the pledge were:

"I do promise to abstain from all intoxicating drinks, unless used medically, and that I will discountenance by advice and example the causes of intemperance in others;" the Rev. gentleman adding, "God bless you, and enable you to keep the promise."

This remarkable work was the great theme at our Anniversary in May, 1840. It was most graphically presented by Dr. Heman Humphrey, President of Amherst College, who had himself just witnessed the scene; also by Rev. Dr. Kirk of Boston. Said Dr. H.:

"An insurrection, a glorious insurrection in Ireland! It began in the South, and rolling on, like an irresistible torrent, it has broken out all over the land. Even the capital is in the hands of the revolutionists.

The priests and the highest dignitaries of the church are in the revolt, the magistrates are favoring it, and the army is infected. Was there ever such an electric shock? Let the shouts of green Erin for once drown the voice of our own politics; for the greatest tyrant that ever lacerated her skin, laid bare her sinews, and consumed her flesh, is routed, and in a fair way to be expelled from her coasts. Alcohol, the personification of all evils, physical, political and moral, there maintained dominion over mountains and valleys, rivers and lakes, with iron hand, marble heart and pestiferous breath. But in a little while more all Ireland will be free."

Not a few of our good people viewed it all as a mere Roman affair, designed to increase the power of the priests by the pledge, and their wealth by the sale of medals. In publicly contending with a most eloquent and powerful enemy of Rome, the Rev. Dr. Brownlee, I drew upon myself much reproach as a disturber of a Lecture, but I was too well informed of the facts in the case, and too much interested in the temperance cause to hold my peace. We expected in our efforts at saving the world to be the "song of the drunkard," but not the ridicule of the pulpit; and we bade our good Protestant friends hold their peace, and let Father Mathew, if he could, destroy the great dragon which was drawing millions of Catholics and Protestants down to destruction.

While we were astounded and delighted at tidings from abroad, a new wonder appeared in our own land. The powerful appeals of Drs. Hewitt, Edwards and others, and the general attention to the cause, had not been lost upon that class of men known as drunkards. In the seventh Report of the American Temperance Society, 1834, Dr. Edwards, a gentleman who seldom committed errors, stated that 10,000 drunkards had, in five years, ceased to use intoxicating drinks. And in his appendix a most interesting letter was inserted from Gerrit Smith, Esq., of Peterboro', N. Y., a gentleman of remarkable intelligence and philanthropy, giving a minute account of the reform, in that village, of thirty-eight lost men. In England the temperance reform had commenced, not as in America, among the more intelligent and virtuous classes to save others, but among the lower and drinking population in Lancashire, to save themselves. At Preston numerous and most interesting meetings had been held and conducted by men of that class, many of whom related their experience, as long lost and hopeless drunkards, who had now reformed; and these extraordinary changes had greatly moved the public mind. Accounts of these marvellous reforms were transmitted to America, and were published in the Report of 1835. But a general belief was spreading through the community, that there was little or no hope for the drunkard, especially while the traffic existed in its public and enticing forms.

At this moment of hopelessness and despair, however, six intemperate men in the city of Baltimore, who were accustomed to meet almost nightly for drinking purposes, were strangely led to the resolution that they would drink no more spirituous or malt liquors, wine or cider. A pledge was drawn, which in a few days all signed. This was in the month of April, 1840. They formed themselves into a society, which they called the WASHINGTON TEMPERANCE SOCIETY, after the Father of his Country and great Liberator from tyranny. These six men immediately exerted themselves to induce their bottle-companions to unite with them. In a short time they numbered an hundred; and by the 1st of December, about three hundred; two thirds of whom were drunkards of many years' standing, and some notorious for their abandonment. Their meetings, which were weekly, were exciting, and made more so and increased, by a relation which each member gave of his own experience, or the history of his drunkenness and its ruinous effect upon himself and family. In less than a year, over one thousand drunkards were thus gathered in.

The first knowledge we had of these extraordinary events in New York, was communicated to me in a letter by John Zug, of Baltimore, dated December 12, 1840, which was published in the Journal; but to many, this story also seemed incredible. Soon after, I had a letter from Christian Keener, giving an account of a speech by John H. W. Hawkins (a reformed man, who, in the month of June, had joined the Washington Society) before the Legislature at Annapolis: "He commenced his speech," said Mr. Keener, "by letting them know that he stood before them a reformed drunkard, less than twelve months ago taken almost out of the gutter; and now, in the Senate chamber of his native State, addressing hundreds of the best-informed and most intelligent of men and women, and they listening with almost breathless, I was going to say, but certainly tearful attention."

These accounts led the friends in New York to invite a delegation to come to this city and tell their story. Mr. Hawkins and four others immediately came. A meeting was announced for them in the Greene St. Methodist Church, as a meeting of reformed drunkards, to be addressed by them. Instead of being repulsive, as it was feared it would be, it attracted a large crowd. Anson G. Phelps, Esq., presided. Mr. Hawkins made the first speech; and while relating the story of his reform, a trembling voice in the gallery asked: "Can I be saved, too?" "Yes," said Mr. Hawkins; "come down and sign the pledge." He came, amid the plaudits of the assembly. Another uttered forth his feelings from the gallery, and was led to come down and sign the pledge. Five or six others of this miserable class followed, with thirty or forty other hard drinkers and drunkards. The victory was now gained in New York. In two weeks, immense meetings were held daily in the largest churches, and, finally, in the Park, addressed by Messrs. Hawkins, Casey, Pollard,

Wright, and Shaw. In that time 2,500 individuals were induced to sign the pledge as intemperate men bent on reform.

To these meetings I devoted all my time and attention; and being somewhat of a reporter, I took notes of the speeches and published them in the Journal. Anxious that other cities should enjoy the same blessings with ourselves, I early wrote an account of the meetings to my friend Mr. Sleeper, of Boston, who read the statement in a public meeting, and published it in the Mercantile Journal. No time was lost in securing the blessing. On the 10th of April the first public meeting was held in Boston; and soon not Faneuil Hall would hold the people that gathered together. There, at an immense meeting, the Hon. Theodore Lyman, ex-mayor, presided, and gave an address of welcome; and John H. W. Hawkins made a speech of remarkable appropriateness and power, winning all hearts. He said:

> "When I compare the past with the present, my days of intemperance with my present peace and sobriety, my past degradation with my present position in this Hall—the Cradle of Liberty—I am overwhelmed. It seems to me holy ground. I never expected to see this Hall. I had heard of it in boyhood. It was here that Otis and the elder Adams argued the principles of Independence, and we now meet here to declare ourselves free and independent; to make a second declaration, not quite so lengthy as the old one, but it promises life, liberty, and the pursuit of happiness. Our forefathers pledged their lives and fortunes and sacred honors. We, too, will pledge our honor and our life, but our fortunes have gone for rum. Poor though we drunkards are, and miserable even in the gutter, we will pledge our lives to maintain sobriety."

Large numbers of intemperate men were at once induced to sign the pledge. Wives and parents brought their lost and hopeless ones to the meetings, as the relatives of the sick brought their diseased and afflicted to the Saviour to be healed; and by the 1st of October the

Boston Washington Society, which was almost at once formed, had sent out two hundred and seventeen delegates to one hundred and sixty towns, in five different States, on errands of love.

Learning that the General Association of Congregational Ministers of Connecticut were to meet in New Haven in June, and that there was no small unbelief in that quarter, I invited Capt. Wm. A. Wisdom and four others, all reformed men, to accompany me thither, promising them an opportunity to tell their tale. We were received respectfully, but manifestly with the feeling that there was a great distance between them, a highly educated and professedly sacred class, and men, for the most part uneducated, and from the grogshop and the gutter. But such was the humility and meekness of Capt. Wisdom, such his fulness of confession, sense of unworthiness, gratitude for reform, and desire of the prayers of the ministers and churches, that he and his brethren might be kept from falling, that the entire body were overcome, and all were ready to exclaim: "It is the Lord's doing, and it is marvellous in our eyes."

The citizens of New Haven and vicinity at once sympathized with them, and crowded meetings were held for several evenings. Many miserable drunkards came forward, signed the pledge, and at once became blessings to their families. A Washington Society was organized on the 29th of June. Nearly all the officers had been intemperate men. The whole number reformed in that season, was one hundred and fifty, and most of them heads of families, and hopeless cases. Five able-bodied men, who had spent days and nights in the almshouse in deep degradation and misery, came forth to respectability and hope. Two of them had been educated merchants, and were well connected. In gratitude for what they had experienced, numbers left their home and went forth to save the miserable and the perishing abroad. In twenty out of twenty-two towns in the county they proclaimed deliverance from the rum power with great success. In less than a year they had held in New Haven alone sixty public meetings and obtained 1647 signatures to the pledge. Everything conspired to hold these miserable men and their families in bondage; but the power of the reformation was irresistible. And as they yielded, their whole soul and body were filled with new joys, and the community around them united in thanks to God; and, in war with vice and degradation, took courage.

When the first meetings in New York were past, I was induced to go to Baltimore, to attend, on the 5th of April, 1841, the first anniversary of the Washington Temperance Society, and there saw ONE THOUSAND men stand in a line as reformed men, and moved in procession with thousands more about the city. It was a most interesting spectacle as their wives and children stood on the sidewalks, many of them weeping for joy as they beheld their husbands and sons marching onward in sobriety and moral dignity. In proof of the genuineness of the work, it was ascertained that the whiskey inspections for the city were reduced in six months 40,582 gallons, a decrease of twenty-five per cent., and that great peace and quietness everywhere prevailed.

These extraordinary movements at Baltimore and elsewhere, among our drunken population, filled all hearts with joy, at our sixth Anniversary, and at the third National Convention at Saratoga Springs. In the Annual Report, which I presented in May, I condensed as far as possible the wonderful events which had transpired, and which will be contemplated when these generations have passed away as almost incredible; but never to be surrendered as wild enthusiasm and profitless hallucination. Never, probably, was there a large body of men, of high intelligence and business character, so melted into gratitude, joy and love, as were the attendants on that National Convention at Saratoga Springs in the month of August, at the relation of their experience by several of the reformed, and the relation of numerous, most affecting, incidents by others. As chairman of the Business Committee, I found no difficulty in framing suitable resolutions for the occasion; and where there was such a prevalence of love and gratitude, the presiding officer had no occasion for force to control the meeting. It was a sort of millennium to thousands who had hoped and prayed that sin and sorrow from intoxicating drinks might be done away. "Never before," said a venerable member, "did 560 men assemble, and continue days as a deliberative body, without one unkind look or action."

As the Convention dissolved, the reformed men scattered in all directions in their work of mercy; and wherever they went, they met with a cordial welcome, and became instrumental in reclaiming multitudes who were bound in the drunkards' chain. Messrs. Pollard and Wright went through Central New York, New Jersey and Pennsylvania, and took 22,300 names to the pledge. Mr. Hawkins and companions went through New England. Vickars and Small from Baltimore set their faces to the West, first lighting on Pittsburg, where over 10,000 took the pledge. Through the summer and autumn, the whole country was in a blaze. In the State of Ohio 60,000 were reported as having signed the pledge, and many of them hopeless drunkards. In Kentucky, 30,000; in Richmond, Va., 1,000; in Petersburg, 1,000; in Columbia Co., N. Y., including Hudson, 18,000; in Pennsylvania, 29,000; at Portsmouth, N. H., 30,000, of whom 100 were confirmed drunkards; in Springfield, Mass., 1,100. In New York the Parent Washington Society, in a year, consisted of 4,000 members, with twenty-two auxiliaries, with 16,000 members. In Syracuse, 5,000; one society of reformed men alone of 400. In Illinois more than 10,000; at St. Louis, 7,500. All classes gave their names to the pledge to countenance the work, but there was good reason to believe that 150,000 decidedly intemperate men took the pledge and abandoned their cups.

How far the subjects of this work remained steadfast, the judgment only will reveal. For a time, they held to it with wonderful tenacity. If they violated it, they hastened to a renewal. Their character and condition were wonderfully improved. From the deepest degradation, poverty and shame, they came, at once, to respectability and comfort. Men, who were tottering over the drunkard's grave, were, at once, strengthened in their physical organization. Men, who would make their bed with the swine, who would lie and steal, and be the vilest of the vile, were seen well-dressed and taking a place among the respectable and good. Homes that had been abandoned, were sought out and loved. Families neglected, were again provided for. Husbands and wives that had long been separated, were again united; and parties divorced for intemperance, were remarried. Two reformed men became Mayors of cities; one, Governor of his State; several, members of Congress. Many who had been ejected from Christian churches for their intemperance, were, on repentance, restored. One in New Haven, Conn., Mr. Abel Bishop, who for three years had drank a quart of rum a day, who had suffered his family to fall into the deepest want, and who himself had often raved in horrid delirium, imagining that men were about him to flay him alive, who saw them begin to cut his flesh with saws, and pull off his skin in strings, and hang them on wires; who often thought his breast was full of animals to be drawn out, one after another, amid horrid faintness, was so restored, as to become a blessing to his family, a member of his church, and a public advocate throughout the State.

Judge Smith, of Medina, Ohio, an able jurist, had been so debased that his wife had taken advantage of the law and obtained a divorce, after which he sunk to deepest depths. On the coming of the reformed men, he nerved his arm and took the pledge. He soon came up to his former condition, sought out his wife, and, in presence of thousands, was remarried, and then became a public advocate of the cause. In Massachusetts, Joseph J. Johnson; in Maine, Joseph Hayes; in New York, George Haydock, were among the most degraded and debased of men, who all became most signal instances of moral power, extensively reclaiming inveterate drunkards and breaking up most profitable liquor establishments. Mr. Johnson, for a time, regenerated Mobile and caused New Orleans to shake to its centre.

Ministers and churches everywhere saw that the great barrier between them and a large population, who never came to the house of God, was broken down, and rejoiced in it. Said the Rev. Dr. Joel Parker, in a sermon before the New York Presbytery:

> The great change that has been produced within the last few months in the reforming of poor, lost inebriates, is a wonderful phenomenon. The church had passed them by as hopeless. God raised up reformers from among themselves, and now the multiplied and moving tales of the woes and sins, and recoveries of poor, lost drunkards, are telling with amazing power upon hearts that were accounted to be beyond the reach of the Gospel. These reformations are bringing thousands of new subjects under the means of grace. Nor are they merely brought to listen while under a powerful impulse of self-improvement. Good influences are upon them as the nand upon the helm and the breeze upon the sail of a ship under a good headway, to guide and propel it into a good harbor. Nor is their conversion to God the chief good to be hoped for from this remarkable movement. The greater part of them have families, wives and children, brought out of degrading poverty, to hold a place in the sanctuary, in circumstances to awaken gratitude to the Giver of their mercies.

The results of this mighty movement to many individuals were not as happy as they would have been, had the States stepped in and closed the dram shops. The reformed men, influenced by love and kind feelings, were hostile to law in the suppression of the traffic, believing they could, in due time, induce the liquor dealers to abandon their business; but, alas! the venders were too shrewd and hardened to be drawn away from their spoils. The reformed, being often without self-control, decision of character, and moral and religious principle, the old appetite revived; and, ere long, not a few went back to their old habits; yet many became not only confirmed in sobriety but eminent in piety, and died in the triumphs of Christian faith. With some such, I was intimately acquainted till they departed to sing, not only the praises of temperance, but of redeeming love, in glory.

With none had I greater intimacy and for none a higher regard than John H. W. Hawkins. He was surely a remarkable man, most devoted to the last, to his work of reforming and saving inebriates. This was his great concern wherever he went, and, as has been truly said, "His wonderful success in inspiring the victims of intemperance with hope and a belief in the possibility of their reform, and in leading them to pronounce the words I WILL, can be attested by hundreds of living and grateful men."—*Dr. Jewett.* As a man of industry, few equalled him. He never asked for rest. He ever felt that he must be about his Master's business. In eighteen years, he had travelled two hundred thousand miles and delivered over five thousand addresses. Though a Washingtonian, he was a strong prohibitionist; clear in his views of the enormity of the traffic and the wickedness of Legislatures in licensing it. He died in Pennsylvania, August 28, 1858, aged 60. At his death, many tributes were paid to his memory, but none more beautiful than one by Wm. H. Burleigh, not only a true poet, but himself one of the most eminent temperance lecturers:

Shall we not drop a tributary tear,
Oh, champion of the fallen! on thy bier?
Not for thy sake, for thou hast found thy rest
Among the many mansions of the blessed,
Where pours no fiery desolating flood
Swollen with tears, incarnadined with blood;
Nor ribald song, nor drunkard's jest profane,
Nor horrid oath shall vex thine ear again!

Oh, who thy perfect blessedness can tell,
As lauds and hallelujahs round thee swell,
While angel hands sweep over quivering wires,
To wake the music of a thousand lyres,
And angel voices tuned in sweet accord,
Welcome thee home, thrice blessed of the Lord.

Nay, not for thee, thou habitant of heaven,
But for the wine-enthralled our tears are given.
Thou art not dead! for still thy name shall be
Heard in the songs of those thou hast made free.
The wife, whose husband thou didst toil to save,
Not vainly from the drunkard's yawning grave,
Shall teach her little ones, in coming days,
To tell thy story and to lisp thy praise.
The child, redeemed from all the shames that fill
A rum-cursed house from woes that blight and kill,
Lisping thy name, shall link it, morn and even,
With the sweet prayers that tremble up to Heaven.

In his daughter Hannah, the instrument, when twelve years old, of his reformation, I ever took a deep interest; and, for the benefit of the young, wrote and published a small memoir of her. HANNAH HAWKINS, or The Reformed Drunkard's Daughter, has passed through sixteen editions, and is in most Sabbath-school libraries. Strongly sympathizing with the victims of vice, in the early stage of this work, I also wrote and published "The Pool of Bethesda," or the unfortunate drunkard's call for help, now that the waters are troubled by an angel of mercy, that he may be taken to the pool and not be discouraged and driven away.

My home in Baltimore was with Christian Keener, a warm-hearted and devout member of the Methodist church, who took the deepest interest in all moral reforms. At his own expense he established the Maryland Temperance Herald, and continued it many years with great ability. He was from the first, one of our Executive Committee. Whether at home or abroad, in church or legislative meetings; among the aged, or in Sabbath-schools and Cold Water armies, his voice and heart were for perfect temperance, the reform of all inebriates, and, above all, the prevention of drunkenness, as, in his view, infinitely preferable to cure. When he died, temperance in Maryland lost its strong supporter; and many an individual a precious friend.

CHAPTER VII.

Change in our Committee—Dr. Sewall's Plates of the Stomach—Excitement of Thomas F. Marshall—Signs the Pledge—Speech of G. N. Briggs—Visit Washington—Great Meeting—Procure Messrs. M. and B. for our Anniversary—Great Meetings in New York—Soirée at Centre Market—Sixth Anniversary—Mr. Marshall's Speeches—Duel—Depraved Morals of Reformed—T. B. Segur on Sabbath-schools—Croton Water—Seamen—Sons of Temperance—Issues of the Press.

On the 18th of January, 1842, Mr. Delavan, being compelled to go to Cuba with his invalid son, resigned his office as Chairman of the Executive Committee of the American Temperance Union. His extraordinary liberality, his uncommon zeal and devotedness to the cause, his ability to reach the higher classes, to set great wheels in motion and unexpectedly effect great results, caused his resignation to fill me with fearful apprehensions. Deeply sympathizing with him in his expected affliction, I bade him adieu. The Committee were fortunate in inducing the Hon. Theodore Frelinghuysen, Chancellor of the N. Y. University, who, for years, had been a tower of strength, to take his place; he promising to give as much of his time and counsel as his other occupations would permit.

About the same time, my friend and fellow laborer (though differing a little on the pledge), Robert M. Hartley, resigned the office of Secretary of the New York City Temperance Society, having, in thirteen years, been active in forming 174 auxiliaries, calling 1,400 temperance meetings, and obtaining 179,624 pledges. From this he passed to the Secretaryship of the N. Y. Association for the Relief of the Poor, where, by his efficient labors, he has drawn upon him the blessing of many thousands ready to perish.

At Washington, much excitement was produced at this time by a delineation of the effects of Alcohol on the human stomach, by Dr. Thomas Sewall, in a series of drawings:

1. The human stomach in a state of health.
2. The inner surface of the stomach of the temperate drinker of intoxicating wine or other alcoholic drinks.
3. The confirmed drunkard's stomach.
4. The drunkard's stomach in an ulcerous state.
5. ———————— after a debauch.
6. ———————— in a cancerous state.
7. ———————— after death by delirium tremens.

These drawings were taken with great care, by Dr. Sewall, after dissections; and were first exhibited in Washington, with a lecture upon the pathology of drunkenness, before an assembly of three thousand. The reformed men of the city, thankful for their deliverance, and feeling deeply for others, yet victims to the cup, held, nightly, public meetings, which were often attended and addressed by members of Congress. Of those, one, a highly talented gentleman, Hon. Thos. F. Marshall, of Kentucky, nephew to the distinguished Chief Justice, was fearfully awakened to his own condition, as on the very brink of ruin, while admonishing others. Entering the House, on the evening of January 7, 1842, he found himself nervously affected to a degree that alarmed him, as the sensation was accompanied by a raging thirst for strong drink. Terrified at his condition, he called for Mr. Briggs, of Massachusetts, to bring him a pledge, that he might at once sign it and place himself in a condition of safety. Mr. Briggs came with a pledge, which he signed on the spot. But he said he must go to the temperance meeting, make a public confession, and put himself beyond the power of temptation. Mr. Briggs and others accompanied him. The meeting was at the Medical College. "I was present," said Dr. Sewall, in a letter shortly to me, "and saw him sign the pledge of total abstinence, after which he made a most touching speech. Several other members followed his example. Mr. Marshall's step has astonished Congress. There is no man who compares with him in debate." The National Intelligencer, the next morning, spoke of the occurrence as one of the most interesting which ever took place in Washington. Mr. Briggs closed the meeting by saying: "From this day a new era in the cause of temperance may be dated. The high and commanding talents of his friend, would give it a new impulse. His name had gone over the country once; and it would go over it again, leaving a trail of light behind. He rejoiced that he had seen this night and congratulated the Society on the happy event which he had witnessed in that hall."

I, at once, in the name of the American Temperance Union, sent Mr. Marshall my congratulations; and, in reply, he said: "The great cause in which you are engaged and in which we will be co-workers, as far as I can aid you, has my most ardent wishes." Under the powerful impression made, measures were immediately taken to reorganize the Congressional Temperance Society, and, if possible, get the whole body to take the pledge. A meeting of members friendly to the object was called on the 9th, in the Capitol, and the Society was reorganized, under the presidency of the Hon. Mr. Briggs, and a day appointed for a large public meeting in the Hall of Representatives. Believing that the presence of Mr. Marshall, the most eloquent man in Congress, would, under these circumstances give great interest to our May anniversary, I at once resolved on going to Washington, to attend the great meeting, form an acquaintance with him, and induce him, if possible, to come to New York. I was soon in his room, and on terms of intimacy and friendship with him. The meeting came off on the 25th; the Hall was crowded to excess, in expectation of a speech from Mr. Marshall. Mr. Briggs presided. It was a day of triumph and joy with him. He gave an account of the old Congressional Society, which was formed on the ardent spirit pledge, and which, with the pledge in one hand, and a bottle of champagne in the other, had a name to live, but was guilty of suicidal acts. A temperance society had perished by intemperance. In compliment to my office, I was put forward to make the first speech after the President's address; in which I gave a summary of the present extraordinary movement and its results, so far as I had been able to collect them. My statements were confirmed by William K. Mitchell, of Baltimore, who was President of the Washington Society of reformed men, and the first who signed the pledge. The meeting was then addressed by Hon. Mr. Riggs, of New York; Mr. Fillmore, of New Jersey; Mr. Gilmer, of Virginia; Mr. Burnell, of Massachusetts; Mr. Giddings, of Ohio; lastly by Mr. Marshall, who spoke more than an hour, in a strain of unsurpassed eloquence. He was often received with bursts of applause.*

* Mr. Marshall's appreciation of the pledge he had taken:—Sir, the pledge I have taken renders me secure forever from a fate inevitably following habits like mine; a fate more terrible than death. That pledge, though confined to myself alone, and with reference only to its effect upon me, my mind, my heart, my body, I would not exchange for all earth holds of brightest and of best. No, no, Sir; let the banner of this temperance cause go forward or backward; let the world be rescued from its degrading and ruinous bondage to alcohol or not; I, for one, shall never, never repent what I have done. I have often said this, and I feel it every moment of my existence, waking or sleeping. Sir, I would not exchange the physical sensations, the mere sense of animal being, which belongs to a man, who totally refrains from all that can intoxicate his brain or derange his nervous structure—the elasticity, with which he

Having secured his attendance with Mr. Briggs at our anniversary, I set my face homeward, to record the interesting events I had witnessed, in the Journal, and prepare for the Anniversary.

On the 22d of February, the birth-day of Washington, a grand Festival was held, by the reformed men of our city, at Centre Market Hall, a floor of 275 feet by 40, whose appropriate decorations, crowds of people, mutual congratulations, supplies of table, and eloquence of orators, had not before been known amongst us. Here the rescued men met with their happy families, and received the congratulations of some of our first citizens. And a month later, on the 29th of March, their Anniversary, they moved in procession, 3,000 in number, with four teetotal fire com-

bounds from his couch in the morning—the sweet repose it yields him at night—the feeling, with which he drinks in through his clear eyes, the beauty and the grandeur of surrounding nature; I say, Sir, I would not exchange my conscious being as a strictly temperate man—the sense of renovated youth—the glad play, with which my pulses now beat healthful music—the bounding vivacity, with which the life-blood courses its exulting way through every fibre of my frame—the communion high, which my healthful ear and eye now hold with all the gorgeous universe of God—the splendors of the morning, the softness of the evening sky—the bloom, the beauty, the verdure of earth, the music of the air and the waters—with all the grand associations of external nature, reopened to the first avenues of sense;—no, Sir, though poverty dogged me—though scorn pointed its slow fingers at me, as I passed—though want and destitution, and every element of earthly misery, save only crime, met my waking eye from day to day; not for the brightest and noblest wreath that ever encircled a statesman's brow—not if some angel, commissioned by heaven, or some demon, rather, sent fresh from hell, to test the resisting strength of virtuous resolution, should tempt me, both with all the wealth, and all the honors, which a world can bestow; not for all that time or earth can give, would I cast from me this precious pledge of a liberated mind, this talisman against temptation; and plunge again into the dangers and the terrors which once beset my path. So help me heaven, Sir, as I would spurn beneath my very feet all the gifts the universe could offer, and live and die as I am, poor, but sober.

panies, and more than sixty splendid banners, and several bands of music, from Hudson Square to the Park, and up Broadway to Washington Square, where they were dismissed, to attend a large meeting in the Broadway Tabernacle in the evening. Indeed, temperance was now the all-engrossing topic. Fifty-two public meetings, many in large and well-lighted halls, were regularly held, and as many as 1,200 pledges were taken weekly. The traffic, the drinking, and the drunkenness were much diminished, and there was great joy in the city.

The sixth Anniversary, held in the Broadway Tabernacle, in May, surpassed, in interest, our highest anticipations from the presence of Mr. Briggs and Mr. Marshall. In absence of the President, the Hon. Theodore Frelinghuysen presided. My Report was filled with interesting facts which few other years had presented. From our office we had issued 10,000 Journals, 45,000 Youth's Temperance Advocates, 40,000 Almanacs, 10,000 Hymn Books, numerous tracts and hand-bills; more than 700,000 publications in all. The number of pledges taken this year in the United States, was estimated at half a million. Many details were given of the public sympathy in this movement, especially in the readiness of the Martha Washington Societies to clothe the naked, and sustain the reformed, and in the enthusiasm expressed in numerous and often magnificent processions in cities, towns and villages. All the large distilleries in Philadelphia were reported as stopped; all, or nearly all, in Brooklyn. Breweries were closed; tavern bars taken down. In 1831 seventy-two million gallons of ardent spirits were consumed by twelve millions of people; but, in 1840, only forty-three million gallons, by seventeen millions of people; such had been the operations of temperance.

Mr. Briggs did not arrive at the first meeting on Anniversary evening, but Mr. Marshall poured forth, before an immense and highly intellectual audience, such strains of eloquence as had not before been heard in our city. His speech was fully reported in the Journal, and now stands before the world, as unsurpassed for interesting and effective oratory. For several days these two gentlemen remained, addressing, every afternoon or evening, some public meeting. At one Lecture, they were preceded by Dr. Nott, of Union College, who gave an explanation of Dr. Thomas Sewall's plates of the human stomach under the ravages of Alcohol. Another meeting was devoted to the Washingtonians. Another, filling to overflowing the Tabernacle, to the Firemen. Another, to ladies.

These effective speakers were earnestly solicited to go to Boston and other cities, but his duties in Congress called Mr. Briggs back, while, unfortunately for himself and the cause, Mr. Marshall remained entangled in some political controversies, which resulted in a duel with James Watson Webb; unhappily blasting the good influence of his temperance speeches, and putting an end to farther operations. By some of our clergy, I was made to bear the whole sin in bringing to the city as moral instructors, men who feared not God, and in the violence of passion could shed a brother's blood. I replied, temperance had no concern with duelling, and I was not responsible for it; we only brought forward the testimony of men, who knew in their own experience, the evils of strong drink, and who were willing to raise the warning voice to young men, and to testify to the practicability and blessedness of reform. But I was not readily forgiven.

Over the subsequent history of this gentleman, though often displaying his great talents, humanity wept at this loss of moral power; and all learned, more than ever, the curse of the traffic and drinking usages. And yet this gentleman had much in him, that, at times, drew toward him the religious community. On receiving the thanks of an aged mother, for saving her son, he said:

"I too have a mother, and if she knew a man through whom I have been plucked, as a brand from the burning, how would her prayer go up for him to the throne of God night and day. And she does offer up her blessings to the Most High. She writes in her letters to me, that she considers my reformation as through the direct agency of God himself; and her voice is raised in continual thanksgiving and praise to the Father of mercies. Oh, to be instrumental in doing just such good to others, I do believe, I would quit Congress, the bar, and every thing else, and just turn circuit rider, and preach through the country."

In justice to the temperance cause, and as a warning to temperance lecturers, I would say, that it must have the whole man, or it has no security. From the first I was distressed at the amount of tobacco which Mr. Marshall used, and I often felt and said, no good would come of it. When remonstrated with and warned, he would ever say, it was for his life, and how could he give it up? still he knew he ought to; and yet if he perished, temperance men could be held responsible! Said Colonel S., one of our first citizens: "Mr. M., why don't you give up this extravagant use of tobacco?" "I will," replied Marshall, "if you will give up your wine." But this he could not do; and on went the victim under this excitement to the field of blood. From our proud Anniversary season I turned away in sadness, and many a rich devotee of the weed and wine cup, almost persuaded, turned back and went on to ruin.

Anniversary over, I made an excursion to Boston, where I beheld on the 26th of May an immense Washingtonian procession, and attended a Washington Convention in the Representatives' chamber, in the State House, which sat two days, for the organization of a "Washington Total Abstinence Society." An immense public meeting was held at the Odeon. This Convention adopted moral suasion, in opposition to prohibitory law, as the true and proper basis of action with the traffic. Numerous interesting letters were daily laid upon my table, giving reports of large meetings and great reforms in Charleston, S. C., Cleveland, O., Mobile, Ala., Pittsburg, &c.; also from England, Ireland, the Sandwich Islands, and Missionaries in China. Their publication gave great interest to our Journal.

The celebration of the Fourth of July this year was distinguished for juvenile movements; one of the most beautiful of which was in New Haven, Conn., where six thousand children gathered from all the surrounding towns, beautifully robed, with badges, banners, and music, marched through the principal streets to Hillhouse Avenue and Sachem's Wood, and there, amid appropriate exercises and addresses, the minds of all were forestalled for temperance.

In the summer of 1842, there was an evident depression in the moral state of the reformed; a lack of readiness on their part to acknowledge their dependence on God, no small desecration of the Sabbath, and a painful unwillingness, in not a few professed Christians, to connect the temperance cause, as now seen, with religion; all which, within a few months, had extensively shown itself, and led me to prepare and publish in the National Preacher a sermon, entitled God's Hand in the Reformation of Drunkards. I had reason to believe that it led some of our reformed friends to see to whom they were indebted for their deliverance, and to consecrate themselves to the divine service. But, alas! Satan was let loose. Good men, who had gloried in the work, became alarmed. Said Dr. Edwards, in a public meeting in Massachusetts, "If this mighty movement is destined to go onward, the glory of it must be given, not to men, but to God. He was its author; He has been its continuer; and He must be its finisher. The glory of it does not belong to any man, or body of men. Everything good about it was from him; and let all who attempt to carry it on, in all their ways acknowledge him, and then He shall direct their paths."

My friend, T. B. Segur, Esq., of Dover, N. J., addressed me, in September of 1842, a letter of much feeling, on a juvenile temperance effort in connection with Sunday Schools. He had for some time been most deeply interested in it. Said he:

"I am absent from home almost every Sabbath; sometimes visit several schools the same day; and I love children. No man of my information and ability can love Sunday-schools more. My object is, among other things, to make temperance a branch of Sunday-school teaching and training. The way it is done gives no offence. All denominations, to whom it has been presented, have approved; scruples and objections have vanished like the early dew. Let the plan and manner of carrying it out be fully understood, and such must always be the case, for its principles, purposes, and sympathies, are those of the Bible."

No man in his State was more efficient in the cause of temperance than Mr. Segur. No dramshop or liquor-seller could live in his village. He was a great friend to the Youth's Temperance Advocate.

"The object, dear sir, is worthy of your best efforts. Let its influence be for the healing of the nations. In New Jersey, there are over one hundred and eighty thousand, under twenty years of age; in the State of New York, more than one million two hundred thousand; and in the United States, more than nine millions. What a field for moral and religious effort! How interesting! How promising! Go in and possess it."

In Mr. Segur I had a firm and independent friend. He was ever hopeful when others were desponding; cheerful, when others were depressed; fully confident that the cause was right, and would prevail. When he died, New Jersey lost, in her temperance effort, her greatest support.

On the 14th of October, the vast population of New York and vicinity welcomed the introduction of the Croton

Water, and it was felt to be a great event for temperance. While multitudes of temperance men were in the civil, military, and firemen's processions, numerous societies were out with their banners and badges welcoming the coming guest. "The Croton Ode," written by George P. Morris, Esq., was sung, in front of the Park Fountain, by the New York Sacred Music Society:

"Hail the wanderer from a far land!
Bind her flowing tresses up,
Crown her with a fadeless garland,
And with crystals brim the cup.
From her haunts of deep seclusion
Let intemperance greet her, too,
And the heat of his delusion
Sprinkle with the mountain dew.

Water leaps, as if delighted;
While her conquered foes retire;
Pale contagion flies, affrighted,
With the baffled demon, Fire;
Safety dwells in her dominions,
Health and beauty with her move,
And entwine their circling pinions
In a sisterhood of love." &c.

Samuel Stephens, Esq., President of the Water Commissioners, in his address, viewed it as the greatest help to temperance. Said he:

The more good water that is conveniently supplied, the more temperate will be our people; because we shall now no longer afford the poor apology for mixing brandy and rum with water—that of making it drinkable—and we may hope the temperance cause, with pure Croton Water, and a Croton Banner floating to the breeze, will, on the present system, so successfully carry on the warfare in all future time, as to make it impossible for them to find subjects to fill up that part of their corps which now consists of reformed drunkards."

On the 18th October, I went to Hartford, Ct., and with

others addressed the State Temperance Convention—a body of more than 200 delegates. The report of reformed-drunkards' and cold-water armies was most heart-cheering. Hartford reported six hundred reformed drunkards, and scarce any relapses; Norwich, seventy-two; Fairfield, fifty; Suffield, seventy-five. Sixty-five divisions of the Cold-Water army had been formed, numbering 14,000 children. The Convention united with the Hartford Washington Society and the Catholic Society, and marched from the Centre Church, where they had met, to the front of the State House, where several speeches were made, and resolutions adopted on the Cold-Water-army enterprise; on the Washingtonian movement, and that the sale of intoxicating liquors, to be used as a beverage, ought to be prohibited (for a great change had come over the Washingtonians in this matter) by law. It was a proud day for Connecticut.

The Cold-Water armies which were now formed, much under the labors of my friend, Rev. Charles J. Warren, at this time, were a most interesting portion of the temperance reform. In many towns, they embodied the children of nearly all religious families, and often drew in the children of the poor drunkard; and they laid the foundation of temperance among the youth of both sexes, who, in a short time, would be the controlling power in Church and State. Many a temperance man, in these days, has looked back to his stand in the Cold-Water army of 1842 as the foundation of his temperance, in principle and practice.

Great attention was paid also to the condition of seamen in all our ports. The Mariners' Society in New York had been organized, and interesting meetings were held weekly in the Mariners' Church, in Roosevelt street. Usually, from two to three thousand pledges were there taken in a single year, much to the annoyance of the vile groggeries—the bane of the noble tars. Few meetings did I attend with more pleasure; and, on the Fourth of July, 1840, I had the opportunity and pleasure to deliver, before this Society, an address, entitled THE BOW OF PROMISE, which was printed, and widely circulated among the seamen. This Society still flourishes, under its excellent President, Captain Richardson, and has on its roll-book 43,000 members. The change it was enabled to effect among seamen was great. Out of its operation grew the "Sailor's Home," which became a most influential establishment. Both in England and America, a strenuous effort was made to induce ship-owners to dispense with the spirit ration in merchant vessels, and to lower the premium on ships sailing on temperance principles. In this work, Mr. John Dougal, of Montreal, was long actively and successfully engaged.

A large proportion of the reformed men were in destitute circumstances—a natural result of their intemperance—and so much was the sympathy of the community excited for them, on their signing the pledge, that extensive beneficial societies were established, in which they could find clothing, fuel, food, support in sickness, and burial in death. These were most numerous in Philadelphia. But in New York, one was established among themselves, on the plan of the Rechabites in Great Britain, and called the "Order of the Sons of Temperance." Its avowed object was to shield its members from the evils of intemperance, afford mutual aid in case of sickness, and elevate character. It held its meetings with closed doors, with forms and pass-words. It proposed local, State, and national organization.

It soon manifested an *esprit du corps*, which gathered into it a large portion of the reformed; inasmuch as, on paying a small weekly or quarterly due, they were sure of a useful remittance in case of sickness or death. An imposing initiation gave the order impressiveness, brotherhood, and attachment; and a regalia, a distinction from other temperance men. Soon, divisions and grand divisions, based on total abstinence principles, were found springing up in every quarter. Old temperance societies lost such of their members as were reformed men; and where there was a revival of temperance, young reformed converts were allured hither, often in large proportions. The chief agent was the New York Organ, a paper published by Mr. J. W. Oliver, which obtained a large circulation among them, giving all the details of business, and reports of progress. They also published a spirited and popular address to the friends of temperance throughout the United States. Their pecuniary basis was admirable and worthy of imitation. General S. F. Cary, of Ohio, a gentleman of great eloquence and power, became one of their chief advocates and supporters.

At this time Mr. Delavan gave to the public eight large drawings of Dr. Sewall's, on a grand lithograph, nine times the size of a common stomach. They were extensively taken at ten dollars a set, and hung in public institutions and temperance halls, for the use of public lecturers. He also commenced a preparation of a small set to be placed in every school in the State, confident that no parent would withhold his mite for such an object.

My table had, in the last two years, been furnished with many important documents. "Examination of Bacchus," by John McLean, Professor of the College in Princeton, N. J.; "Bible Temperance," in three discourses, by Joseph Carroll, D. D., Newburg; "Proceedings of the National Convention, 1842," with an address, by General Cocke; "Moral Principle of the Temperance Movement," addressed to the students of Harvard College, by Henry Ware, Jr.; "Pathology of Drunkenness," by Thomas Sewall, M. D., of Washington City, with drawings of the human stomach, as affected by Alcohol; "The Inquirer," devoted to free discussions of the kind of wine to be used at the Lord's Supper, by E. C. Delavan; "Reminiscences of a Ruined Generation," by Rev. Daniel A. Clark; "The New Impulse, or Hawkins and Reform;" "A View of the Excise Law of the State of New York," by Gerrit Smith; "The Respondent," an answer to the Inquirer of E. C. Delavan; "The Cold Water Army," by Rev. J. C. Warren; "Address to the Merchants' Temperance Society of New York," by Hon. Theodore Frelinghuysen; "An Historical, Scientific, and Practical Enquiry on Milk," showing its destructive nature, when derived from feed in the distilleries, by R. M. Hartley, Secretary of the New York City Temperance Society; "Six Nights with the Washingtonians," a series of original tales, by T. S. Arthur; "Connection between Intemperance and Religion," an address before the Home Temperance Society, Philadelphia, by Rev. Albert Barnes; "The Temperance Lecturer, or Investigations in the Poor Houses and Jails of the State of New York," by Samuel Chipman; "Importance of Female Influence," by S. J. Grosvenor; and several Hymn and Song Books; all showing that the cause of temperance had a strong hold of the public mind.

CHAPTER VIII.

Letters to Friends Abroad—Pierpont's Song of the Reformed—Incidents in the Work—City Traffic—Alexander Welsh—Firemen—Merchants' Society—Mr. Frelinghuysen's address—Pennsylvania State Society—Toast and Water Dinner—Barnes' Sermon—Liberal Donations—Foreign Correspondence—Seventh Anniversary, A. T. U.—Change of Presidency—Hon. G. Catlin's Speech—Hutchinson Family Introduced to New York—Inquirer, Sacramental Controversy—Controversy with Dr. Hun on Stomach Plates—High Appreciation of Plates—Feeling of Drunkards—Missionary Reports.

So impressed were they with the magnitude and blessedness of this work, that I was directed by our Executive Committee, to draft a full account of it and send it, as from the Committee to the friends of temperance in England, Scotland and Ireland, that they might sympathize with us, and have no misapprehensions. The statement was well received and widely circulated.

Ever ready with his pen to aid the good work, the Rev. John Pierpont, of Boston, indited a spirited song for the reformed:

A SONG.

We come, we come! that have been held
  In burning chains so long;
We're up! and on we come,
  Full fifty thousand strong.
The chains were snapp'd, that held us round
  The wine vat and the still—
Snapped by a blow—nay, by a word,
  That mighty word—I WILL.

We come from Belial's palaces,
The tippling shop and bar;
And as we march, those gates of hell
Feel their foundation jar.
The very ground that oft has held
All night our throbbing head
Knows that we're up, no more to fall,
And trembles at our tread.

From dirty den, from gutter foul,
From watch house and from prison,
Where they, who gave a poisonous glass,
Had thrown us, have we risen;
From garret high, have hurried down,
From cellar cold and damp,
Come up, till alley, lane and street,
Echo our earthquake tramp.

To God be thanks, who pours us out
Cold water from the hills,
In crystal springs and bubbling brooks,
In lakes and sparkling rills;
From there to quench our thirst we come,
With freemen's shout and song,
A host, already numbering more
Than fifty thousand strong.

Many incidents in that great Washingtonian reform come to my recollection, which should not be unknown to those who come after us. One was a great diminution in hospitals in cases of insanity from intemperance. Another was a great diminution of the common accidents of life from drinking. Another was diminution of crime. Judge Humphrey, of Ohio, said it was too palpable to escape observation; and it was publicly spoken of by the Recorder of the city of New York. In the State prison at Charlestown there was, in 1842, a diminution of 46 commitments. Of 192 discharged convicts, 148 had taken the pledge, and of these, only three were ever recommitted. Another was, of pauperism and family destitution. Many children of drunkards, who were in alms-houses, were taken away by their reformed parents, a thing never before known. Another was, that, in revivals of religion, reformed men were apt to become the first subjects of the work. In a letter to me, from Lewiston, Pa., in February, 1843, the Rev. Thomas P. Hunt said:

> I have been from home since the 6th of November, 1842; I have lectured and preached upwards of two hundred times. The blessing of God seemed to follow my temperance lectures, and a glorious revival of religion now exists in every place where I have lectured since I left home. Many, very many of reformed men, are now converted. In one place, more than one hundred and fifty, many of them hard cases, now belong to different churches. I do not know the number that profess conversion in all the places, but it is somewhere in the neighborhood of a thousand.

In Lockport, N. Y., where seven hundred and eighteen persons united with the church, the Rev. Dr. Wisner said:

> As an event which prepared the way, I would mention the wonderful temperance reform which has been in progress for some time past, under the direction of the Washingtonians, as they are called. Many of this class of our citizens, having broken off from a life of profligacy, are peculiarly susceptible to the influence of divine truth; and a large number of them have opened the door of their hearts to admit the Saviour as a permanent guest.

The free and frank confessions of these men, of the connection between their habits of drink and infidelity, were often very impressive. Said one:

> There are infidels plenty made in public houses, and it must be so, for they are driven to it to reconcile themselves to their wicked practices. Not nine out of ten can meet a sick bed and a dying hour with their principles. I know more of infidelity than they do, and have been more determined than they all, never to yield to the truth of divine revelation. Ah! many a time have I sat up an hour together, three parts drunk, to defend Infidelity, and a poor shattered thing I made of it.

Still another mark was, that a great degree of worldly

comfort accrued to their families; and this was of no short continuance. Said Gov. Baldwin, in his address to the Legislature of Connecticut, in 1844:

In our own State it is gratifying to know that this glorious reformation, though retarded perhaps by legislation, still maintains its onward progress. Its fruits are everywhere apparent. Within the past year, poverty and crime have sensibly diminished. The tears of the broken-hearted have been dried up; and joy and gladness are diffused through many a family circle to which they had long been strangers.

Few knew what was the character of the rum traffic in our city before that time, nor what it is now. Its internal horrors, and the part our leading citizens had in it, were fully revealed in the conversion of Alexander Welsh, who had been considered the head of rumsellers, and who, when converted, became one of the most substantial of the reformed men. I knew him well, and was on terms of great intimacy with him. The following was the account he gave of himself, in a public meeting, March 22, 1842:

"I am called 'King of the Rumsellers' (and I suppose I am), in the way of ridicule. I stand before you, one of an unfortunate, or fortunate, class of reformed drunkards. I have been nine months on the list, and I have had a new life of it. I never attended a temperance meeting in all my life. I said it was all a humbug. I was converted at home, in a rumshop where more rum has been sold than in any place in New York. I was sitting there, at twelve o'clock at night, with friends—I called them friends—drinking friends. I had drank, that day, twenty-five glasses. Few know what is going on in New York after twelve o'clock at night; and no man could tell the extent of his drinking. It is only when a man has drank twelve glasses, that he begins to get dry. I was asked to drink, that night; but I had made up my mind to drink no more. But I would not come out then; for I kept a rumshop, and had to ask men to drink rum—but that is a poor business; it will always end in making the rumseller himself a drunkard. I would not drink, and the drinkers began to suspect me, that I had been among the teetotallers. They do not love to have a teetotaller among them. Some have advised me not to go into the rumshops. I do not go much, only when I see a poor fellow there, I go in and say, 'Come, now, this won't do; come and sign the pledge.' I don't want to hurt the rumsellers; but they had better quit, now the cause is going on. I met one to-day, and he said, last night he had a ball at his house, and he took only twenty-seven dollars for liquor, whereas, last year, he took ninety. And, said he, if you want my room for a temperance meeting, you may have it for nothing, and I will light it up. I stuck to my plan. Two months before, I made up my mind to sign the pledge; and I'll tell you how I came to: I was invited among gentlemen of distinction, the Governor, Corporation, Mayor, and four hundred others, to the opening of the New York and Erie Railroad. There is drinking in high places as well as in low. Some are here to-night who were along with us—I see you, gentlemen! Soon after we left the dock, I went to the bar to get some lemonade, but it was all crowded full. When we arrived at Goshen, I went out and got my dinner, and two glasses of water. When I came back to the cars, I saw a dozen of Champagne brought in. I was asked to partake. I said, No. I had not signed the pledge, but I had made up my mind not to drink. Soon a second dozen came, and was drank up; and then a third, and a fourth, and a fifth, all drank by men in high stations and some of your old pledged men, too. Then came the result: one hanging his head out of the car, like a dead calf; another tumbled over on to his neighbor; then settling all manner of subjects, politics, religion, railroads, all mixed up, hurrahs and shouting. I then saw what liquor would do with gentlemen. I made up my mind to sign the pledge."

At the commencement of 1842 there was great excitement among the fire companies of the city. On the 5th of January there was an immense meeting at the church in Chrystie street. I was called to open it with prayer; after which, several spirited speeches were made, when Engine Company No. 2 and Hose Company No. 13 came in under escort of No. 18, and over fifty fine-looking men went up to the table and signed the pledge. They then sang with great spirit the Temperance Firemen's Song:

When, in the night,
The skies grow bright
With the flames of the poor man's dwelling,
The fireman springs
As the Hall bell rings,
The burning district telling.

Hark! the cry, Fire! Fire!
As the flames rise higher,
The gallant firemen fly
At the sleep-dispelling cry,
Fire! Fire! Fire! Fire!
And we'll dash on the water till the flames expire.

Thus, in the height
Of his drunken plight,
If the tippler falls in the gutter,
The fireman kind,
Who the pledge has signed,
Plies him with good Cold Water.
He puts out rum's fire,
Drags him out of the mire,
Nor leaves him there to die,
'Neath the cold and stormy sky;
On rum's curst fire
He pours cold water till the flames expire.
&c., &c., &c.

Five companies had joined in New York and two in Brooklyn.

On the 27th of January, 1842, our chairman, the Hon. Theodore Frelinghuysen delivered an address in the Tabernacle, before the Merchants' Temperance Society. This had been an important institution, and Mr. Frelinghuysen was the man from whom, of all others, they would best take counsel; a man of distinguished talent, of the purest character and warmest benevolence. His address was worthy the occasion. At the close, he said for their encouragement, and the record should not be lost:

The Mayor of our city—it is grateful to honor his name for it—in the late New Year salutation of his fellow citizens, received and entertained them without any intoxicating drinks. The Chief Magistrate of our State, with like examplary regard, also excluded them from his mansion on the last New Year's day; and has since given still more decided proof of his personal approval, by enrolling himself as a member of the total abstinence society. The American Institute, an association of gentlemen of first respectability and usefulness, in their late anniversary supper, with no loss of wit or enjoyment, abstained from all exciting liquors. And very recently, the New England Society of this city celebrated their anniversary in like manner; they banished wine, and introduced the ladies to their dinner party, and who could quarrel at the substitution? It was worthy of their name. It well became the sons of New England, that home of their principles—that cradle of liberty, and spring of an enterprise that never tires—that is now pushing its settlements into the untrodden forests of the West, and will soon plant its institutions, and open the spelling-book and the Bible, beyond the Rocky Mountains. To conclude with another affecting incident: Within the past week two hundred seamen of one national vessel, and three hundred of another—the ship Columbia—with her captain and purser, have associated as members of a total abstinence society. To the merchants this voice from the sea is full of meaning, and, I think, will be heeded and responded to by them. The merchants of this city hold a position of most commanding and extensive influence. New York is the heart of this great community; a throb felt here, creates a pulsation at the remotest extreme of the country. Think, gentlemen, of the precious interests you may preserve and promote. Your example will reach your country merchants—the sailor—every harbor where your commerce floats, and every sea where the flag of your country waves. Let your example be lofty as your position. Let it go forth in its power to reform the tastes and purify the sentiments of the whole earth.

At a New England Cold Water Festival a leading member of the largest Insurance Company in Wall Street, proposed that all intoxicating liquors be removed from the office. The President seconded it, since intoxicating liquors were the cause of more shipwrecks than anything else. And it was accordingly done from that time.

On the 14th of January, 1842, the Pennsylvania State Convention met at Harrisburg; 250 members. On invitation both houses of the Legislature adjourned to take their seats in the Convention as honorary members. They came in a body, headed by the Governor and Heads of Department. The speaking was deeply interesting and important.

On the 4th of March, 1842, a committee of the two

Legislatures of New York and Massachusetts met, and dined together at Springfield. The Hon. Mr. Quincy, President of the day, congratulated them, that as they were drinking their toasts without any wine, they were dining on toast and water.

In July, 1842, Rev. Albert Barnes of Philadelphia, delivered an admirable sermon before the Howard Benevolent Society, on the connection between Temperance and Religion, which I gladly inserted in my August Journal, and which should be a permanent tract of the Tract Societies.

Long was it my heart's desire to reach many minds with our publications, besides regular subscribers and purchasers; and in 1842, I was gratified with a donation from Chester Bulkley, Esq., of Wethersfield, Conn., of one hundred dollars to send two hundred Journals for a year to as many home missionaries; and of the same sum from Orin Day, Esq., of Catskill, to send two hundred to the foreign missionaries of the American Board. The first named gentleman afterward gave one thousand dollars for general purposes, and the latter and his family have continued their donation to 1865. And it has ever since been a great source of happiness to me, when I have met returned missionaries, to have them take me by the hand, and say, "Sir, we know you well. Your monthly Journal has been a source of great pleasure and profit to us." Oh, how little do men of wealth know of their ability, by a small contribution, to dry up the fountains of wickedness, and bless the world.

I was brought by my position much in contact with distant parts of our globe, to see and know what were the ravages of the alcoholic fiend, and what were the commencement of counteracting influences. The following letter reached me from Lodiana, India, dated May 21, 1841:

Rev. J. Marsh:

Dear Sir:—The temperance publications despatched on June 20, 1840, together with your note, arrived here two days ago. The soldiers are greatly delighted with them. The whole troop is now engaged in reading them. Societies are formed in nearly all the large stations. Some number hundreds, and others fifty, twenty, and so on. The soldiers are in advance of the officers. Abstinence from ardent spirits would generally be approved of, but the wine and the beer, that is the stumbling-block. Our prayers are with you; your success is indispensable to our own. You fight on the side of Omnipotence and must prevail.

W. S. Rogers.

From Pontlanck, Borneo, Dr. Pohlman, American Missionary to China, wrote me, November 12, 1841:

As the American Temperance Union is laboring for the whole world, it cannot be unmindful of the vast family of the Chinese. Myriads of eyes are now turned toward China. The Christian sees a train of events which is to eventuate in pouring the light of the Gospel day upon that great portion of the human race. But before that happy period arrives all obstructions must be removed. The greatest of these obstacles will no doubt be found to arise from the use of opium, arrack, wine, &c. Whether there is more intemperance from opium or from liquors of various kinds, it is difficult to ascertain. The disastrous effects of intemperance in a country so thickly peopled as China, must be great beyond all conception. Will you not try, my dear Sir, to enlist the sympathies and prayers of the friends of the cause in America, in behalf of their antipodal brethren.

Yours truly,

Rev. J. Marsh. W. J. Pohlman.

A letter in 1842 from the Secretary of the Temperance Society for foreign residents and visitors at Lahaina, in the Sandwich Islands, said:

The visit of the French frigate in 1839, demanding and enforcing the introduction of French brandy into the Islands, broke the salutary laws of that feeble nation, and let in a fiery flood. On the foreign residents and seamen its burning power has been dreadful. But through counteracting influence the native population have been saved. At Lahaine the king, and all the high chiefs of the nation, with 1,500 people, have united in a total abstinence society, and the king takes pleasure in addressing temperance meetings, which he does with great success.

Frequent letters from Germany assured me that, while the temperance societies at Berlin and other places were strong against all distilled liquors as a poison, wine and all fermented drinks were viewed as nutritious and promotive of health. But these were opposed by Berzelius, the distinguished chemist of Sweden, who vindicated the existence of the intoxicating principle in all vinous and fermented drinks. With him German Professors were in a spirited controversy.

The Temperance Society of the New York College of Surgeons and Physicians held its tenth Anniversary, at the Medical Hall in Crosby Street, February 15, 1843. Two hundred students had attached themselves to it in all. Letters were read from Professor Krauschfield of Berlin, giving an account of the progress of temperance in Germany, and from Baron Berzelius, Professor at Stockholm, containing cheering news from Sweden. Rev. Robert Baird, D. D., gave an interesting account of the progress in the North of Europe. This Society was considered one of the most important of any in the city.

At the seventh anniversary of the American Temperance Union, General Cocke, of Virginia, resigned the presidency, much to our regret. He was a very gentlemanly man of the old school, of great liberality, and much devoted to the cause; but so exceedingly diffident, that he could never be induced to attend an Anniversary meeting, where he should be expected to preside and make a speech. In his resignation he said:

"While life lasts, I shall never cease to work and pray for our common cause; and, I trust, more effectually in a private station than in the high and conspicuous one which all the partiality of friends, and the kindness of coadjutors, never released me from the consciousness of my unfitness for, and which, the progress of our blessed enterprise, under God, has now rendered more disproportionate to my qualifications than ever."

The Hon. Reuben H. Walworth, Chancellor of the State of New York, was elected in his place; and at once consented to fill it, bringing me into frequent conference with him, in which I have long had the greatest satisfaction. Said he, in his letter of acceptance:

"Although my heart has long been engaged in the cause, my official duties, for the last fourteen years, have deprived me of the power to lend much aid to the many efficient men who were devoting their time and their talents, and contributing of their substance, to carry the blessings of temperance to the palaces of princes, and the splendid dwellings of the wealthy of the world, as well as to the more humble habitations of the poor. After duly considering the subject, however, I have concluded to accept the office, and to hold it, at your disposal, until some one shall be elected who is entitled, by his standing in the Union, and his devotion to the cause of temperance, to the honor of being at the head of the Temperance Associations of the United States."

The state of public feeling required that our meeting should be principally addressed by some reformed man; and I was fortunate in procuring one who, from the very lowest debasement, through intemperance, had attained to the elevation of a Member of Congress for Connecticut, the Hon. George S. Catlin. For more than an hour, he spoke with great appropriateness and effect. He was not unwilling to look back to the rock from whence he was hewn, and to the hole of the pit from whence he was digged. In his speech he said:

"To the temperance principle I am indebted for the physical power which has brought me here; to it I owe my life. Had it not been for this, my voice would long since have ceased to be heard among men. I have known long years of cruel bondage to a fearful folly. I have known long years of poverty and of deep suffering. My spirit struggled to throw off its chains, but I saw open no way of escape. The dangers thickened around me. I was ready to fall crushed into the grave. But the world was told there was hope. I heard of the triumphs of temperance in the Monumental City. I signed the pledge, and the struggle for release from the wretched thraldom was at an end: I was myself again."

He was followed by Rev. Dr. Patten, of New York; Rev. John Chambers, of Philadelphia; John H. W. Hawkins, and the venerable Dr. Lyman Beecher, of Cincinnati, who, when at Litchfield, Connecticut, had so caused his battle-axe to ring on the walls of King Alcohol. The Doctor was introduced, amid much applause, as Father Beecher. He looked around upon the immense assembly, and exclaimed, "I am alarmed; for I never expected to have so many children." But he made one of his pithy, characteristic speeches.

Having heard of a family of rare vocalists, who were singing temperance songs, and doing good service to the cause in New Hampshire, I wrote to them, and invited them to come to our Anniversary. They replied, in an unwillingness to appear before a New York audience, being fitted only for the country village. Again pressed, they consented to come, and they gave us such a musical entertainment as had not been heard on any former occasion. Such was the introduction of the HUTCHINSON family to New York. It was never forgotten by them.

Two great events occurred in June, 1843. The Corporation of the City of New York resolved they would provide no intoxicating liquors, at the reception of the President of the United States; and none were provided in Boston, at the magnificent Bunker Hill Celebration. With 300,000 people abroad, no booths or stalls were provided for liquor, and at a dinner for the chief men of the State, not a drop of the bewitching, fascinating poison was visible.

A singular event, attracting the attention of all concerned, was, that the ship John G. Carter, Capt. Barlow, went to sea, for India, with a crew of twenty-eight men, direct, without hauling off and waiting for the men to become sober, as all went on board sober and orderly. The Journal of Commerce remarked upon it, as a rare occurrence. Once, it was necessary to haul off the vessel, so that the men would not get back on shore. "Now," exclaimed Capt. Hart, "we can go on board all sober, ready to meet the storms of the ocean."

While I was devoted to the Journal, Advocate, and tracts, as the great instruments of advancing the cause, Mr. Delavan, unwilling to have its progress obstructed by the Sacramental controversy, commenced, in 1841, a publication called The INQUIRER, which should be devoted to free discussion as to the kind of wine to be used at the Lord's Supper. A reform in the Communion cup, from the highly brandied, drugged, and factitious wines of commerce, containing from forty to fifty per cent. of proof spirit, to the new wine of the Bible, he thought the duty of all Christian Churches, and very important to the temperance cause. He was met in a publication called the RESPONDENT, in which he was charged with a desire to substitute water for wine at the communion, or at least unfermented juice-grape, which could not be obtained, and, if it could be, would not be acknowledged as wine. The controversy, for a long time, caused much warmth of feeling throughout the community. But he was attacked, not only on this subject, but on the truthfulness of the plate No. II. of the drunkard's stomach, by Dr. Hun, Registrar of the Albany Medical College. Dr. Hun denied that there was any effect visible from the use of alcoholic liquors in the stomach of the moderate drinker, and affirmed that there was nothing, therefore, in the moderate use of such liquors which called for condemnation. Mr. Delavan promptly replied, and the controversy was warmly maintained in the Albany papers. But not only the testimonials to the correctness of the plates of scientific men, such as Drs. Mott, Warren, Horner, Green, and others, but the common sense of the community, put down Dr. Hun; for, if the stomach of the drunkard is a ruin, when did that ruin commence—with ten glasses, or with five, or one? With immoderate, or with moderate use? The appreciation of the drawings continued greatly to increase. General Scott desired that they might be furnished to every military post. The Hon. Samuel Young desired they might be hung in every common school in the State. The presidents of the Marine Insurance Companies expressed a wish that they might be put on board of every vessel on the ocean, on our rivers, and on our lakes, counteracting the peculiar temptations to which mariners and emigrants were exposed. Testimonials from lecturers were often of a most affecting character. "It is very frequently the case," said one, "that, after all the facts I could present, or the appeals I could make, seem to fall powerless on the ear of the drunkard, his head up and apparently entirely unmoved, when these *pictures* are shown, his cheeks turn pale, and his head droops." "I have heard," says another, "the unfortunate drunkard exclaim, when looking at them—and particularly at the one representing the stomach after a debauch—*they look as I have often felt!*" Missionaries in foreign lands, at Constantinople and other places, were found to be exhibiting the plates with great effect. "I will drink no more," said a gentleman in that city, after gazing at the pictures, "how can I, when I see the effects of this habit on the constitution, and when I remember I must give account to God for the manner in which I deal with my body, as well as my soul?"

CHAPTER IX.

Fifteenth Anniversary New York State Society—New Jersey—Visit Washington—Reorganization Congressional Society—Gov. Briggs in Massachusetts—Eighth Anniversary A. T. U.—Progress among Seamen, and in Navy—Great indignation against the Traffic—Uselessness of Moral Suasion—Opinion of L. M. Sargent—Dr. Bacon—John B. Gough introduced to New York—Great Popularity—Travel with him through the State—Great Washingtonian Meeting at Boston—Excursion with Mr. Gough, south—Letter of Dr. Beecher.

The Fifteenth Anniversary of the New York State Society was held at Albany, on the 14th February, 1844. One hundred and seventy-nine delegates were present. The indefatigable chairman of its executive committee, Elisha Taylor, had retired; and Philip Phelps was now occupying his place. The Report related chiefly to the effort for the circulation of Dr. Sewall's plates of the stomach. The public meeting was addressed by Rev. S. Pritchett, of Washington county, L. S. Parsons, Esq., of Albany, and myself. I felt peculiarly happy in addressing this venerable society, which had performed an immense amount of labor in sustaining numerous agents, and sending more than fifteen millions of publications abroad; and, now that it was drooping under a debt of $3,000, and feeling unable to sustain longer its State organ, I could not but call loudly on the people, to whom it had saved millions, to come to its support. I said, One thing was certain, the rich cannot keep their money. If they do not give it to us to reform and save the drunkard and suppress intemperance, they must soon give it to support the paupers and criminals which the bloody traffic will make. Like the powerful locomotive, this society once moved forward with mighty energy, and I desired to see it thus moving again. In the language of General Cass, our late minister to France: "If the temperance enterprise could be carried forward to its completion, it would be a monument far prouder than the genius of antiquity had bequeathed to us, and more useful than any which modern wealth or power had erected, for the generations that are to follow us upon the theatre of life."

The society, at this meeting, resolved to discontinue their paper, the "Recorder," and to adopt the "Journal of the A. T. U." as their organ, thus bringing me into closer connection with them, and increasing my responsibilities.

On the 18th of February, I was invited, with Lewis C. Levin, to address, at Trenton, the New Jersey State Temperance Society. The Governor and Legislature, with a large number of citizens, were present. In one hundred and eighty towns, 30,892 had, during the year, signed the pledge; of these, one thousand eight hundred were reformed drunkards. Yet two hundred and seventy-nine taverns and fifteen stores were still engaged in the ruin of the people.

In the month of January, I went to Washington, by request, to aid once more in reorganizing the Congressional Temperance Society. The change of members rendered it very difficult to sustain an organization. Mr. Briggs, the strong tower, had left, and become Governor of Massachusetts. But a meeting of temperance members was collected, and the Hon. Charles Hudson, of Massachusetts, was chosen president. A public meeting was held in the Capitol, February 15, and, as a result, a resolution was adopted in the House, by a large majority, excluding from it all intoxicating liquors.

In Massachusetts, Mr. Briggs at once brought all his

influence to bear upon the cause. The Legislative Temperance Society made him their president. On taking the chair, He hoped, before the session closed, every name would be enrolled under their constitution. For, he said:

"Such a course would be a benefit to the Commonwealth. We shall not do as much for the public good by legislating, as we should by contributing to the temperance reform. If we should lend all our exertions, we might soon say, there is no drunkard in Massachusetts, and there is no wretched family in our State. We could live then with but little legislation. And the citizens of Boston have the power to produce such a state of things. The plan is simple; the easiest on earth. Let no one drink himself, nor offer it to others, and the triumph is complete."

Governor Briggs had power with the people. Simple in his habits, honest and determined in his purpose, and full of pity and compassion for the lost, few could stand before him in their vindication of the wine-cup. Early in life, returning from Court, he found a demand of the stomach for an ordinary drink before dinner. "What is that?" said he. "A demand? It shall not be granted; no, not while I live!" And it never was. In the Saratoga Convention of 1836, as has been related, he took strong ground, though a young man, for the true principle. Wherever he spoke, he made a deep impression. At a meeting in Albany, he related the story of the mysterious woman who appeared before the licensing commissioners, in Pennsylvania, and defied them to give license, if they dared, in view of her husband and sons, who had, all four, filled drunkards' graves; and there was given a unanimous *No!*—a story which has probably been read by more people, and made more impression than any other. At a Presidential dinner, where many drank, and a gentleman next him said, "I do not drink, I only make believe," Mr. Briggs said, "I do not make believe, sir." And he told me himself, that, in all circles, and all companies, he never had the least difficulty in maintaining, openly, the total abstinence principle.

On our eighth Anniversary, in 1844, I was enabled to report much cheering information from seamen in harbor and on the ocean, from sailors on boats and canals, and, more especially, from our gallant navy. At Charleston, South Carolina, over twelve hundred seamen had, during the year, signed the pledge. The captains of British vessels in that port acknowledged, with gratitude, the extraordinary change there was both in officers and crews. On board the revenue-cutter stationed in that harbor, the captain, officers, and entire crew signed the pledge, which only two of the ninety were known to violate. On board of the U. S. frigate Cumberland, under Commander Foote, between two and three hundred had refused their grog. All intoxicating drinks were excluded from the ward-room and steerage. In Boston, not less than one thousand persons connected with the navy signed the pledge. The Brandywine, on a cruise to Bombay and the Indian seas, signalized herself by her temperance spirit. The English residents declared she should change her name, as her officers neither drank brandy nor wine. And in the Pacific, a commodore (Jones) issued an address to all the officers and seamen of the U. S. naval forces in that section, inviting them to abandon entirely the use of all intoxicating drinks, and to unite with him in memorializing Congress to withhold at once the spirit ration from the navy.

It was the constant, terrible exposure of our pledged seamen, as well as reformed men, to destruction, from the licensed and unlicensed dram shops, that was rapidly changing the public sentiment from a reliance on moral suasion, for the removal of temptation, to a demand for law. On this subject no individual expressed himself more truthfully and powerfully than did Lucius M. Sargent, Esq., author of the "Temperance Tales." Said he:

"I believe moral suasion alone, as a means of ridding the world of drunkenness, would prove about as effectual as a bulrush for the stoppage of the Bosphorus. In spite of the expectations of the most sanguine suasionists, unless opposed by some more powerful barriers, this river of rum and ruin will flow on to eternity.

'Rusticus expectat dum transeat amnis, at ille
Labitur et labetur in omne volubilis ævum.'

The Gospel openly recognizes the civil rule. The moral suasionist of modern times, though not always inspired, presumes to accomplish, without the aid of law, more than was achieved in the days of the Apostles, by the power of the law and Gospel combined. The rumseller steals the widow's son, the stay and staff of her old age. The rumseller knows all this; he listens heartlessly to her importunities for mercy; he will not pity; he will not spare, until he has stretched his miserable victim in the grave, and left that lone woman the heart-broken mother of nothing better than a drunkard's corpse."

But the community needed something more than the reasoning and declarations of powerful intellect to array them against the deadly traffic; even the full sufferings, from their own lips, of the deluded victims. They had already heard it from the lips of the reformed men. They had had it in the eloquence of a Marshall, who had stood on the brink of the burning crater, and who had started back affrighted, and raised his warning voice to all young men who would venture near; though his testimony was sadly blighted by the unfortunate duel. Something now was needed, which before had not been granted, though we knew not what; but, in an overruling Providence, it was sent in one who, in the morning of life, had been thrown to the bottom of the crater, and had been surprisingly brought forth to tell an experience which should touch all hearts. I heard of him as addressing crowded school houses at the East, to the surprise of all who could gain admittance; and last as addressing the prisoners in the State Prison of New Hampshire, throwing all the prisoners into tears, and causing almost the entire company to raise their hands in the declaration, that when once at liberty, they would never take into their lips the intoxicating drink. I immediately wrote to Deacon Moses Grant, the devoted friend and patron of temperance in Boston, to find him, and bring him to our Anniversary, that we might hear him. He did so; and in the afternoon of the day, he stood before me, with JOHN B. GOUGH. I could scarce give credit to reports that he, a still, quiet, unimpassioned man, had a power of eloquence to move millions. But the evening came; the Broadway Tabernacle was filled, as usual on those occasions, to its utmost capacity, when, after the reading of the Report, and a lengthy and able speech by the Rev. Leonard Bacon, D. D., of New Haven, Ct., highly satisfactory, the young orator was introduced. In a simplicity and modesty promising nothing, in less than three minutes he struck a chord in every heart, and drew tears from many an eye. Said he:

"God forbid that I should boast of my degradation! Oh, there is a dark spot upon my past life; and if, by any efforts of mine in the temperance cause, I can wipe it out, I shall feel that I have attained the height of my ambition. A bright star of hope now gleams upon my pathway, and the dark pall which has hung over my existence for a few past years is looped up, and I can see in the distance the gleaming of that bright star; and I thank God who has plucked a brand from the burning, and that I am deemed worthy to raise my voice in this cause, which I love."

His relations, showing the hardening influence of the traffic, first in the case of the lady, a maniac in the Worcester Insane Hospital, whose reason reeled as the rumseller asked her, if he should say to her father, that she had requested him to sell him no more rum;—of the poor woman, once in affluence, but now sadly reduced, husband and two sons wasting their all in a tavern, who on the terrible death of one of her boys petitioned the rumseller to spare the rest, but he rolled up the petition into matches to light cigars with, as father and son came in for their drink, and then boasted that he had made the husband and son burn up the pious petition of the old woman;—but more of the poor widow in Oxford, Mass., whose son Frederic returned from a long prodigal absence, having signed the pledge, but was induced by the heartless rumseller to drink before going home, and in the morning was found dead in the rumseller's barn—the rumseller helping to carry him to his mother on a board, when the mother cursed him as the murderer of her son. He acknowledged he had given him the liquor, but did not know it was her son. She told him he did; "and it was wrong," she said, "but I cursed him; I did it. Heaven forgive him and me!"

This remarkable young man, remarkable for a natural eloquence, seldom surpassed, came from England with a stern farmer when he was twelve; but, at fifteen, he left the farm for a more congenial employment in the city, where he labored at the book-binding business to support himself and his poor mother and sister, all suffering the most cruel privations; but soon he fell into the debasing habits of a drunkard, wandering about to gain his living, now by a little work, and now by singing songs, and performing at low theatres, till he was reached by a kind friend in Worcester, Mass., who induced him to sign the pledge, and then to attend temperance meetings, and relate his sad story. In New York he remained a few evenings, filling every house where he would speak. I felt that such an instrument of rousing the public mind should not be lost; and I made arrangements with him to go through the State of New York, and speak with me in all the principal towns and cities.

In the mean time we went together to Boston, to attend on the 28th of May a vast Washingtonian encampment on the Common. On the steamer, Mr. Gough made an address, for which he was well rewarded by the numerous passengers. On the Common by eleven o'clock from 20 to 30,000 were gathered from all parts of the State; 9,500 came by the Eastern Railroad. At twelve, an immense procession of military and temperance societies started from the State House—Governor Briggs leading the way in a barouche, with four white horses—passing down the Mall, through two long rows of beautiful children, under direction of Deacon Grant, and around the principal streets, magnificently decorated with flags and banners, and lined with crowds of spectators, who, with joyful voices and waving handkerchiefs, cheered us. Riding with the Governor, W. K. Mitchell and Mr. Gough, I had a fine opportunity of seeing the whole. Arriving at the Common, the Governor, from the stand, made an appropriate address. "The cause," he said, "is a glorious one; one which was near his heart, and it should have his entire influence and strength as long as Heaven preserved his life. He was glad to state from that platform, and on that day, that the Chief Magistrates of six States of the Union were pledged teetotalers, who would give all their influence in favor of the cause." The Hutchinsons sung some of their happiest songs. The Banks were closed. Most business was suspended, and in the evening an immense meeting was held in the Tremont Temple.

On the 24th of June, I commenced my tour, with Mr. Gough, through the State of New York. Announcement had been made of every meeting; and, as high expectations had been raised, we found every place of assemblage entirely full. About thirty meetings were before us—first, at Hudson; next, at Albany. Mr. Gough, after a short introduction by myself, gave full proof of his ability to sustain himself. At Schenectady, President Nott received us most kindly, at the College; and released the students from their evening studies, that they might hear the young orator, who admirably adapted himself to such an audience. Anxious to be at the Auburn State Prison on the Sabbath, we hastened on to that important post. Eight hundred prisoners stood before us, for the most part, the victims of rum. After prayer and singing, Mr. Gough addressed them for an hour. Few were unmoved; many wept freely, as he told them all the evil they did, and under what influences they had conducted; and when asked for an expression of their determination to drink no more rum, a forest of hands was raised. Two pulpits were opened to us in the day and evening; and on the next morning, at ten o'clock, the laboring classes, and the *polloi*, gathered in front of the Exchange, where other speaking, save that required by the sacredness of the Sabbath, was freely indulged in. At Geneva, Palmyra, and Canandaigua, the people gave themselves up to the occasion, and expressed great satisfaction. Rochester claimed, and had us, on the Fourth of July—the glorious day of Independence. In lieu of military display, we had, on the public square, a monster temperance meeting, which we addressed as the occasion required; and, in the evening, the large Methodist Church was entirely full, and the same was true, the succeeding evening, of the Presbyterian. The minister came forward, with the acknowledgment that he had never signed the pledge; but now he was ready to do it, and did so, several following his example. Geneseo and Mount Morris gave us good audiences; and on our return to Rochester, we had the largest and most enthusiastic meeting we had had since we left home. At Batavia, four hundred citizens had just petitioned the authorities not to sign a license, and they were determined so to do. Speaking to them was pleasant. Niagara Falls and Lockport next had our attention.

At the former, we saw much wine-drinking; and here, Mr. Gough learned one simile, which he ever after used with power, of the moderate drinker commencing moderately, carelessly, and playfully; but, as he advanced, cries reached him from the shore; cries for help rose up in the boat; but on he pushed, with terrible fury, till he went over, and knew no more. Buffalo threw open its largest buildings to us, and gave us deeply interested audiences. A general meeting of children, on Saturday afternoon, foreboded the attendance we should have of parents the next day. A large ladies' meeting was held in the afternoon of Monday, succeeded by a great crowd, at Dr. Lord's Church, in the evening. The people of Buffalo seemed determined on an exterminating war.

Oswego and Syracuse, Utica, and Rome, all gave us a good hearing on our way back. Saratoga Springs was a world in miniature; and most fashionable people, from all quarters, rushed to hear the young temperance orator. A meeting in the Temple Grove was also addressed by Messrs. Hawkins, Stainsby, Huntington of Salem, and others. At Troy, the greatest preparations were made to receive us, by military and fire companies, and temperance processions, and Cold-Water armies; but the rain drove them from the streets; the churches were quite inadequate. In Albany, a mass meeting was held in the State House yard, and Mr. Gough spoke from the steps. But, in the evening, the very elite of the city were gathered in the North Dutch church—for fashion had no power now to make the most refined stand aloof; and in all my travel with Mr. Gough, I never saw so much weeping as in that meeting—by far the happiest effort of his mind and soul. Here ended our tour; a complete success. The whole of the Empire State which we traversed was roused to thought and action. The rich put away their wine, and the poor their whiskey and beer. The open infidelity, and radicalism, and abuse of ministers, by some reform-speakers, had kindled up in many minds an opposition to all temperance effort, especially on the Sabbath; but Mr. Gough took such decided ground on religion, as the basis of all temperance, and the great security and hope of the reformed, as entirely reconciled them, not only to the meetings, but to his occupying the pulpit, on the Sabbath, as most profitable to the spiritual interests of men.

Mr. Gough proceeded to Springfield, and I returned to New York, to the duties of my office. But so valuable were his services, especially among the religious and wealthy classes, that I procured them, the following winter, in New York city, for more than thirty consecutive meetings, in crowded halls and churches; took him to Hartford and New Haven, in Connecticut; to Newark, Patterson, New Brunswick, and Trenton, in New Jersey; to the city of Philadelphia, where we had eleven enthusiastic and powerful meetings; to Baltimore and Washington, where we had eight meetings, which were attended by members of Congress and numerous strangers assembled at the inauguration of the new President; and as far South as Richmond, where a great impression was made. In all this action, we were well sustained by the liberality of friends, and had the countenance and prayers of the ministry and churches. Though himself an uneducated man, Mr. Gough deeply interested the officers and students of Harvard, Yale, Princeton, and other colleges, and induced many to pledge themselves against the use of intoxicating liquors. In what consisted his peculiar power, was the subject of much speculation in the press. In my own Journal, I spoke of his eloquence as Antenor, in the Iliad, spoke of the eloquence of Ulysses:

" 'When Ulysses arose, his eyes were cast down. He used no motion with his staff, but held it motionless, after the manner of a clown. You might have taken him for a simple fellow. But no sooner had he begun to give vent to his sonorous voice, uttering flakes of words gently falling like winter snow, than it became evident that, in eloquence, no man could cope with Ulysses.' "

The Journal of Commerce said:

"Mr. Gough is certainly a wonderful young man. He is worth studying as a model of natural eloquence, as well as of Christian fervor and kindness. No man, or woman, can hear him without rising in moral feeling."

"It is impossible," said the New York Sun, "to convey anything like an adequate idea of the powers possessed by, or to tell what there is about him so fascinating. A close critic, in nine cases out of ten, attending for the express purpose of picking flaws in his address, would, in five minutes, forget the nature of his errand."

Said the Tribune:

"Mr. Gough has no system about his lecturing; he never uses notes. He does not stop to sermonize, but feeling that his story has gone home, and that it will do its own work, he dashes off on another theme, depicts the wife of the drunkard as she sits in her destitution and misery, in the cold damp cellar, or the rickety garret, working her fingers to the bone, that she may gain a morsel of bread for her band of half-starving, half-naked, shivering children; hearing no sound but their cries for food and fire. The scene of early days and her youthful bloom—the time when she pledged her all to the man who has now deserted her—his broken promise—his progressive steps in vice—his waning love—his brutality—his indifference to her wants—and the deep, utter midnight darkness that has settled upon her hopes and happiness, are all brought before the mind, as though they were daguerreotyped upon the wall. And then the sketch of the drunkard—the husband, as he sits in his apathy in the groggery within a hundred yards distant, carelessly steeping the little left of his sensibility in the damning bowl:—you can almost hear the sigh, the cry, the voice, the low jest—almost see the thin wife and the bloated husband—the days of light, and the days of darkness, and the scenes of happiness, and the midnight despair; all are touched as by the hand of a master who has not been taught in the schools of others, but in his own."

Such is my clear and pleasant recollection of the introduction of Mr. Gough to New York. From every quarter

I was asked for his services. The following characteristic letter was from the temperance veteran and orator, Dr. Lyman Beecher, at the West:

CINCINNATI, *January* 21, 1845.

DEAR BROTHER MARSH:—You must come out here, and without fail, with Mr. Gough, and as soon as you can. The flood of Coffee House opposition has rolled over us, and though the Washingtonians have endured, and worked well, their thunder is worn out. The novelty of the common-place narrative is used up, and we cannot raise an interest which will command the respect and attention of those who have been restrained and half convinced, but have not joined us, or wholly given up their wine, and are now beginning to turn against us by open transgression in high places. We must open a new campaign, and you and Mr. Gough must come. I long to see you, and once more buckle on the harness.

Affectionately yours,

LYMAN BEECHER.

To such as may be desirous of knowing what Mr. Gough actually said in these addresses to excite such emotion, I here quote the close of one which, delivered in his impassioned tones and action, will never pass from my memory:

"What fills the almshouses and jails? What brings yon trembling wretch upon the gallows? It is drink. And we might call upon the tomb to break forth. Ye mouldering victims! wipe the grave dust crumbling from your brow; stalk forth in your tattered shrouds and bony whiteness to testify against the drink! Come, come from the gallows, you spirit-maddened man-slayer, give up your bloody knife, and stalk forth to testify against it! Crawl from the slimy ooze, ye drowned drunkards, and with suffocation's blue and livid lips speak out against the drink! Unroll the record of the past, and let the Recording Angel read out the murder indictments, written in God's book of remembrance! aye! let the past be unfolded, and the shrieks of victims wailing be borne down upon the night blast! Snap your burning chains, ye denizens of the pit, and come up sheeted in the fire, dripping with the flames of hell, and with your trumpet tongues testify against the damnation of the drink.

"Of those who began this work some are living to-day, and I should like to stand now and see the mighty enterprise as it rises before them.

They worked hard. They lifted the first turf; prepared the way in which to lay the corner-stone. They laid it amid persecution and storms. They worked under the surface; and men almost forgot that there were busy hands laying the solid foundation far down beneath. By-and-by they got the foundation above the surface, and then commenced another storm of persecution. Now we see the superstructure, pillar after pillar, tower after tower, column after column, with the capitals emblazoned—'Love, truth, sympathy and good will to all men!' Old men gaze upon it as it grows up before them. They will not live to see it completed, but they see in faith the crowning cope-stone set upon it. Meek-eyed women weep as it grows in beauty; children strew the pathway of workmen with flowers. We do not see its beauty yet; we do not see the magnificence of the superstructure yet, because it is in course of erection. Scaffolding, ropes, ladders, workmen, ascending and descending, mar the beauty of the building; but by-and-by, when the hosts who have labored shall come up over a thousand battle-fields, waving with bright grain, never again to be crushed in the distillery—through vineyards under trellised vines, with grapes hanging with all their purple glory, never again to be pressed into that which can debase and degrade mankind; when they shall come through orchards, under trees hanging thick with golden pulpy fruit, never to be turned into that which can injure and debase; when they shall come up to the last distillery, and destroy it—to the last stream of liquid death, and dry it up—to the last weeping wife, and wipe her tears gently away—to the last little child, and lift him up to stand where God wills that mankind should stand—to the last drunkard, and nerve him to burst the burning fetters, and make a glorious accompaniment to the song of freedom by the clanking of his broken chain—then, ah, then will the cope-stone be set upon it—the scaffolding will fall with a crash; and the building will start in its wondrous beauty before an astonished world.

CHAPTER X.

Changes in the Advocacy of Temperance—Experience Meetings give Place to Argumentative—Dr. Charles Jewett—W. H. Burleigh—A. W. Riley—Dr. Sewall's Death—Excitement on the Traffic—Trials before U. S. Supreme Court—Webster—Choate, Liquor-dealers' Counsel—Prohibition demanded in New England—No License in New York—Ninth Anniversary A. T. U., 1845—T. P. Hunt on Rights of Liquor Dealers—Six Months' Action for no License—Glorious Results—Tenth Anniversary, 1846—Rev. A. Barnes—Commodore A. H. Foote—Cold Water Army—Yale College Temperance Society Literature.

As years rolled on, many and important changes were called for in the temperance meetings. They were for a time almost entirely experience meetings. No individual had been called for or expected to speak, who could not relate an experience as a reformed man. This excluded almost entirely all clergymen and the early temperance speakers from the platform. The popularity of the reform speeches was, for a time, great; and as many of their experiences were both of the comic and tragic character, they were very exciting. But ultimately there was much of a sameness in them, and as there would be often five or six at a meeting, the interest in them waned, and the public sentiment demanded something scientific, something on the moral basis, and the religious obligation. But so had speakers of this class retired from the platform, and such was their sense of unpopularity with the masses, that it was difficult introducing them again. Some, however, were to be found that were highly acceptable to all classes. Such an one was Dr. Charles Jewett, early in life a skilful physician in Rhode Island, but who had been so impressed in his practice with the evils of strong drink, that he every where commenced war against it; and in 1832 he delivered a public address in the town of Exeter, which was published and extensively circulated. So much were his services here demanded that, in 1839, he gave up a lucrative practice, and devoted himself for life to the public advocacy of the temperance cause. Various departments he has since filled; sometimes State agent, sometimes editor and conductor of the press, bookmaker, &c., but always pre-eminent as a lecturer. As Hawkins by his appeals touched every fibre of the soul, and Gough gave beauty, life, and a charm to all he touched, so Dr. Jewett now began most deeply to interest the thinking community by the well-prepared lectures on the medical points, the pathology of drunkenness—its destruction of the physical, intellectual and moral powers of men—its insidious advances—the connection between temperance and the educational, agricultural and commercial interests of the State, and the abominations and deadly influence of the traffic in all its branches. With a vein of humor seldom possessed, both in poetry and prose, he made the lecture hours pass rapidly, and has proved one of the mightiest instrumentalities of advancing our great cause.

William H. Burleigh, Esq., was another mighty advocate, both in poetry and prose, who followed on after the Washington reformers, and coped with high intellectual power and true eloquence, with all who would sustain the drinking usages, and the traffic in intoxicating drinks. For a time he was Corresponding Secretary and Editor for the New York State Society, masterly both with his tongue and pen. His poem, THE RUM FIEND, is one of the standard works of true genius.

General A. W. Riley, of Rochester, also early entered the field as a lecturer *sui generis*, who has, perhaps, travelled more miles, and delivered more off-hand lectures than any other individual of the class; always battling tremendously the rum-seller wherever he could meet him, and even offering him pay, so much an hour, if he would give him his attendance; and not sparing the church and the ministry, where they were holding back from the cause, and countenancing the drinking usages of society. To him I was long indebted for large subscriptions to the Journal.

Mr. J. P. Coffin, himself a reformed man of an early date, was long an able agent of the New York State Society, and a lecturer most able, powerful, and acceptable.

Thurlow Weed Brown, editor and publisher of the Cayuga Chief, was excelled by none on the platform in instructive, soul-stirring speech. With a beauty and power of thought and language, and a two-edged sword, giving the liquor-dealer his due, he moved on through his hour with great force, charming all by his diction, except those who were resolved not to be saved themselves, nor to save others.

G. W. Bungay, a gentleman of unusual genius as a writer, both in prose and verse, and talented in speech, took the field, and did much service. In Ohio, Gen. S. F. Cary, a prince of orators, visited, and spoke in all cities and villages, with great effect.

On the 10th of April, 1845, I heard of the death of my friend, and the friend of humanity, Dr. Thomas Sewall, of Washington, at the age of fifty-nine. Few had done so much for the cause of temperance. Few had seen so much of the ruins of intemperance as he had, connected as he was with Congress and its members. In most glowing and expressive language, did he ever express himself on the subject. I quote his emphatic words:

"Intemperance has swept over our land, with the rapidity and power of a tempest, tearing down everything in its course. Not content with rioting in the haunts of ignorance and vice, it has passed through our consecrated groves, has entered our most sacred enclosures; and oh! how many men of genius and of letters have fallen before it! how many lofty intellects have been shattered, and laid in ruins by its power! how many a warm and philanthropic heart has been chilled by its icy touch! It has stalked within the very walls of our capital, and there left the stains of its polluting touch on our national glory. It has leaped over the pale of the Church, and even reached up its sacrilegious arms to the pulpit, and dragged down some of its brightest ornaments."

His drawings of the stomach will ever remain a monument of his philanthropy and genius.

Leaving the reformed, the attention of the community was now beginning to be turned much toward the traffic, as blasting all the good work which had been done; and the question was rising in every State, has the liquor-seller a right to carry on his destructive business; especially is it right for the State to grant him a license to do it? With the general burdens all were acquainted, the people paid their heavy taxes imposed by the traffic, without complaining; but when there was blood and murder in the streets, they would stand it no longer. In the spring of 1845, a respectable mechanic of Pittsfield, Mass., was made drunken by liquor sold contrary to law, and was torn to pieces while lying on the railroad-track, in the darkness of midnight. A public indignation meeting was at once held, and indignation speeches were made, and resolutions adopted by some of the first citizens which thrilled the country. Gov. Briggs, after narrating the destitute condition of the family of the deceased, the aggravating circumstances of his death to his family, and the desolation and woe it had brought to the hearts of his wife and children, called upon every friend of humanity to come forward and lend his aid in drying up the prolific fountain of wretchedness. He asked:

"Who did the deed? Who robbed those children of a father, and made that wife a widow, perhaps a maniac? It was not the ponderous engine, rushing with whirlwind speed over its iron road. It was the vendor of intoxicating drink, the man who, in defiance of all laws, human and divine, scattered around him the seed of temporal and eternal death."

The Hon. Thomas B. Strong said:

"It was demanded by every feeling of self-respect, by every dictate of pride of character, by every impulse of generous humanity, that our village be purified from this unhallowed traffic. Woe to him who putteth the bottle to his neighbor's lips. It was all the same to him, whether the victim of his avarice were crushed under the ponderous wheels of the railroad engine, or swung from the gibbet, or died amid the horrors of delirium tremens, or eked out a miserable existence in a dungeon, or, outliving health and fortune, and friends, and respect, and home, staggered over his last years down to a drunkard's grave. Judas sold his master for thirty pieces of silver; but the rum-seller sells his victims for one. The piece of money would canker in his posssession; and, if he died in his unhallowed traffic, like Judas, he would go unrepented and unforgiven to his own place."

Said Rev. Dr. Todd, minister of the place:

"For what would you be the man who sold that bottle of spirits? For what would you own that money? Oh! if the man be here who owns it, and has got it, let him look at it! Don't you see the blood on it? In your bar-room, by the cask, don't you see that mangled body? Don't you hear the steps of the naked feet of the orphans? Don't you see the wild eye and the pale face of the broken-hearted widow? Can you look up, and see written on those heavens, 'No drunkard shall inherit the kingdom of God,' and then rejoice that you have cut one more such off from life, and hurried him to judgment? Where will you hide that money, from which the blood will not wash?"

But how should the evil be suppressed? The liquor-dealers now demanded the right to sell. They appealed to the Supreme Court of the United States against the unconstitutionality of the license law of Massachusetts, which made it criminal for any person to sell without license. They engaged for their counsel the two first lawyers of the State, Hon. Daniel Webster and Hon. Rufus Choate, U. S. Senator, men whose sympathies were always with the moral community. But the State was defended by a gentleman of adequate power, Asahel Huntington, Esq., of Salem. Mr. Webster argued "that the right to import implied the right to sell—to the unrestricted use of all the channels of commerce, even the most minute—to the consumer." But it was replied, "the men who made the Constitution never thought of giving it such a construction; but were continually, with their descendants, regulating commerce as circumstances demanded." Mr. Choate relied chiefly on the position, that the license law interfered with our treaty with France. On the question, the court were divided, and the decision was deferred to a full bench, in 1846.

But, throughout the country, a spirit was rising for an entire suppression of the traffic. At large conventions, in Maine, New Hampshire, and at Boston, the high ground was taken: 1. To grant no license for the sale of intoxicating drinks as a beverage. 2. To provide, by fine and imprisonment, for the effectual suppression of the traffic. In the State of New York, great efforts were made to give the question of LICENSE or NO LICENSE to the people, to be decided at the ballot-box. A bill to that effect was passed unanimously in the Assembly; but it was stayed in the Senate, unless the city of New York could be exempted. Against this, a remonstrance was made by 25,000 citizens. But the Assembly yielded, and, in this form, the bill passed on the 14th of May, 1845. The day fixed for the vote was the last Tuesday of April, 1846. Great was the exultation of the temperance men, though it threw upon them a vast amount of labor to secure the desired result. It was at once resolved that there should be two State Conventions, one at the east and one at the west; and a county meeting in every county. My Journal was to be devoted to the enlightenment of the people; and from our office was to go forth a large amount of tracts, handbills, etc.

At our ninth Anniversary, May, 1845, I made a strong effort to secure the presence and aid of Gov. Briggs, of Massachusetts, and Gov. Slade of Vermont. Both declined, owing to their press of business, but manifested great interest in the cause. Said Gov. Briggs: "I believe, under God, the cause is advancing all over the land; its mighty currents are growing deeper, and wider, and carrying away one obstacle after another. Benevolence, patriotism, and religion must slumber, before it will cease to advance." And said Gov. Slade: "The present is a very important crisis in the Temperance Reform, as the transition is being made to Legislative action, a resort which every intelligent friend of the cause must see is indispensable to its final triumph."

The meeting, which was very large, was ably addressed by Rev. Dr. Pohlman, of Albany; Rev. J. P. Thompson, of New York; and Rev. Thomas P. Hunt of Pennsylvania. Mr. Hunt supported a resolution:

> "That while the whole community is groaning under the evils which flow from the traffic, it is incumbent upon the friends of humanity to pursue firmly and unflinchingly every measure to relieve society of it, consistent with the liquor dealers' rights."

Mr. Hunt became well known by his attacks upon the rum-trade in Wilmington, N. C., even before his amusing and striking speech before the National Convention in Philadelphia. No man was ever more fearless in his attacks on iniquity, or master of a more stinging satire. His numerous publications, and arduous labors in the pulpit and on the platform, have long entitled him to the gratitude of the country. On this occasion he was for guarding carefully the rights of the liquor-seller:

"But what were the rights of the liquor-seller? The same as the rights of any other man, the right to carry on his business without injury to others, and none other. If he can carry on his business without injury to others, he may do so. But can he? The liquor-seller may say he has a right to carry it on, provided he makes the damage good that his poison makes. I say to him, 'You cannot do it, if you try. You cannot bring back the dead from the grave and the damned from hell, put there by your business. You cannot dry up the widow's tears, nor be the father to her children, as he was before he fell in among you. The liquor-sellers' business cannot wipe away from the country the disgrace of their business, nor remove its curse from the land. Your business has filled hell with groans unutterable and despair never dying, while the earth has been heaving and mourning and groaning, filled with the widows and the orphans' voices, from the time your business has commenced to the present moment; and you cannot deny it.'"

The two State Conventions designed to prepare the people of the State of New York to vote on the license question, met, the one, in June, at Albany, and the other in October, at Rochester. Both were very full and spirited. To me it was allotted, as one of the business Committee, to prepare a series of resolutions, which were to be discussed as the basis of action, and which drew out many spirit-stirring and powerful speeches. Great indignation was felt in both Conventions, at the omission of the city of New York from the law, but yet all felt the importance of bringing the rest of the State to a bold and decided action against the license system. An able address to the people was prepared and issued by Vice-Chancellor Whittlesey, of Rochester. In presenting the resolutions at Rochester, I remarked, "That we were not in this cause strangers to deep and solemn responsibilities; but we were now in a peculiar position. Year after year we have asked the Legislature to permit the people to carry the question of license or no license to the ballot-box. With the unreasonable exception of the city of New York, they have granted the desired privilege to every town and city. And in April next, are to go up all our electors throughout this vast State—with the exception of New York city—and say whether they will or will not legalize this most demoralizing and desolating business. Never, it is believed, has there been a more important crisis. Not only have we to act, and act rightly, ourselves, but on us it rests to prepare the electors of these States to do their duty in the matter. There is a noble field of action before us; the eyes of the world are upon us, and philanthropists are everywhere awaiting the issue."

For the remaining six months, the subject engrossed all hearts. My own and other Journals of the day were filled with short and pithy appeals to the people. Tracts, handbills and pictorial illustrations were scattered over the State. Messrs. Delavan, Bradford, R. Wood, Azor Taber, Dr. Pohlman and O. Scovil were a Central Vigilant Committee, who issued through my Journal a series of articles on the license question, addressed to various classes, to farmers, to manufacturers, to the Irish, to laborers, to ladies, &c., and a general address to the people.

To bring out the strength of the State, I addressed a letter to a number of distinguished citizens; Judge Smith of Genesee, Mr. Delavan, Alvan Stewart, Gerrit Smith, General J. J. Knox, and others, asking them for a written opinion, which, when received, was printed in the Journal. Conventions were held in most of the counties, and an immense amount of reading was circulated among the people. And when the day came in which the Empire State was to cast its vote, (it had been changed to the 19th of May,) many a heart went up to Him, in whose hands are the hearts of all, that the people might be led to a right decision.

But little doubt was there of a favorable result; for great had been the change of public sentiment throughout the land. In Connecticut the previous year, a similar election had given temperance commissioners in about 200 of 220 towns. In Michigan, the question had been given by the Legislature to the people; and in Detroit, and a large number of towns, the vote had been No License. But the result in New York exceeded all expectation. More than five-sixths of the towns and cities gave overwhelming majorities against license. Several whole counties voted No License. Of 856 towns, 528 voted No License; of the 528 thus voting, 382 gave majorities of 48,101; of the 104, voting License, 63 gave majorities of 2,623. Excess of No License majorities 45,478.

Great rejoicings were manifested by the friends of humanity and reform throughout the country. The licensed dealers, wishing for license, not merely to give them liberty to sell, but respectability to their vocation, held large meetings to give vent to their indignation; but it was biting a file. A congratulatory State Temperance Convention was called at Albany, July 15, to express public thanks, and to consider what measures should now be taken to gain the greatest possible good from the vote of the State. Two hundred and eighteen delegates were enrolled as members. The Governor of the State, Hon. William C. Bouck, was called to the chair, and thanks were rendered to Almighty God for the glorious advance the cause had made, evidenced in the extraordinary vote of the people for No License. Much gratitude was expressed to Mr. Delavan and the central Committee, for their arduous labors in placing a copy of the State Address, at much expense, in every family; also to Azor Taber, Esq., for his able Report, and to the lecturers and agents: General Riley, of Rochester, Rev. R. S. Crampton, W. H. Burleigh, Mr. Coffin and others, who had been untiring in their labors. The Convention resolved that, in view of the overwhelming majority for No License, any attempt to secure the return of a Legislature hostile to the Excise law, and secretly pledged to repeal it, would be an outrage upon Republican principles and a palpable endeavor to subvert the will of the majority, by mingling the question of temperance with politics, from which the new Excise law had separated it.

As our Tenth Anniversary preceded, a few days, the great vote, and was held in an hour of anxiety and uncertainty, it was without the enthusiasm which would have attended it in another week; but it was an excellent meeting, being ably addressed by Rev. Albert Barnes, of Philadelphia, on the resolution "That, in promoting the temperance reformation, while it is proper to invoke the aid of the laws of the land, and the principles of science, the ultimate reliance must be on the religious principle, and the coöperation of the religious community; and that every friend of religion should be the friend of the cause of temperance." He showed that the religious principle, be it right or wrong, is the most powerful agency in the world; that, in a community under the influence of religion, no reform can succeed that does not call religion to its aid; that the temperance reformation has ever had close connection with religion, and the religious community have the deepest interest in its success.

"The cause of intemperance opposes religion, with the boldest and most open front. All other evils put together have not robbed the Church of so many distinguished men as that. Why then should the Church stand aloof from so good a cause as this? It makes no infidels, disrobes no minister of religion, bars out no prayers from heaven, infuses no pestilential air in the way through life; wherever its friends go, it accompanies them as a blessing to the end of their days."

I had made special effort to get my friend, Captain Andrew H. Foote, to address the meeting, as he had just returned from his late temperance cruise in the Mediterranean, but I was left only with the following letter, which I read to the meeting:

CHESHIRE, 10*th May*, 1846.

MY DEAR SIR:—I regret exceedingly that orders to the Boston Station, and suffering from ophthalmia, will prevent my being present and making some remarks at the Temperance Anniversary. I hope that the friends of temperance will petition Congress until the whiskey-ration shall be abolished, as this must be the basis of any permanent reform in the service.

The frigate Cumberland, during her late cruise, fairly tested the experiment; and conclusively proved, that discipline, efficiency, good morals, and everything requisite to render a man-of-war creditable to a nation, at home and abroad, are only to be secured by the discontinuance of intoxicating drinks. Some officers of the Navy are, no doubt, still opposed to abolishing the whiskey-ration; for a large portion of the crew of the Cumberland, at the outset of the cruise, regarded it as impracticable, but experiment changed the sentiment entirely, when the commissioned officers and two hundred and fifty of the crew petitioned Congress for the abolishment.

Respectfully and truly yours,

A. H. FOOTE.

To the Corresponding Secretary American Temperance Union.

Captain, and afterwards Commodore, and Rear-Admiral Foote, was an excellent platform speaker, and ever ready to throw his influence in behalf of the temperance cause. His mind was much bent on the abolition of the spirit-ration in the navy, and he lived to see it accomplished. Noble man! he fought heroically, both moral and civil battles, and died full of honors, amid the lamentations of millions.*

* The following was from a letter written by a seaman on board the Cumberland, dated Port Mahon, February 8, 1844:

"The Society met in the sail-loft, at Mahon's Navy Yard. Lieutenant Foote took the floor, and for twenty minutes addressed the meeting, in his usual happy way, and concluded by inviting all to sign the pledge who had not done it. Forty new names were added. We muster now two hundred and ninety-three strong; and, next week, our Commodore talks about breaking up the spirit-room, and storing water in it instead of rum."

After the Albany Convention, in June, came to a close, most of the members adjourned to the new and magnificent Delavan House, which had just been opened, on strict temperance principles, where a splendid entertainment was provided by Mr. Rogers, the keeper, at which one hundred and fifty ladies and gentlemen sat down, and where was, also, "a feast of reason and a flow of soul." Numerous speeches, of wit, humor, and powerful eloquence, were made by Dr. Jewett, Rev. G. H. Ludlow, C. W. Dennison, and the Mayor of Boston, who was present. It was considered a great triumph of temperance over the system which had consecrated everywhere the traveller's home to drunkenness.

The President of the United States, Mr. Polk, was reported as having travelled to Washington and opened his house without wine at his table; and at the inauguration of the Hon. Edward Everett as President of Harvard College, six hundred distinguished citizens of Massachusetts, with numerous literary gentlemen from other States, sat down to dinner, without any intoxicating drinks; and all the rejoicings of the students were without any ruinous excitement. Indeed, leading minds, in all departments, were giving the temperance cause their decided approbation. The venerable John Quincy Adams, at a meeting in his own county, not long before, had said:

> He had been an attentive and rejoicing witness of the successful movements in favor of temperance, throughout the world; although he had not entered on the arena, as one of its enthusiastic advocates and apostles. He regarded the temperance movement of the present day as one of the most remarkable phenomena of the human race; operating simultaneously in every part of the world, for the reformation of a vice often solitary in itself, but infectious in its nature as the small pox or the plague, and combining all the ills of war, famine, and pestilence. Among those who had fallen by intemperance, were included untold numbers who were respected for their talents and worth, and exalted among their neighbors or countrymen. He had read an excellent discourse by Rev. Albert Barnes, show-

ing the connection between temperance and religion; and he thought a small portion of time might not be unprofitably spent in inquiring into the principles of total abstinence, and the doctrine of pledges, as sanctioned by the writings of the Old and New Testaments, the laws of Moses, and the doctrines of Jesus Christ.

Under the auspices and activities of the Rev. C. J. Warren, secretary, more than sixty thousand children had now been enrolled, in the State of New York, in the Cold-Water army. In Boston, also, under Deacon Moses Grant; and in Pennsylvania, under the Rev. T. L. Harman, this organization was securing the most important results. Said Mr. Warren, in his enthusiasm, in a letter to me:

"You, my dear sir, are among the few privileged persons, that have been led up to the mount, and there have gazed upon the lovely prospect that will gladden the eyes of happy millions, when this Juvenile Temperance movement shall become universal. The 2,500,000 boys who are now under fifteen years of age will sway the destinies of this vast Republic when it shall contain fifty millions."

A circular was addressed by the officers of the New York Juvenile Association, to all the county and town superintendents of common schools, soliciting their coöperation, and proposing that each teacher should be furnished with a pledge-book, in which children, with consent of parents, should enrol their names; and that there should be in every school a monthly meeting, for the Report to be read, for recitation of speeches, dialogues, singing, and an address by the leader; reports for all the schools to be made annually to some central society. Such a system could not fail, if carried out, of being eminently successful.

As the year 1841 drew to a close, the third anniversary of the Yale College Temperance Society was held, Professor Silliman in the chair, and Professor Goodrich offering prayer. Professor Silliman stated that, thirty-five years ago, he had abandoned the use of all kinds of liquors; and his hale and hearty look, as he stood, with his eye flashing with pleasurable excitement, bore ample testimony to all who saw him, that none of his faculties had been injured by the abandonment. Professor Goodrich had frequently stated that much of the drunkenness of college was chiefly on wine. The society now numbered two hundred and sixty-four members, being more than three fifths of all the undergraduates.

The social and civil benefits of the temperance reform were now looming up from every quarter; but in nothing did they appear more signal than in the diminution of crime. From returns from twenty county, and twelve State, prisons, it appeared that there had been, from the commencement of the work to the close of the year 1844, a constant diminution of crime, with an amazing increase of population; which was uniformly attributed by men in official stations to the temperance reform.

The temperance literature, if not as voluminous as in some earlier days, was not less valuable. Lucius M. Sargent, Esq., author of the Temperance Tales, was like an overflowing fountain. No productions were read more extensively, or with better effect. Between the first, "My Mother's Gold Ring," and "The Temperance Meeting at Tattertown," they met every want of the community, overthrew every false principle abroad, and established our scientific and moral principles on a solid basis.* The Rev.

* The following tribute to the value of these tales was sent to Mr. Sargent, by a female missionary in Siam:

DEAR SIR:—A short time since, an English ship came in here, and I went on board, and offered, if needed, a supply of the officers and men with Bibles, which were coldly, but politely declined. The next day, I sent a dozen of the "Temperance Tales," with a note, requesting the captain to induce all his men to read them attentively. In answer, I received the following: "The title-pages of the little books are such as will entice

Thomas P. Hunt also gave the public some moral and instructive works, chiefly from his own observation and experience: "Wedding Days of Former Times" "Jessie Johnson," "Death by Measure," "It will not Injure Me"—books which may well be in every Sunday-school-library, and should never be out of print. The "Annual Reports of the American Temperance Society," by Dr. Justin Edwards, were invaluable documents—the Sixth Report especially, which entered into a full discussion of the license question;—a discussion that was submitted to several of the first statesmen, lawyers, and divines of the land, and received their hearty approbation. "The Investigation in the Jails and Poor-houses of the State of New York," by Samuel Chipman, was brought out in 1841; "Hannah Hawkins," and "Fourth of July Address," by Albert Rhett, of Charleston, in 1842; Dr. Tyng's "Address to Medical Students," and "Inquirer" No. 1., in 1843; "Life of J. B. Gough," "The Voice of Blood from the Grave," by Rev. Edwin Hall, of Norwalk, in 1845; and Dr. Nott's "Lectures," in 1846; all books to be held in lasting remembrance.

my sailors to peruse them carefully, and they may, I trust, instil into the minds of myself, officers, and crew, that knowledge which is requisite to make us happy here, and to enjoy everlasting life in a future state." A request for Bibles soon followed, with a promise that they should be carefully read. Here, the whole current is evil, but I have never seen one of these tales rejected; and I have seen the whole crew of a vessel seated on the deck, bent in eager attention over one of these little works, while the rough hand was ever and anon drawn hastily across the weather-beaten cheek, to stop the course of the falling tear.

CHAPTER XI.

World's Temperance Convention—Retrospect—Foreign Operations—Formation of London Society—Mr. Buckingham's Report—Spread of the Cause in Britain and North of Europe—Pacific Ocean—Australia—Call for a World's Convention—Letter from Mr. Compton—Appointment of delegates—Reception Meetings and Speeches—Covent Garden Theatre—Visit to Father Matthew—Attendance on the Christian Alliance—Meetings at New Castle, York, Edinburgh, Glasgow, Liverpool, Huddersfield—Return to America in Great Western—Incidents Abroad—Dr. Beecher on Sunday-schools—Extracts from Speeches—Response in Broadway Tabernacle.

The little seed carried across the water by Rev. Mr. Penney of Rochester, and planted and watered by Rev. Mr. Carre, of New Ross, in Ireland, in 1829, was destined to spring up and become a great tree, under whose shade the nations, burned and cursed by Alcoholic fires, should find life and peace. In less than two years, numerous temperance societies had sprung up in all the three kingdoms. Many temperance publications had been issued from the press; and a general expectation was raised of some great and wonderful moral reform.

On the 29th of June, 1830, the London Society was formed, much through the agency of the Rev. Dr. Hewit, of America. His Honor, the Mayor, had promised to preside, but was prevented. Able addresses were made by the Solicitor-General of Ireland, Professor Edgar, Dr. Hewit, the Bishop of Chester, and Mr. Carre, of New Ross. Thirty societies had then been formed in England, and

10,000 tracts put in circulation. By this meeting, in connection with a Report of a Parliamentary Committee of six hundred pages, prepared by James Silk Buckingham, giving a minute account of the extent and evils of intemperance, the attention of the higher classes was widely arrested; while the other extreme of society, in Lancashire, at Preston, and other places, had been moved, in 1831–2, to great and noble efforts to burst the chains which had long held them in cruel bondage. A large number of miserable, worthless men, who had been ten, twenty, and even thirty years cast off as hopeless drunkards, became reformed, signed the total-abstinence pledge, and related their experience in public meetings, in a manner similar to the reformed men afterwards in the United States. Dr. Baird, our countryman, had kindled a temperance flame in the north of Europe; and, in 1846, scarce a place was known among civilized men, where the temperance banner had not been unfurled. In Ireland, Father Matthew was holding on his way, with great power. Large national institutions were well established, and in successful operation, in England and Scotland. In Holland, Silesia, Poland, Germany, Prussia, Sweden, Norway, Denmark; at the Sandwich Islands, Tahiti; in Australia, in Africa, China, India; wherever missionaries had lifted up the standard of the cross, there men and women were combining to rid the world of the monster evil.

At this time, there was a demand for a World's Temperance Convention, that the advocates of temperance might come from the East and the West, the North and the South, and by consultation, in London, the world's capital and the fountain-head of religious and philanthropic influences, might bind themselves together, and become more resolute and engaged in their blessed enterprise. In December, 1845, I received the following notice:

WORLD'S TEMPERANCE CONVENTION.

The National Temperance Society, London, to the Corresponding Secretary of the American Temperance Union:

LONDON, 18*th Nov.*, 1841.

DEAR SIR:—I have the pleasure of handing you the enclosed circular, by which you will perceive that a WORLD'S TEMPERANCE CONVENTION is at hand. I have to request your kind attention, in giving all possible information, throughout the United States, and arranging for delegates to be appointed.

I have to call your particular attention to the desirableness of securing the most ample and correct statistics of the state of temperance, the numerical strength of the societies, the number of houses for the sale of liquor, open and closed, the total consumption, the drinking customs, and other facts bearing upon the subject. We hope to be provided with such information, on our part, and shall do our best to procure it from all parts of the world.

I am, dear sir, yours sincerely.

Rev. J. MARSH. THEODORE COMPTON.

A Meeting of the Committee was at once called; and it was resolved, that we cordially respond to the proposal and invitation: and that as many State and local societies as conveniently can, be invited to appoint and send delegates. How much the world needed the influence of such a Convention, could not easily be told. In France, Great Britain, Sweden, Prussia, and the United States, the annual consumption of intoxicating liquors was officially reported at one thousand nine hundred and seventy million, nine hundred and sixty-three thousand, nine hundred and eighty-eight gallons, valued at $546,268,880. Under such a terrible machinery, the greater part of the world's degradation and woe was caused. The number dying of drunkenness, in Great Britain alone, was estimated at 60,000 annually; the number in the United States, at 30,000. To arrest such an evil, was felt to be one of the greatest objects for which a Convention could be gathered. But the distance, the expense, and the dangers of the sea, with some threats of war, prevented a large delegation from America. Only thirty-one were found ready to go; but among these, were gentlemen of high respectability and influence.

FROM NEW YORK.

Rev. Samuel H. Cox, D. D.,
Rev. Wm. Patten, D. D.,
Rev. John Marsh, D. D.,
Henry Wager, Esq.,
Rev. A. Wheelock,
Rev. Gorham D. Abbott,
William Brown, Esq.,
W. A. Passavant.

MASSACHUSETTS.

Rev. E. N. Kirk,
Daniel Safford, Esq.,
H. E. Wright,
J. D. Ross,
Henry Clapp, jr.,
Wm. Lloyd Garrison,
Elihu Burritt,
Rev. Joshua V. Hines.

RHODE ISLAND.

Rev. Dr. Elton,
Rev. H. S. Osborn.

MAINE.

George Webber, Esq.,
Rev. S. L. Pomroy.

PENNSYLVANIA.

Rev. J. Andrews,
Professor Caldwell,
Rev. Dr. Pressly,
Rev. S. S. Smucker, D. D.

OHIO.

Rev. Lyman Beecher, D. D.,
R. D. Mussey, M. D.,
Dr. Cappell.

MICHIGAN.

Charles Galpin.

VIRGINIA.

Frederic Douglass.

KENTUCKY.

Gen. T. C. Flournoy.

Letters of regret at their inability to attend, were received from Presidents Wayland and Olin, Rev. Dr. Tyng, Gen. S. F. Cary, E. C. Delavan, and others.

In England, there were high-raised expectations from this gathering of the friends of reform.

"As a mere matter of curiosity," said the Teetotal Times, "there will be much to interest. Who does not wish to see the founders of great systems, the originators of wise plans, the first apostles of important truths? We pray that the spirit of wisdom and charity may shed his choicest influences on the assembly, and that its deliberations may prove instrumental, through the divine blessing, in accomplishing a vast amount of good."

Through a kind Providence, several of us were favored with a safe passage in the packet-ship Victoria, Captain Morgan. On our arrival in London, I was welcomed to the house of G. W. Atwood, an American merchant, but one of the Convention Committee. It being Saturday evening, he proposed giving me the best exhibition I could have, in the week, of the doings of Alcohol. I had seen them pictorially; but oh! the crowd of squalid poverty and vice presented to the eye at the gin-shops! Rotten men, and rotten women, rushing up to get their glass of gin, or sitting packed in large rooms, with their pots of ale; listening, for a moment, to shameful songs, from abandoned women—"How," I inquired, "is a World's Temperance Convention to reach these people?" I gladly escaped, looking forward to a peaceful, Christian Sabbath, when I was gratified to hear Dr. Campbell, editor of the Christian Witness, and Rev. James Sherman, of the Surrey Chapel.

The next morning, several of our delegates were introduced to the Convention Committee, with whom we were politely asked to coöperate, in preparing for business; but as I had a week to spare, I improved it in visiting Paris, and seeing its sights—its palaces, its gardens, hospitals, and scientific establishments; and witnessing, with my own eyes, its wine-drinking customs. Drunkenness was not in France—as in England and America—a prevailing vice; and yet every Frenchman, with all his meals, drank wine. In a single year, the thirty-four millions of France consumed 748,571,429 gallons of wine, but only 11,000,000 gallons of spirits, 221,000,000 of cider, and 74,000,000 of beer; while England consumed, of beer, 500 millions.

The café and hotel keepers were disposed to pay me

but little attention, when I refused to order a bottle of wine. But the merriment of those who drank freely satisfied me that it was a powerful exciter. I found a glass of iced water tasting as delicious in Paris as in America; though Americans often complained, when abroad, that they could not drink the water. In the suburbs of Paris, where were the brandy-shops, I saw in plenty the bloated face, the bleared eye, the staggering gait.

On Tuesday morning, August 4, it was my happiness to meet, in the Theatre of the Literary Institute, the World's Temperance Convention. Two hundred delegates were present. Ladies filled the galleries. It was delightful to us to look upon men whose writings we had read, with whom we had corresponded, and who were everywhere known as the pioneers in the cause—Dr. Grindrod, Rev. Benjamin Parsons, John Dunlop, Joseph Sturge, James Teare, Mr. Buckingham, Dr. Campbell, Rev. William Reid, Samuel Bowley, John Cassell, Wm. Janson—and to be recognized, and taken by the hand, in cordial welcome. After organization, Joseph Sturge, of Birmingham, rose and offered a welcome address. He said:

"A few months ago, they were alarmed at the probability of a war with America; but now, thank God, those fears were altogether dispelled. They now saw their American brethren crossing the Atlantic, for the purpose of assisting them in their efforts, and mingling with them, on the present occasion, to endeavor to crush and abolish one of the greatest evils that ever afflicted humanity, the use of intoxicating liquors." "The Secretary of the American Temperance Union (said the report) seconded the resolution. From the time that he first heard of the Convention, he felt desirous of coming to it. The clouds of war, however, hovered over us, and the voices of our wives and children said 'You cannot go; there is danger.'

But we did not believe that the dogs of war would be permitted to hinder us; and, by the time ships were ready to bring us, the voice of peace was heard, and we came away, amid the congratulations of many. God, in his good providence, had permitted us to come to England; and it delighted his heart, to see the faces of men of whom he had heard for years, and who had gloriously aided in this good work."

I was followed by Rev. Dr. Beecher, the object of much curiosity and veneration, in a speech full of emotion and power.

The Convention sat five days, listening to able papers which were prepared for the occasion; to discussions of important resolutions; to reports from distant countries, and to projects of reform, and greater extension of the temperance cause. Dr. Beecher and myself were made members of the Business Committee, and were often much occupied in its deliberations. Wednesday morning, a rich breakfast was given to the American delegation, at Guildhall, at which one hundred and fifty were present; and in the evening, meetings were held in the city chapels. On Thursday evening, a large meeting was held at Freemasons' Hall; but the crowning meeting of all was, on Friday evening, at Covent Garden Theatre, which was filled to its utmost capacity. Such a meeting for temperance had never before been held in London. Members of the American delegation spoke, and did credit to themselves and to their country. The Hon. Lawrence Heyworth, M. P. for Liverpool, brought forward, from the Committee, the great principles of the temperance reform, which were ably discussed and unanimously adopted; and, from the same committee, I brought forward a plan for a Temperance Union for the World, to have its seat in London, and a powerful press and agents for all countries.

The discussion continued a long time; but at last it was laid on the table.

I regretted to see so few of the clergy of England and Scotland in the Convention. It would not be so now. I regretted also not to find Father Matthew there. An unwillingness to mingle with so many of the Protestant creed, was supposed to prevent his coming. After preaching in London on the Sabbath, I set my face at once to see him. On my way, I spent a night with Rev. Benjamin Parsons (author of "Anti-Bacchus"), at Stroud, who, knowing I was coming, had assembled his people in a temperance tea-party, in his session-room, to whom I was introduced. The next morning, I called on Rev. Wm. Jay, of Bath; and in the evening, addressed a large meeting at Bristol, which was got up in honor of the American delegation, of whom several were expected. A steamer took me roughly to Cork, where I had no difficulty in finding Father Matthew. He was living in a very plain house. A large company were about the door, waiting to receive the pledge. As I entered, he gave me a cordial welcome, for we had corresponded. He gave the pledge to some forty, with his blessing on each individual, kneeling. These retired, and another batch came in. He then took me up to his parlor, and insisted upon my dining with him. While dinner was preparing, he took me into the street, and showed me a large number of liquor-shops, all empty. "These," said he, "were formerly crowded." On the afternoon of the next day, the Sabbath, I attended with him the funeral of one of his juvenile band of music, and walked with him, next to the bier, with a thousand people following, but without order. We went to the cemetery, which he had purchased and fitted for the poor. In the evening he took me to a temperance meeting, where I was introduced to the Mayor, and called upon for a speech. The next morning, after introducing me to

William Martin, the Quaker friend, who was the means of his temperance conversion, and whom he called his Temperance Father, I left him, for Dublin. I was impressed with his simplicity, humility, kind-heartedness, and regard for the poor; and, before I left him, I extracted a promise from him that, God willing, he would come to America. His roll-book was before me, with from five to six million names. On my way to Dublin, I witnessed the awful desolation of the potato rot;—but not of men. But one drunken man met my eye. Even in Kilkenny, I saw no quarrelling.

On my return to London, I spent some time with the World's Evangelical Alliance. But there, we American delegates were pained with seeing a sad amount of drinking, among ministers. Our white glasses were subjects of much merriment. But we knew we were right, and that they, one day, would see and acknowledge it. A violent effort was made to shut out of the Alliance the slaveholder; but not the manufacturer and vender of intoxicating drinks.

On Monday evening, October 24, a closing temperance meeting was given to the American delegation, in Exeter Hall. It was an immense one, and well sustained. The press highly complimented the speakers. The Patriot gave many of the speeches in full.

Leaving London, I visited the excellent Richard Dykes Alexander, at Ipswich, the publisher of the Temperance Tracts; and then I set my face homeward, by York, Newcastle, Edinburgh, Glasgow, Liverpool, and Huddersfield, where temperance meetings were in readiness for the American delegation. Both at York and Glasgow, I delivered, on the Sabbath, temperance sermons; and, at the latter place, I witnessed, on Saturday evening, those scenes which had led the Mayor to say that thirty thousand people went, Saturday night, in Glasgow, drunk to bed. Only one of the ministers, Dr. Brown, could I then find, who sympathized with us in our doctrine of total abstinence; though things have, since then, much changed. At Liverpool, with Dr. Beecher, Dr. Mussey, and several others, I took the Great Western, for America. Most mercifully were we preserved, on encountering one of the severest of storms. Our steamer was much broken; but much prayer was offered, and we were permitted to come safely to the desired haven. "Oh! that men would praise the Lord for his goodness, and for his loving kindness to the children of men."

While in England, I spent not a little time and strength in kindling up a civil war. I saw there the beer and brandy-god wringing out the life-blood from thousands and tens of thousands of her sons. And yet it was England's greatest benefactor! Everywhere, the god was praised, as bringing vast revenues to the crown; as the life of the army and of the navy; as the source and spring of all mental energy and social happiness. The licensed victuallers of London alone, paid the Government eleven millions annually. So I proposed in my speech, at Exeter Hall, that, as London was full of statues to distinguished benefactors, a statue should be erected in Hyde Park to England's greatest friend, the beer and brandy-god, higher than any statue ever conceived; and to carry it out as it should be, I would have, on one side, carved by the most eminent sculptors, groups of miserable drunkards, raving in delirium tremens, tearing the hair of their wives, beating their children; and, on another side, I would have paupers, lunatics, and criminals, in chains and on gallowses, through strong drink; on another, parents pressing into the horrid temple, and leading their children up to their god, to drink early of his cup. But not ridicule, it was found, could move England in her self-complacency. There must be war—exterminating war. "Down with the tyrant!" I cried; so we found it in America; and as I said this, I was received with shouts and applause. The public press responded, and said: "These Americans have put some new thoughts into our minds. We confess we are converts to their views; and we are greatly mistaken in the signs of the times, if the late interviews which the teetotallers have had with the Americans have not produced similar results in the minds of others. Hence, a crusade against the traffic has already commenced."

A large Sunday-school meeting was held, and the formation of temperance associations in all the Sunday-schools was strenuously urged. My beloved colleague, Dr. Beecher, made a powerful speech on the occasion.

He compared the instructor of youth to a person standing at the rise of some mighty river, having in his hand two phials, the contents of which were capable of impregnating the whole of the waters. One, if imparted to the stream, would cause it to roll along the instrument of disease, and pain, and death; and the man who thus impregnated it would be justly execrated through life, and would sink into the grave amidst the maledictions of thousands. But if he uncorked the other phial, filled with the elements of life and vigor, fruitfulness and beauty, what happiness would he not be the means of communicating, and with what gratitude and delight would not thousands bless his memory! Sunday-school and other teachers stood at the head of such a river; each teacher had the water of life or death; if he poured in the death-water, the river would roll along with disease and death; but with life and health, if he poured in the life-giving liquid—which he powerfully applied to the dispensing of intoxicating drinks, on the one hand, and the temperance agency, on the other.

Rev. Dr. Cox, of New York, offered, in the Convention, a resolution expressing entire confidence in the practicability of the reformation of the most confirmed drunkards, both in England and America.

He expressed regret that the clergy, instead of impelling the movement, retarded its advance, by holding on the traces of its progressive and triumphant chariot. There could be no objection to a glass of water, when it was recollected that our common father, Adam, had nothing better for a wedding dinner. He deprecated despair of the conversion of the most confirmed drunkard, as well as the most hardened sinner. His colleagues in total abstinence sounded the blessed word "hope," in the ears of the most desponding drunkard. The worst was reclaimable, and capable of being made a zealous and effectual apostle of the camp, which was the camp of religion as well as morality, and would be the means of diffusing Christian civilization, on catholic principles, through the world. Heathenism and Mahommedanism were antipodes to temperance. Our reformed men claimed no glory for themselves. They laid the crown assigned to them at His feet to whom all power, and honor, and glory belonged.

Rev. E. N. Kirk, of Boston, offered a resolution on the shamefulness and wickedness of exporting intoxicating liquors from Christian to Pagan countries, especially in ships which carried out missionaries of the cross; and made a very effective speech. He said:

While wine and beer were sent out in our missionary ships to the castes of India, the mission produced as much evil as good. He was not extreme in identifying Christianity with total abstinence. The latter was a negative, the former a positive medium of reformation. But, of one thing he was well assured, that Christianity did not approve or sanction the existence of gin-palaces, and the degrading train of vices, miseries, offences and crimes, which they engendered. They struck at the root of Christianity.

Rev. Dr. Patton, of New York, offered a resolution on the late signal triumph in the State of New York, on the license question, commending it as an example to all who were suffering under the burdens of the liquor traffic.

Dr. Patton gave a history of the progress of the cause in America, from the first commencement of temperance by Dr. Rush, in 1804, till the movement reached the high-pressure form, in 1836, dwelling on the glorious refusal of license by the trial of the ballot-box—five sixths of the towns pronouncing against licensing. He eloquently urged England to imitate America, in abolishing the whole system. They should sing "God Save the Queen" and "Yankee Doodle" in concert.

Frederic Douglass, formerly a slave in Virginia, was

received at the Covent Garden Meeting with great applause.

"He was not a delegate from America, for those who would be anxious to send him there, in that capacity, were themselves slaves. He was sorry to say, there were three millions of his brethren in a state of slavery. He loved the Americans; but they had neglected their duties towards their fellow creatures, because they had a skin not colored like their own.

In 1842, when the temperance movement was making such immense progress among the white men, a great number of the black men had the wisdom and courage to declare in favor of the movement. They walked in procession though Philadelphia, on the first of August; but they were met with shouts of contempt, with hurled brickbats, and other missiles, upon them. He did not mention the fact with a view of insulting his brethren here; but he wished that, when they went home to America, they would themselves, while advocating the cause of their white brethren, also seek to rescue the black man from the pit of slavery into which he was thrown." (Great cheering.) Here the chairman whispered something into the speaker's ear, when a voice from the gallery cried out, "Don't interrupt him! Don't dictate to him!" This caused the most tremendous cheering for several minutes, when the speaker assured the audience the chairman had only told him his time had expired. "He concluded by calling on the ministers in England to aid in effecting that progress in the cause which it had reached through the instrumentality of the American clergy in the New World."

Mr. Kirk asked if Mr. Douglass had intimated that the temperance men of America were in favor of slavery? He said he had not. Then Mr. K. had nothing to say.

An able letter, full of important suggestions, from Mr. Delavan, in America, was read to the Convention; and an address was sent out from the Convention to the friends of temperance throughout the world.

A pleasant response to the World's Convention was held, on the 29th of December, in the Broadway Tabernacle, Anson G. Phelps, Esq., presiding. As Secretary, I gave an account of the Convention, and offered a series of resolutions, to be adopted and sent to our friends who had so hospitably entertained us, the first of which was:

"Resolved, That the World's Temperance Convention, held in London, on the 4th of August last, was one which met the views and designs of the friends of temperance, in all countries; that it was a noble convocation of brethren—reformers and reformed—who, in various countries, had long toiled in the cause; that its harmony of principle, and unity of action is the subject of devout gratitude; and that its various resolves and acts, its appeals and counsels, should inspire us with new zeal and devotion in our blessed enterprise."

Animated and brilliant speeches were made by Rev. A. Wheelock, Dr. Patton, and Dr. Cox, returned delegates, and by Rev. Dr. Tyng; and the following hymn, composed by Rev. Dr. Hatfield, was sung by the choir, the congregation all standing:

"They come! see, they come, from the land and the sea!
The friends of the world, to the world's jubilee;
They come from the north, from the east, and the west,
To save the inebriate, to help the distressed;
While floating on high, is their banner unfurled,
Inscribed with the motto, THE HOPE OF THE WORLD.

They meet, to rehearse what Jehovah hath done;
To tell of the triumphs by temperance won;
To joy for the drunkard from ruin reclaimed,
And weep for the millions by liquor inflamed;
While floating on high, is their banner unfurled,
Inscribed with the motto, THE HOPE OF THE WORLD.

Now, praised be the God of the winds and the waves!
Who rescued our brethren from watery graves,
Who gives us the blessing to meet them once more,
His wonders to hear, and his grace to adore;
While floating on high, is our banner unfurled,
Inscribed with its motto, THE HOPE OF THE WORLD.

CHAPTER XII.

Decision of Supreme Court of the United States, on the License Question —Repeal of the New York Law—Dr. Nott's Lectures—The Nott Controversy—Famine in Ireland—Instructive Lessons.

The friends of temperance entered on the year 1847 in great solicitude relating to the forthcoming decision of the Supreme Court of the United States on the license question. Should it declare, as Messrs. Webster and Choate were arguing, that the States had no constitutional right to regulate or suppress the traffic in intoxicating liquors, there would be an end to all hope of protection from that great evil, excepting through moral suasion. All law would be for the protection of the traffic, rather than the people. It was with great joy, therefore, that they heard on the sixth of March, that the unanimous decision of the Court was, that "the States have a right to regulate the trade in, and licensing the sale of ardent spirits." Six of the nine judges were upon the bench, viz.: Taney, McLean, Wayne, Nelson, Woodbury and Grier. All gave full written opinions, which were very instructive and satisfactory to all reflecting men throughout the country. In Portland, Boston, Providence, New York, and other cities, large public meetings were held, in which the decision was joyfully received, in full confidence in its justice and its important connection with the future progress of the temperance cause, and the welfare of the people.

But in the State of New York joy was almost immediately turned into grief and indignation by the vote of the people, in a large number of towns, reversing their former decision on the license question; and by the act of the Legislature repealing the law of 1845, and throwing the State back under the old Revised Statutes. The magnitude of the temperance victory in 1846 had placed the friends of temperance at their ease, and led them to feel that their work was accomplished. The facilities of obtaining drink in towns which voted license, by adjoining towns, especially the open trade of the great city of New York, which did not come under the law, made the NO LICENSE vote in many places almost a nullity. Many politicians were most active to make capital for themselves; and now the decision of the Supreme Court of the United States had extinguished all hope, in the thousands of manufacturers and venders, of resisting license law as unconstitutional. So that, with a desperate effort, in two hundred, out of three hundred towns, which had voted no license, the decision was reversed, and in many cases by large majorities; and the Legislature, chosen much with this object in view, in a summary manner gave a quietus to all the temperance expectation. Great was the exultation among the manufacturers, venders, and consumers of strong drink, while the friends of truth and humanity were taught to be still, and put their trust in the power of truth and love, and the overrulings of a righteous Providence. They had nothing to regret in all they had done. The law was as successful as any reasonable man could have expected. Said the report of the minority of the Legislature in resisting the repeal:

In the country towns where the vote was no license, to a great extent the traffic has been abandoned. Many dealers have acquiesced in the public sentiment of the State and of their towns, and, in good faith, obeyed the law. Many others have apparently done so; and if they have not yielded implicit obedience have closed their bars, or withdrawn their liquors from the public gaze, and thereby removed a great temptation to the young, the idle, and the community at large.

Other States, however, held to their integrity. Maine had enacted a law prohibiting the traffic altogether, and empowering the heirs, or widow and orphans of the drunkard to recover back the money paid for liquors—the first law, thoroughly prohibitory, ever passed by a Christian State. Vermont, voting on the license question, gave 8,091 majority against all license. In New Hampshire, many towns had elected boards of excise, who had refused to grant license. In Rhode Island, every town but three, had, for two years, voted no license. In Massachusetts, commissioners, elected by the people, had, with one or two exceptions, withheld all license. In Connecticut, the Legislature gave the license question to the people, who, in three-fourths of the towns, voted no license, but in 1846 they repealed the law, and enacted another countenancing and sustaining the reputable vender in his business. In New Jersey, the license question was given to the people, and twenty thousand petitioners had asked that all sale might be forbidden on the Sabbath. In Pennsylvania, the license question was given to all who desired it, being eighteen counties, and these generally voted NO LICENSE. In Indiana, Michigan, Iowa, and Wisconsin, the question was given to the people; about half the towns voted NO LICENSE. In Iowa, every county but Keokuk. Ohio and Michigan made it unconstitutional ever more to grant license. Such progress had been made throughout the country against licensing and sustaining the traffic. Its ruinous tendencies were everywhere demanding prohibition. From the first of May, 1846, to April 30, 1847; 12,876 persons had been committed for intoxication in New York city. The minority report of the committee of the New York Legislature, just quoted, remonstrating against the repeal, said:

> Within the last ninety days, and since we have been here convened, and engaged in legislative duties, our ears have been pained, and our sensibilities aggrieved almost by the cries of twelve human beings sacrificed in the counties of Albany, Schenectady, and Schoharie upon the altar of this inhuman traffic. Four men perished in the highway from drunkenness; two children from drunkenness, in presence of their drunken parent. One mother and five children burned alive. One boy stabbed by drunken men in the street, and his bowels gushed out; and a man in Rochester killed by a blow on his head, by a billet of wood, by boys inflamed by whiskey.

And yet the license law, as given in New York, in 1845, was not satisfactory to temperance men, inasmuch as it gave towns which voted LICENSE opportunity to enrich themselves on the miseries of their neighbors who voted NO LICENSE; and especially New York city, to flood the whole State with rum and ruin. They, therefore, held themselves, when it was repealed, in hope of something better in future, but in great indignation at the indifference of many professedly good men, and the arts of base politicians.

The following language in the Report of our committee, at the May Anniversary, expressed the feelings of the temperance community:

> "The right of self-defence none can question. It is a primary law of nature. It lies at the very foundation of civil government, and is the great object of government. All laws are enacted in self-defence, to protect the community from existing or threatened evils. But what evil is greater than the traffic in intoxicating drinks, which brings with it such a train of wailing, lamentation, and wo? War, famine, and pestilence are trifles compared with it. Let a son be brought wounded or slain from the field of battle, and it can be endured; let him come home with the plague of Smyrna or Egypt, and it can be endured; let him pine away with hunger, and die like the sons of Erin, and it can be endured; but let him come from the shop of the vender, a drivelling drunkard, and curse

his father and his mother, and fall into a drunkard's grave, and it *cannot* be endured. The question is between the people and the manufacturers and venders. It is not between the people and the Government. The people demand protection. The vender says: 'You shall not have it; no law shall intervene between me and my business. If I fire my gun, and send my shot through your streets, and kill your sons, no law shall prevent me.' Yea, the vender says more: 'I'll have protection; I'll be licensed to do it.

'Licensed to do my neighbor harm,
Licensed to kindle hate and strife,
Licensed to nerve the robber's arm,
Licensed to whet the murderer's knife.

Every law shall be repealed which takes away my license; and if I can't have license, I will sell without license; and take vengeance on the man who interferes with my business.'

"Here is the conflict in the Empire State, and in almost every other State in the Union. The acts of a legislature in relation to the two parties, are much as they are swayed by the parties themselves, and are, by no means, the index of truth. In giving to the people the liberty of saying at the polls whether they wished protection, they sided with the people. In taking away that liberty, they sided with the venders. The vender, even while he claims immense majorities, and says the people are with him, and he wants no protection, is not willing to trust the question with the people. He dare not. He knows, if he has a majority with him, it is a forced majority, a bought majority, a miserably deluded majority; and that, as soon as they are unshackled, and come to the light, the people will drive him from them, with burning indignation. The plea is offered that no law suppressing the traffic can be enforced, and therefore none should ever be enacted. Why not say the same of laws against murder, arson, theft, and counterfeiting? Who says the law cannot be enforced, but the rum-seller? And what a spirit is his which refuses obedience! He is the cause of all the difficulty—the only nullifier. And are the people never to be defended against unendurable evils, because the doer never chooses to regard punishment or law, or to cease doing injury? Surely, a government that would wink at this could not be ordained of God, for good; but for evil of the basest kind."

My excursion to England deeply impressed me with the importance of sustaining the cause in America; for I saw that our friends there looked much to our operation, and success here, as their great impulse and encouragement; and therefore forbade all despondency from the momentary triumphs of venders and political aspirants who would improve the moment for revolutionizing the State.

In 1846, the temperance lectures of Dr. Nott, President of Union College, which had been exceedingly admired in their delivery, in various places, were published; attracting then, as they ever must and will, much attention. Few productions in the English language had excelled them in eloquence; but some portions of them drew forth severe animadversion as incorrect in their quotations from classical authorities, while other portions were thought to be at variance with the fundamental principles of true temperance.

By most temperance men, Alcohol was considered, as described by Dr. Mussey, to be "a thin, colorless fluid, produced only by the decomposition of vegetable and animal substances in a state of fermentation, and the intoxicating principle of all fermented liquors, as wine, beer, cider, &c;" in no direct sense, therefore, the creation of God, or existing in natural fruits, and, as an intoxicating principle, to be shunned by all who took the pledge of total abstinence from all intoxicating liquors. It might, indeed, be so mixed and mingled with other things, and so diluted, as to produce no visible effect; still if it was in the cup, it gave it character. Dr. Nott was understood by many to affirm that the wine of the Bible, which was pronounced "a blessing," while it was not intoxicating, had in it still the intoxicating principle; that this principle was united to it by God with other elements of the pure blood of the grape, and that the beverage thus formed was not only innocuous, but nutritious and renovating, until, increasing in potency, it became in Bible language, a "Mocker," when it must no longer be used. His language was:

"The wine (the wine of the cluster) must be good wine, for it was approved of God; and, however it may now be spoken against, we believe it to be not the less worthy of commendation on that account; because we believe it still to be what it then was, unintoxicating wine. Not that we affirm the pure blood of the grape, as expressed from the ripened cluster, to have been absolutely untouched by fermentation, but only slightly and healthily affected by it. I am aware that there are those who consider the question of fermentation in wines a question not of degree, but of totality. 'Pure alcohol,' say they, 'is poison; and because it is so, every beverage in which alcohol is contained, how minute soever the quantity, must be poison also.' This, though plausible, is not conclusive; and were it so, the water we drink, nay, the very air we breathe, would be poison, for oxygen and nitrogen are so. In like manner, though alcohol be poison, and though every mixture of it in any greater proportions than that in which God has united it with those other elements in the pure blood of the grape may also be poison, it does not follow, if so united, it must be so. On the contrary the beverage thus formed may be not only innocuous, but nutritious and renovating; as the noble Cannaro found it when he drank the fresh new wine of the recent vintage; and yet this same beverage, so bland and healthful while its original elemental proportions are maintained, may increase in potency as its contained alcohol is increased by progressive fermentation, till, changed in its nature, it becomes what the Bible significantly calls it, 'a Mocker,' executing on those who drink it a vengeance, which the Bible no less significantly describes by comparing it to the bite of the serpent and the sting of the adder."

The objection to the Doctor's theory was, that it supposed Alcohol to exist in the pure blood of the grape, and to be placed there with other elements by God himself; that it helped form a beverage, nutritious and renovating, which it was right to use until its alcohol increased in potency, and so changed the character of the wine that it became a "mocker;" that this would always furnish an excuse for drinking alcoholic beverages until men became intoxicated; and that, if practicable to obtain the wine which, though alcoholic, was innocuous, no man could ever draw the line between the good and the bad, the intoxicating and unintoxicating. Our only safety, it was believed, was in total abstinence from all alcoholic liquors, because such liquors had in them the intoxicating principle which might commence a ruin, not to be checked or retarded.

A controversy on these several points was long continued in the Journal. Several distinguished gentlemen, as Dr. Mussey, Dr. Tyng, L. M. Sargent, Esq., Dr. Calvin Chapin, Chancellor Walworth, Mr. Delavan; as well as Dr. Nott himself, and the Editor, taking part in it. Dr. R. D. Mussey, then of Cincinnati, said, that he regretted that Dr. Nott had taken so much pains to show that the declarations of Scripture necessarily imply the existence of alcohol in the ripe grape.

"The wine of the cluster is without alcohol, and the taking of it as soon as it is pressed from the fruit, is the same thing as eating the grapes. A sound ripe grape is as destitute of alcohol as a ripe peach, or a grain of wheat; should a peach or an apple be mashed or have its skin broken, so as to expose its juice to the atmosphere long enough for a partial decomposition, and for the generation, either of alcohol or of vinegar, or of what is commonly called rot, the fruit is none the better for it, but the worse, and should not be eaten. The notion that a little alcohol makes the juice of the grape wholesome for a person in health, strikes me singularly."

Rev. Dr. Tyng, of New York, expressed himself greatly interested in the Lectures, and affected by their persuasive eloquence; but he should be greatly mistaken, and should rejoice to be so, if they were not perverted by those who would covet the use of such authority to a use most foreign from the purpose of their venerable author and abhorrent to his feelings. "How direct," said he, "is exposure to perversion in the following passage:

"'It is enough if wine be placed on the same footing as other articles of *diet*, with respect to each of which the question in relation to deleterious qualities is a question of degree, and not of totality. If we procure the best article in our power, it is all that can be required of us.'"

Said Mr. Sargent, author of Temperance Tales, in a letter to me:

"You believe, I presume, that total abstinence means total abstinence. So do I. Dr. Beecher, Dr. Edwards, Professor Stuart, and some others, I presume, are of the same opinion. This simple opinion is very intelligible and very safe; this abstinence from all that will intoxicate—all, as I have understood it, that contains alcohol. All chemistry agrees that decomposition and fermentation, without which there can be no alcohol, readily and speedily take place, at a temperature of about 60 Fahrenheit. New or old, fermented or unfermented, are ticklish questions. The result of incorporating such novel doctrines with our system, will inevitably be that every individual will profess to be cautious that he drinks nothing but good wine, containing a very little alcohol, so carefully proportioned that it will not intoxicate."

Professor Stuart, the most eminent Biblical critic of his age, said:

"I have read Dr. Nott's addresses with great pleasure. My opinion is, that it would be better to modify them, or make them less equivocal. The cause cannot be supported on any distinction between wines"—doubtless meaning alcoholic.

Chancellor Walworth sustained Dr. Nott. He said:

"His lectures will have the effect to relieve the minds of many who cannot believe, and who ought not to believe, that the Scriptures commend as a blessing, or that our Divine Master ever made or used that which it is sinful for his erring followers to manufacture and use themselves, or to commend for the use of others. I think, too, he has succeeded in showing, that the pen of inspiration only commends as good, the pure and unintoxicating blood of the grape before the vinous fermentation has progressed so far as to render it inebriating, and absolutely hurtful to man."

The Chancellor made a distinction between alcoholic and intoxicating liquors. If the former were not of sufficient strength to intoxicate, they were not to be classed with the latter. This had been his decision on the bench.

The recollection of this controversy is still fresh in my

mind, as it was painful to me then to come into collision with one so venerable and beloved as the President of Union College, and his numerous friends. It was consoling, however, to have the President of the Union say:

"I cannot regret the publication of your strictures upon these lectures, as I believe it will be productive of great good to the cause of which you are such a devoted and efficient friend; for their publication in our Journal will induce thousands to examine the Doctor's lectures particularly, who might otherwise have let them pass without a perusal."

To those who were filled with alarm lest the lectures should lead to the free use of new wines, mild wines, home-made wines, etc., it was gratifying to hear President Nott say at the close of the controversy:

"I HOLD TO THE UTTER ABANDONMENT OF THE USE AS A BEVERAGE OF DISTILLED OR FERMENTED LIQUORS OF EVERY SORT; ESPECIALLY OF WINES, WHETHER GOOD OR BAD, HAVING MUCH OR LITTLE ALCOHOL IN THEM."

And here the controversy ended.*

The following eloquent passage is from Dr. Nott's address to venders:

"Brethren, innkeepers, grocers: whose business it has been to sell to drinkers the drunkard's drink, has it never occurred to your mind, that the liquors dispensed were destined, though unseen by you, to blanch some glow of health—to wither some blossom of hope—to disturb some asylum of peace—to pollute some sanctuary of innocence, or plant gratui-

* If any inquire what was the difference between the wine pronounced good wine and a blessing by Dr. Nott, and that which was commended by Dr. Duffield and Anti-Bacchus, be it replied: the latter was the juice of the grape unfermented, and without any Alcohol. "The juice of the grape," said Dr. Duffield, "in an unfermented state, which, being new or inspissated by boiling, possessed no intoxicating properties, but was a cooling, nourishing drink, either taken by itself or diluted by water." "The case," said Mr. Parsons, "is now to me clear, that alcoholic liquors are never spoken of with approbation in any part of the Bible." Dr. Nott, as Chancellor Walworth affirms, considers wine touched with alcohol as good wine, if it has not in it sufficient to intoxicate.

8

tous, perhaps enduring misery in some bosom of joy? Have you never in imagination followed the wretched inebriate, whose glass you have poured out, or whose jug or bottle you have filled—have you never, in imagination, followed him to his unblessed and comfortless abode? Have you never mentally witnessed the faded cheek and tearful eye of his broken-hearted wife—never witnessed the wistful look and stifled cry of his terror-stricken children, waiting at nightfall his dreaded return—and marked the thrill of horror which the approaching sound of his footsteps sent across their bosoms? Have you never in thought marked his rude entrance,—his ferocious look—his savage yell—and that demoniacal phrensy, under the influence of which, father—husband, as he was, he drove both wife and children forth, exposed to the wintry blast, and the peltings of the pitiless storm, or, denying them even this refuge, how he has smitten them both to the earth, beneath his murderous arm?

"And ye, men of fortune, manufacturers, importers, wholesale dealers, will you not, for the sake of the young and the old, the rich, the poor, the happy, the miserable, in one word, for the sake of our common humanity, in all the states and forms in which it is presented, will you not shut up your distilleries, countermand your orders, and announce the heaven-approved resolution, never hereafter to do aught to swell the issue of these waters of woe and death, with which this young Republic is already flooded? Have you never thought, as you rolled out, and delivered to the purchaser his cask, how many mothers must mourn—how many wives must suffer—how many children must supplicate—how many men of virtue must be corrupted—men of honor debased, and of intelligence demented by partaking of that fatal poison? These are evils which God registers in his book of remembrance, and which the day of judgment will bring to light; for at home and abroad, in the city and the country, in the solitude, and by the way-side—it is not blessings, but curses, that the venders of intoxicating liquors dispense to their customers."

The year 1847 furnished two most instructive lessons to the friends of temperance, both in Europe and America, in the famine which was pervading Ireland. While seven millions in Ireland were crying for bread, and thousands had been hurried into eternity amid all the agonies of starvation, sixty-two million bushels of bread-stuffs were devoted in a single year to the creation of drinks which afforded no nutriment; and not less than fifty-two millions of pounds sterling were devoted in the United Kingdom to the craving appetite for strong drink,—a more heartless and cruel appropriation of the bounties of heaven, and the love of gold in man was perhaps never known. The Committee of the American Temperance Union felt themselves called upon to remonstrate against such an awful waste, and such indifference to the best interests of humanity. They accordingly sent out an address to their friends in England and Ireland, exhorting them to improve the distress then felt to show the wretchedness and cruelty of thus wasting by distillation the grain and fruits of heaven, so needful to man.

Another lesson taught was, the value of temperance in a time of public calamity. While the poor drinking population, by the force of habit, wasted their all upon the drink, they had nothing left to buy bread, which was so enormously dear as to be beyond reach of the masses; but the temperance men, having spent nothing on liquor, were now able to give bread and meat to themselves and their children. A most wonderful preparation was the work under Father Mathew, for this day of anguish. At beholding the spectacle, his heart was filled with joy. "Few," said he, "of those who have signed the temperance pledge have been severe sufferers, as they had been led to a provident care of themselves." And again in a letter to a friend:

> "It will delight you to be assured that the sacred cause for which we have so long and successfully labored is progressing gloriously. In the midst of sufferings even unto death, the pledge is faithfully observed; and we now—thanks be to God—number more in the ranks of teetotalers, than at any other period. The temperance society is being tested like gold in the furnace by these calamitous times. Drunkenness will never again, while the Divine assistance is vouchsafed, become the national sin of Ireland."

And another lesson, calling for devout thankfulness, was, that, through the temperance reformation, we at this awful moment, when God was thus afflicting our brethren beyond the sea, had bread enough and to spare.

Had our 40,000 distilleries continued their work of destruction, enriching their owners by the consumption of whiskey among millions at home and abroad, we should have been without ability to aid. But by the great reform of 1841 and '2 they were reduced to 10,000; the bread stuffs were spared, and now, in this year of want, we were enabled to send, and had the heart to send, in less than eight months forty-two million bushels of corn and wheat to relieve the suffering. England's rulers asked how it could be? We told them how. "Our people forbear. We waste not the gifts of heaven on brutal, sensual appetite. Our people are temperate, prosperous, philanthropic and happy." It was an argument for temperance they could neither gainsay nor resist.

So affected was Mr. Brotherton, M. P., that he called on Parliament to encourage, as the best relief, abstinence societies.

"He understood the object of the government measures was to mitigate the distress of Ireland, by providing food for the people. It was proposed to convert sugar, a necessary of life, into spirits and beer; that the barley might be used for food. From returns on the table of the house, it appeared that 27 million gallons of spirits were annually consumed, being at the rate of one gallon for every man, woman and child in the United kingdom. In addition to which, six million gallons of wine and 400 million gallons of ale were consumed, at a cost of FIFTY MILLIONS STERLING. Upwards of 40 million bushels of malt were charged with duty for home consumption. Thus the produce of two or three million acres of land might as well be thrown into the sea; for, in his opinion, intoxicating liquor produced nothing but poverty, crime, disease and wretchedness. If the House would use their moral influence in encouraging ABSTINENCE SOCIETIES, and discouraging intemperance, they would do more to ameliorate the condition of the people, increase their comforts, and elevate their morals than by any other measure whatever. People were very apt to complain of bad government, but it appeared they voluntarily taxed themselves to the extent of FIFTY MILLIONS STERLING."

A manifest change was this year coming over the ministers of Scotland. Sixty ministers of the Relief Secession Church had in a body signed the pledge; and united with 184 ministers of the city and county of Edinburgh, and the provost magistrates and councillors. The existing custom of giving wines and spirits at funerals was abolished. So slow is the abolition of customs which have become seated upon a community; though, once abolished, they appear so perfectly irrational, useless, and even injurious, that they could never be brought back.

But the most important event of Britain, this year, was the obtaining of the signatures of more than a thousand eminent medical men, throughout Great Britain, to the Declaration:

"That Total and Universal Abstinence from Alcoholic liquors and intoxicating beverages of all sorts would greatly contribute to the health and prosperity, the morality and the happiness of the human race." Of these, 184 were in London, 26 in Edinburgh, 184 in Liverpool, 75 in Manchester, &c.

One of the greatest evils, much complained of in America, was the want of such decision and harmony among the medical men on this subject. It was feared that many reformed men were drawn back to drink anew, and many families were entering the path of ruin, through the medical use of wine, beer, and strong drink. As one of the effects of alcohol, Governor Briggs, of Massachusetts, stated that a Committee of the Legislature, after careful investigation, had reported to him that there were from 1,200 to 1,300 idiots in the State, and from 1,100 to 1,200 of them were born of drunken parents. The sixteenth Annual Report of the Massachusetts Hospital declared that intemperance produced a large per cent. of the cases of insanity; that the continued use of alcoholic drinks produced functional, and soon organic, disease of the brain, of itself almost entirely incurable. "'A confused mind, a horrid apprehension of impending evil, timidity and rashness, and a homicidal propensity, were the common symptoms of this form of insanity."

The 21st of October, 1848, was a great and glorious day for the friends of Cold Water in Boston, when the water from Lake Cochituate was brought to that city. Hundreds of thousands witnessed the glad spectacle. But the friends of Temperance considered it their day, and turned out in mass, all their societies, with music, badges, and banners. The numerous bands of children were all marshalled upon the Common, and when the water was let in, sang with their ten thousand voices:

> "My name is Water; I have sped
> Through strange dark ways, untried before,
> By pure desire of friendship led,
> Cochituate's Ambassador:
> He sends four royal gifts by me,
> Long life, health, peace, and purity."

Several other beautiful temperance odes were prepared for the occasion by Pierpont, Tappan, and others. By all it was considered, as was the introduction of the Croton into New York, a great event for temperance.

CHAPTER XIII.

Attention of the Christian Ministry and Churches turned to the Cause—Mr. Wesley's rule restored—New York and New Jersey Synod—Convention of Ministers in Philadelphia—Convention of Ministers in New York—Resolutions of General Assembly Pres. Church—Ministers' Meeting in Boston—Resolutions—Meeting of 200 Ministers at Manchester, in England—Does Teetotalism tend to Infidelity?—Sunday Liquor Traffic in New York, Sermon on—Petition to the Mayor.

If the ministry and the churches were, in a measure, set aside by the Washingtonian movement and its subsequent beneficent Orders, they lost no sympathy with the cause; and when that marvellous action had spent its force, called upon by public sentiment, they came forward to uphold the cause and save the land from the renewed desolations of intemperance. And yet there were difficulties in the way. Influences were at work, with which they could have no sympathy. But necessity was laid upon them. Said the Committee of the American Temperance Union, in their Ninth Report, 1845:

"Without decided aid and support from the Church, the Temperance Reform may struggle on, and press forward, but ultimately, it must languish and die. That aid brought it up from infancy to manhood; when, not from disaffection, but from a mistaken apprehension that it was not needed, it left the cause to the care of others. But she must return, and cast her salt into the fountain, or all will become putrid, and corruption will seize the whole vitality. She must return and give herself to its support, or the strongest hold of Satan can never be vanquished. She must return and cleanse her own garments, and wage a personal conflict for her own sake, and the sake of her own baptized offspring. And if the friends of temperance are wise, they will seek the aid of the ministry and the churches, that, by mutual concession and action, they march on together to certain victory. Let not the hand say to the foot, 'I have no need of thee.'"

Not a little cause of alarm had the Church for herself and her offspring. Errors among the advocates of temperance; false taste, and unauthorized assumptions, had prejudiced many good men against the entire cause; and one whole and powerful denomination—and this among the higher classes—had stood almost entirely aloof, and gloried in it; but not without humiliation, in seeing some of their most distinguished and talented men thrown down by drunkenness, and cast out in open disgrace.

In 1847, an association of clergymen and pious laymen was formed in the city of New York, to be conducted on Christian principles (not antagonistic to other organizations, only to intemperance), on the sure basis of the Word of God, from Christian love; and to be so conducted as to commend itself to the attention and regard of all the friends of religion and pure morality. A similar organization was looked for in every town and city throughout the land. The first meeting of this Society was held in the Broadway Tabernacle, February 2d, 1848. Dr. Peck, of the Methodist Church, President, was in the chair; and the meeting was most ably addressed by Rev. Henry Ward Beecher, and Rev. Dr. Tyng. A fine spirit pervaded the meeting, and there seemed a determination to rally all the Christian feeling in the city, in support of the cause. Said Dr. Tyng:

"In looking around upon our assembly to-night, I cannot but think it is the most magnificent meeting I ever saw in this tabernacle; and that for the cause of temperance. The speaker who has addressed you [Mr. Beecher] has called himself a Son of temperance. There was no need of such an annunciation; for almost the very father of the cause was Lyman

Beecher. In the zeal and activity of other associations, the churches had thought themselves absolved from any great call to be active in the cause. Indeed the book might be found, in which the whole glorious work was represented as the majestical triumph of infidelity. It was when priests and Levites passed by, and the man was left to die on the road, the good Samaritan came along and took him up. We began at the time when the Church was almost staunched with liquor. The 'Royal George,' a noble ship, with eight hundred souls on board, was sunk, with a cargo of rum. The Church was almost in this condition in the early days of the reformation, when the father of my young friend raised the beacon-light; and, like the electric fire, it spread from pole to pole, till the great work was done. We now intend again to raise the standard, in connection with Christianity. Religion perishes without it; and without it every moral cause."

My recollections are very vivid of the joyful anticipations, from this meeting, of a revival of an interest in the cause in the whole religious community; and they were not wholly disappointed.

Among foreign missionaries, of various boards, in heathen lands, and with all the Home-missionaries, at the west, the cause was finding powerful aid; and the American Tract Society published and circulated, within the year, twenty thousand copies of "The Temperance Manual," by Dr. Justin Edwards, an admirable work to put into the hands of all young men.

In 1847, Mr. Wesley's rule was restored in the Methodist Episcopal Church, after many years of hard struggle, to the great joy of many in, and out of, that denomination.

At the regular meeting of the New York and New Jersey synod of the Presbyterian Church, it was unanimously

Resolved, That, as the churches are preëminently permanent and unconcealed organizations, formed under the rules of the Gospel, and destined to operate upon men in every age, the Synod desire to see the cause of temperance fully embodied in them, openly recognized and adopted as the cause of God, of humanity, and sound morals—a practical test of obedience to the self-control and philanthropy of Christianity. And they would recommend it to the pastors of churches under their care, to take, at the present time, such action on the subject as shall make a deep impression on the community around them, and secure the great reformation in all coming generations.

On the 8th of March, 1849, a large convention of ministers, of all denominations, met at Philadelphia, and unanimously agreed in the adoption of the principle of total abstinence as the basis of union and action, recommending to all the ministers and churches that they take efficient measures to gather in all their people, on temperance principles. The general impression and acknowledgment was that, when the ministers and churches were active in the cause, then it advanced; but, when they withheld their action, and, in a measure, ceased to operate, that then temperance, in most of its essentially practical enterprises, was at a stand, and even retrograding.

"They soon organized a city and county society, assuming that the true and efficient method of advancing the temperance reform is by setting forth the Gospel of Christ, and by making appeals to the public on the ground of morality, public good, the present and eternal welfare of man, and the fear of the Lord. They sent out a circular to every clergyman of all denominations, and to superintendents and teachers of Sunday schools, requesting coöperation."

During the Anniversary week, in May, 1849, a large convention of ministers was held in New York. Rev. Dr. Dewitt, of the Reformed Dutch Church, was called to the chair. After prayer and much deliberation, and the free expression of many leading divines relating to the state of the cause, a lengthy and solemn declaration relating to the obligations, duties, and good intentions of the ministers and churches, was adopted, and ordered to be published and extensively circulated. By this meeting, a great and good impulse was given to the cause, in all the churches.

On the 2d of May, the General Assembly of the Presbyterian Church was held at Philadelphia. I attended, on behalf of the Convention, and being invited to address it, I did so; and gave an account of the New York meeting, and read the Declaration; whereupon it was unanimously

Resolved, That the General Assembly do fully approve of the same, and recommend its principles and plans proposed, to all the pastors and churches within their bounds.

On the 31st of May, a large number of ministers met in Boston, and put forth a declaration of sentiments relative to the duties of ministers and churches towards the Temperance cause.

They recommended,

1. Personal abstinence from all intoxicating liquors as a beverage.
2. Preaching on the subject from the pulpit, so long as the evil continues.
3. The circulation of the Temperance Manual and other good publications in every family.
4. Keeping a list of all the families in every congregation who do not use intoxicating drinks.
5. Holding of public meetings.
6. Notices of progress in all annual reports of ecclesiastical bodies.
7. Much prayer in the closet, family, and social circle, for the extension of the cause, with a firm and desperate struggle with the traffic wherever it exists.

While the attention of ministers and churches was thus being raised to the cause in America, no less so had it been for some time in England. On the 13th of April, 1848, a convention of more than 200 ministers of various denominations was held in Manchester, in which a great spirit of harmony, love, and zeal in the cause prevailed. Organizations styled Christian Temperance Unions, formed of ministers and Christians of all denominations, were extensively formed. "The Christian Church," said such, "cannot, ought not, and must not let the subject alone. Her high claims, her divine mission, her benevolent character, her unsuspected consistency, all require that she pronounce her verdict."

As enemies to the cause in England had charged it with pandering to infidelity, or being a substitute for the Gospel, a Circular was there issued to several distinguished ministers, asking for their opinion on the subject. Numerous answers were soon received, denying the correctness of the charge, and upholding the temperance cause as in closest alliance with the Gospel.

The Rev. EVAN JONES, of Wales, wrote:

"I have been connected with teetotalism ever since 1836, and have visited six counties; and in all this time, I have heard of but one single case in which some members of a teetotal society were suspected of infidelity. Temperance, in Wales, is under the guidance of religious men."

Rev. WM. REID, of Edinburgh. "For twelve years, the Temperance question has been the subject of my thoughts and observation, and I have never yet met the individual who has been led to infidelity by the way of total abstinence."

Rev. JOHN PYE SMITH, LL. D., D. D., Hummerton Academy. "I have no knowledge of any facts bearing upon the momentous charge brought against us. Infidels and other ungodly men, though they may profess a wonderful regard for religion and the church, will draw perverse conclusions from the best principles. Our place is to confute them, by practically showing the injustice and absurdity of their reasoning."

S. BOOTH, Surgeon, Huddersfield. "My own observation and experience go to prove the very opposite of that which says that infidelity and teetotalism are connected.

We have one hundred and ninety-five reclaimed characters, honorable and useful members of society, and even of Christian churches."

Rev. Dr. Marsh, Leamington. "There was a Judas among the twelve apostles, and a Simon Magus among the professors at Samaria. There may be also infidels among the Temperance societies. But what has this to do with the principle of duty? Is it not also better for a man to be a sober than a drunken infidel? Here the total abstinence plan has taken several from drunkenness, and brought them to the house of God."

Rev. James Sherman, Surrey Chapel, London. "Although I have been denominated a teetotaller for fourteen years, and have had tolerable acquaintance with teetotallers and their societies, I know not an instance where infidelity has been the result of teetotalism. How can it? I can understand how the drinking customs of England and the habits of intoxication are calculated to lead men to infidelity, and I know men who were once sober and industrious men, who, by drinking, have found it convenient, for the gratification of their appetites, to cast off all restraint, and to rank themselves among the rejectors of heaven and hell. Yet how a drunkard who leaves his swinish herds, and associates with sober men, can be nearer infidelity, is what I cannot understand. I have the pleasure every communion to see at the Lord's table several who were once the curse of their families, the plague of their neighborhood, and the grief of their own souls, now intelligent and devoted members of Christ's church, whom teetotalism first led to the house of God, where the Gospel formed them into new creatures in Christ Jesus."

One of the most devoted of England's sons was Archdeacon Jeffreys, of Bombay. With a heart full of love to God and man, he had devoted himself for thirty years to the cause of temperance in India, satisfied that nothing else would secure the Church of God there from utter desolation. For, as the Hindoo was bound by caste to total abstinence, the moment he became a Christian, he would feel himself liberated from his bonds, and would at once rush into the use of intoxicating drinks.

We all hoped to have seen him at the World's Convention, but were much disappointed. We had from him, however, a letter addressed to the Secretary, in which he said:

> I take the utmost interest in the cause, as twenty-eight years' experience in India with the regiments, and in the hospitals, has convinced me that nothing in the least effectual can be done to arrest intemperance among the British army or the seamen that frequent this port; or to wipe away the disgrace that is daily brought upon our country or upon our common Christianity before the natives of India, except upon this principle. On receiving Hindoos into the Christians' caste, if the missionary does not exhort them to continue in the same principle of pure temperance in which they have been educated from their youth, and set the same example in his own person—if he once loosens the cord, or puts the stumbling-block before their weak consciences by even the sight of intoxicating drinks upon his own table, a flood of intemperance, with all its crimes, will come in upon the infant church and spread over India; and all our missionary efforts will end, on the whole, as a curse, and not a blessing, to this country.

This most excellent man died of the cholera, in England, in 1849. Of his affectionate appeal on the subject to all who love our Lord Jesus Christ, fifty thousand copies had been distributed.

The exemption of the city of New York from the excise law of 1845, and the repeal of that law in '46, threw open the whole State to the cupidity of the liquor-dealers, that multitudes regarded no law of God or man, and were led, for gain, to tread down the Christian Sabbath, in spite of all barriers for its protection. This evil had become so great, at the close of 1848, as to cause alarm among the friends of this holy day. It was found on inquiry, that not less than four thousand houses were engaged in selling liquor on the Sabbath, and that these houses were frequented by from thirty to forty thousand persons; though the greater part of the venders were foreigners, keepers of porter-houses, beer-shops, groceries, etc. If the sales of each Sabbath amounted to ten dollars each (and many, it was well known, exceeded fifty), two millions of dollars were exchanged every Sabbath, in New York, for intoxicating drinks. The results were, not only a great amount of disorder and violence on the Sabbath, but of commitments for intoxication, vagrancy, and crime, on Monday morning, far exceeding any other day.

Having possessed myself, as much as possible, of the facts in the case, extent of the traffic, how far it was a licensed traffic, what were its peculiar traits and evils, and what remedy could be found, I prepared a discourse on the subject, which I was permitted to present in several pulpits, and which was afterwards published and widely circulated. Several of the clergy of the city took a deep interest in the same subject, also many prominent laymen; and, on the 11th of December, a large number of citizens were assembled for consultation, at the Methodist Episcopal Church, in Greene street, where, after much deliberation, and several spirited speeches, it was resolved "to procure as many signatures as possible to a petition to the Mayor, asking him to interfere, and see that the law was enforced which forbade the evil." Forty-two leading and influential citizens, with the Hon. Theodore Frelinghuysen at their head, were appointed a Committee. A petition was drafted, and fifteen thousand names were soon appended to it.

On the 27th January, 1849, the committee met at the Tract House; and, with the petition, and roll of signatures, borne by myself, went in procession to the City Hall, and laid it before the Mayor. It was an impressive spectacle. He received us courteously; and it could have no other than a good effect; at least, every man engaged was thankful that he had done his duty in the matter. During the next July, his Honor issued his proclamation requiring obedience to law in the matter. It was gratifying also to know that, during the year, the Legislatures of Maryland and New Jersey had, by severe enactments, rescued this day from that vile and ruinous desecration.

The same subject was engrossing the attention of the Christian public in England. In the United Kingdom, it was reported, one hundred thousand men were employed in making liquor, and two hundred thousand in selling, and two millions in buying and drinking. In six consecutive years, the number of commitals for drunkenness in London, was twenty-five per cent., and, in the seventh year, thirty-six per cent. of the entire commitments of the land; when, if there were no difference in the days, it should have been fourteen per cent. The friends of temperance and religion, of all classes, earnestly petitioned Parliament for the suppression of the evil; and the result was, the passage of a bill closing all the beer and spirit shops throughout the kingdom, from twelve o'clock Saturday night, until one o'clock, P. M., on Sunday—a measure which, it was estimated by the chief of police in Bristol, would, in a year, cause the diminution of prisoners in that city, a thousand in number.

In the year of which I am writing appeared, a second time, the cholera, that frightful judgment of the Almighty upon our race. The friends of temperance, in remembrance of the past, began to thank God for the temperance reform; which had once proved a good protection, and might be again. But soon their joy was turned into sorrow; for, under a strange delusion, and new medical advice, the very food of the cholera was sought after, as the great preventive and cure. In Albany, in 1832, of three hundred and ninety-six cases, all but sixteen terminated fatally; of these, one hundred and forty were intemperate; thirty-eight, free drinkers; one hundred and thirty-one, moderate; five, total abstainers. In that city, which had a population of twenty thousand inhabitants, eight thousand were members of temperance societies; of these, only two died of cholera. In the ravages of the cholera, in this year, the same discrimination was visible. In the city of St. Louis, in a population of seventy-five thousand, were ten thousand deaths; but of these, only ten were Sons of Temperance—though that association numbered two thousand members. And in the whole State of Missouri, among 6,800 Sons of Temperance, there had been, during the year, but thirty-five deaths from cholera. In New Orleans, among twelve hundred Sons of Temperance, only three had been attacked; while scores of drinking and drunken men were swept off. In New York, where were five thousand victims, only eleven persons in twelve Christian congregations, as testified by their ministers, fell before it. And yet brandy, strange to tell, was the universal panacea, by advice of physicians, who seemed to pander to the appetites of drinkers, and willing to yield to the cry of venders ready to improve the chance to get gain. Even pledged temperance men, to a surprising extent, yielded; and numerous families supplied themselves, to be ready for the terrible emergency. Eminent physicians and medical men, as Dr. John Bell, of Philadelphia, Dr. Samuel Woodward, of the Worcester Insane Asylum, and Dr. R. H. Mussey, of Cincinnati, set themselves firmly against it; but it was like resisting the rolling in of the ocean in a tempest. Said Dr. Mussey:

"Upon boats on the rivers, the increase of brandy-drinking consequent upon the approach of Cholera has been frightful; and the mortality on board those vessels has been terrible and unprecedented. One boat lost forty-three; another, forty-seven; and a third, fifty nine of its passengers and crew. Spirit is not a protection, in any case. To the temperate, it is an active, exciting cause."

Said Dr. Woodward:

"Brandy and water, sulphur and charcoal, laudanum and camphor, Stevens' Specific, and Bird's Specific, and all other drugs and medicines, are useless, and worse than useless, as preventives of cholera. All intoxicating drinks are injurious; and tobacco, which is never beneficial, but always detrimental to health, should be abandoned, and never resumed."

But the temperance cause suffered an injury from which, it is supposed, it never has recovered. Many a family which had banished the brandy-bottle and spirit from their closets, returned them again; and there, in numerous cases, they have remained to this day, ready to step forth on the call of every ailment. The medical faculty, too, lost much of their firmness, and have been far more ready than before to commend the use of alcohol in their practice.*

* During the prevalence of the cholera, a gentleman, a rigid member of a religious society, and who had been a rigid teetotaller, desired his wife to put a tablespoonful of brandy in his glass every day at dinner. The wife was surprised; but, deeming it the result of wise professional counsel, she complied; and the husband filled up the glass with water, and drank it. A week passed by, and he said to his wife while at dinner: "My dear, you have been cutting off my supply of brandy. This has lost its taste. It does not produce the same effect as at first." His wife assured him that she had given him the full amount, and he said nothing more.

Another week passed by, and he repeated to his wife the conviction that she had lessened the quantity of brandy. It did not produce the same effect as at first. He could scarcely taste it, and the effects on his stomach were not perceptible.

"My dear," said the wife, "you have been taking *two* tablespoonfuls every day, for a week past—since you found fault with me for stinting you." He was thunderstruck. He sat a few moments in deep thought, and then desired the decanter of brandy to brought. Seizing it vehemently, he flung it from the window. He saw his danger, and made an end of brandy-drinking.—*Cin. paper.*

CHAPTER XIV.

Father Mathew in America—Reception at New York—Sail up the Bay from Staten Island—Reception at Castle Garden—Speech of the Mayor—Procession through Broadway—Administers the Pledge in Brooklyn—Bishop Hughes not Friendly—Meetings at the Cathedral—Invitation to Boston—Magnificent Welcome—Speech of Gov. Briggs—Operations in Massachusetts—Illness at Worcester—Sets his Face to the South—Compliments at Washington—Reception at Charleston, New Orleans, St. Louis—Return to Ireland—Death—Eulogy.

On Saturday morning, June 29, 1849, I had the pleasure of taking Father Mathew by the hand at the house of Mr. Nisbeth, on Staten Island, whither he was taken from the ship Ashburton, belonging to Grinnel, Minturn & Co., in which he had been brought gratuitously from Ireland. He sprang forward to grasp my hand as he spied me in the crowd; as much as to say, here is a friend I know in this land of strangers. He was not so vigorous and powerful as when I saw him in Ireland; had been suffering at home from illness, and was now wearied with his voyage. His voice had failed, but his eye was bright and his heart warm. On his voyage he held a temperance meeting every Sunday, and administered the pledge to 175 of the 400 steerage passengers.

In New York, there was the same enthusiasm in his behalf as if he had come in the days of his greatest glory; and appropriate measures were at once taken for his reception. On Monday, the city was very much given up to the welcome. At ten o'clock a splendid steamer was in readiness at Castle Garden, to take the Common Council of the city, committees of temperance societies, and invited gentlemen—about 250 in number—with Dingle's Washington Band, to Staten Island, there to take and bring him to the city. Never was a finer day, nor could a sail in the bay be more delightful. In a short space after the boat reached the wharf, he appeared in a carriage, escorted by the "Island Star" division of the Sons of Temperance. As he descended from his carriage, he was addressed by Alderman Haws, on the part of the Common Council, and assured of the hospitalities of the city. In a neat speech he replied, thanking him for the honor conferred upon him; when he was conducted on board, the band playing Hail Columbia and St. Patrick's Day in succession. On the deck, a circle was formed for the Common Council, to whom he was introduced; when Alderman Kelly, as President of the Board of Aldermen, addressed him with a hearty welcome. He replied, saying, "It was the proudest day of his life. He had never done anything but his duty; but whatever sacrifices he had made, he now felt repaid for them all." The committees of temperance societies next advanced, headed by William E. Dodge, Esq., who welcomed him to America in behalf of all the friends of temperance. "You are no stranger," said Mr. Dodge; "there is not a town in the United States where your name is not known. You come a conqueror, but not with the spoils of the battle-field. Your victories are moral—you have overthrown intemperance. We erect, to-day, a monument to you, Father Mathew. It is a monument of gratitude in our hearts."

Mr. Mathew was too much overcome to make much reply. He was then led to the pilot-house on the upper deck, where he was introduced to a large number of gentlemen, and where he had a fine opportunity of seeing the bay and shipping, as the boat steamed up to Williamsburg, and around up the North River to Hoboken. Many of the ships were decorated with flags, and many of the wharves crowded with people. The entire Irish population seemed abroad, to get sight of the apostle of temperance.

Landed by 5 o'clock at the battery, he was conducted to Castle Garden, filled to its utmost capacity, where he was addressed by the Mayor of the city:

"Rev. THEOBALD MATHEW: In the name of the Common Council, and in behalf of the citizens of New York, I welcome you to these shores, and invite you to accept the hospitalities of our city. The story of your life has forerun your arrival, and will secure to you, wherever you may go through this wide country, the high appreciation of good citizens for the eminent services you have rendered to the noble cause in which you have been engaged. The enemy with which you have grappled, is one of the direst of the human race. Frightful are the ravages of plague; but the destroying angel of intemperance has entombed more victims than any pestilence which has ever afflicted humanity. Quarantines and sanitary precautions cannot check its career. Yet there is one human power which can subdue this enemy of man. It is the moral power of a persuasive, earnest, and benevolent heart. It is this power which you have so successfully exercised, and by which you have obtained such astounding results.

"In your progress through this country, we wish you much health and pleasure."

Father Mathew said, in reply:

"I have long wished for the pleasure I now enjoy. I feel prouder on this day than I can give utterance to; gratitude is too swelling to find words of sufficient expression to convey any sense of it. All I can say is, I thank you—from my heart, I thank you. I am only sorry that ill-health prevents my addressing you as I ought; the intensity of my feelings precludes the possibility of giving utterance to them."

A procession was then formed, consisting of numerous temperance societies, with banners and music; several Irish benevolent societies; a large number of carriages, which moved up Broadway, through an immense crowd on the sidewalks, to the City Hall, where he appeared a few moments on the balustrade, and was loudly cheered by the multitude below; after which he was conducted to the Irving House, where he was entertained by the Common Council with a dinner, on strict temperance principles.

The next day, he gave a reception in the Governor's room in the City Hall. An interminable stream of men, women, and children passed by him from 10 in the morning, shaking his hand. Some knelt before him to take the pledge. In the evening he was welcomed at the Broadway Tabernacle by the American Temperance Union. Prayer was offered by Rev. Dr. De Witt. The secretary said it was his usual business to read a report. He now had but a very short one, and that was, FATHER MATHEW HAS ARRIVED (loud cheering). Dr. Cox moved the adoption of the report—that it be printed and spread over the land. In an unique but most happy speech, Dr. Cox then gave him a hearty welcome. This was followed by a lengthy address from the President, Chancellor Walworth, who was unavoidably absent, and which, in his absence, I read. The band then played the national air of Ireland, St. Patrick's Day, the entire audience standing. All eyes were now upon Father Mathew, to hear what he would say. He rose, and uttered himself as follows:

"Mr. Chairman—Ladies and gentlemen: With all the feelings of a warm heart, I thank you for this reception. The greeting which I have already received far exceeded my humble merits. I know my own unworthiness, and little did I anticipate the welcome which was so cordially extended to me by the American people. I had long seen with the deepest sorrow the miserable and degraded state to which my countrymen were reduced by the ravages of intemperance. I knew, in view of this, the difficulties I had to encounter, but, in a trust in that God who always aids the cause of the righteous, I set about the task before me with a zeal and willingness which so far have been blessed with success. I proceeded in the great cause of temperance. I knew that the vices of my countrymen proceeded from their position and not from the heart; they were not wedded to intemperance, and only wanted enlightenment. I went among them, and urged upon them the fearful state to which they were brought by intemperance, and upwards of five millions of them took the pledge. I cannot yet speak of the conduct of their countrymen here. I was sorry to hear of so many hundreds who have been guilty of violating their pledges; and from my intimate knowledge of my countrymen, I feel confident that after my visit, those few who have fallen into the vice of intemperance will return to the path of temperance."

Rev. Mr. Schneller, of the Roman Catholic Church in Brooklyn, followed with a welcome address from his countrymen in America and the city of Brooklyn; when the beautiful ode, "Sparkling and Bright," was sung by the assembly standing, and all were dismissed.

As a little time was required for rest, and he had been afflicted with a slight paralysis, and the cholera was frightfully raging, Father Mathew did not enter immediately into a great field of labor. I soon, however, found that he was administering the pledge to numbers of his countrymen in Rev. Mr. Schneller's church in Brooklyn. The scenes there were much as those I had witnessed in Cork. Large numbers were in a few days enrolled. I called on his behalf upon Bishop Hughes to see what arrangements could be made for him. The Bishop unhesitatingly said he did not approve of his operations, he thought the church had a better way. But the next day he called upon him at the Irving House, and invited him to his cathedral, and to stay with him. But he assigned him only a small room in the basement of the cathedral, altogether too small and obscure. It was filled for several days; much, however, to the chagrin and mortification of Father Mathew, who unhesitatingly said, he would never have gone, had he supposed he should have had a place so small and obscure assigned him.

But an invitation awaited him from Boston, where a great desire was manifested to welcome him; and on the

23d of July he left New York with his Secretary, Mr. O'Meara, for that city. On his arrival in the neighborhood, a large committee of respectable gentlemen met him. On Tuesday he was introduced to the city, which was much given up to the welcome. The multitude of men, women and children that were assembled to see his face, was immense. As he descended from his carriage, Dr. John C. Warren, ever foremost in temperance operations, made him an address in behalf of the Massachusetts Temperance Society. By the Franklin School House, the temperance societies were all forming under the supervision of Moses Kimball, Esq., Chief Marshal of the day. Father Mathew was seated in a barouche drawn by four splendid horses, with Dr. Warren, Alderman (Deacon) Grant, and Mr. O'Brien. Nearly twenty societies with splendid banners and bands of music followed, marching through all the principal streets of the city; arriving at noon at the Adams House for refreshments. At 4 P. M. all were gathered on the Common, where, on a platform, silence being restored, Governor Briggs addressed him:

"His Excellency alluded to the exertions of Father Mathew in the Temperance movement in Ireland, in England, and in Scotland, and hoped that his visit to this continent would be productive of much good. The people of this country sympathize with the Irish in their present sad condition, and deplore that political oppression had brought them to such a pass. But we live in hope, and from you, Father Mathew, said the Governor, we expect much for Ireland and for humanity. Though you make your first appearance in Boston to-day, you are no stranger to its inhabitants, or to the inhabitants of this Commonwealth, who welcome you—not as the warrior, crowned with bloody laurels—but as the chieftain of a noble cause, and the benefactor of your species. By your fair character and reverend name, the hearts of the people of Massachusetts have been drawn out toward the Irish here. In behalf of the people of Massachusetts the Governor welcomed the Christian philanthropist of Ireland to visit the workshops, the schools, and the institutions of learning and charity."

Father Mathew replied in a spirit of humility and

thankfulness, remarking that he had long desired to express the thanks of poor, unfortunate Ireland to the people of Boston—for Boston was the first to send a vessel of war laden with food to the starving Irish. He hoped to aid in the regeneration of his own people, whose happy lot it is to enjoy freedom beneath the wings of the American Eagle.

Several spirited speeches were made from the stand by Dennis W. O'Brien, Rev. C. Waterson, Mr. Leland, of Illinois, Father Taylor, Rev. Lyman Beecher, D. D., and Deacon Grant, who said every body was happy on this occasion but the rumseller.

The next morning Father Mathew was received by the City Government, at the City Hall, and cordially welcomed to Boston, and offered all the hospitality of the city, in a speech from Mayor Bigelow; after which he was taken to the Custom House, Exchange and other public places.

Faneuil Hall was at once opened for the Apostle of temperance, where he might meet his countrymen, and administer to them the pledge. He made no pretensions to oratory, but he had a kind word, which entered into the heart and soul of the Irish more readily than would the highest strains of eloquence. All his speeches and teachings were of a most practical character. He impressed upon them, in a few words, the importance of laying strongly the foundations of temperance, and then avoiding every place and thing which would at all disturb them. He was prompt to urge his countrymen to escape from the toil and drudgery and temptations of cities, and pressed them to remove, as early as possible, to the West, where there was land enough to support countless millions, and where, by honest industry, every man can soon become the owner of the soil he lives on. He pleasantly invited every one who wished, to step forward and take the pledge. He did not require it of every one to kneel; but he preferred it of his own countrymen, also that they should make the sign of the cross, inasmuch as it inspired them with reverence for the solemn promise they made. Often his address was very familiar, as, "Come, my friends, there is room, plenty. I promise you, you will not regret this step. It will be the foundation of your happiness here, and your eternal happiness hereafter." Several were fond of reminding him that they had taken the pledge from him in Ireland, and when and where; and he expressed his joy that they had kept it. In Faneuil Hall no less than 3,000 took the pledge. On the first Sunday he preached at the Cathedral in Franklin Street, and during the day administered the pledge to about 4,000. A great levee was made for him at the Mayor's. The principal citizens of Boston were present, and several of the clergy, medical men and reporters. For him was prepared a splendid supper.

It was soon manifest that Father Mathew had not sufficient vitality to perform the labors expected of him. He visited several of the towns in the vicinity of Boston; went to Lowell and Lawrence, to Providence, Fall River, New Bedford, Woonsocket, Bridgeport, New Haven, Hartford, Springfield; and in all New England he administered about 100,000 pledges.

Deeply was he impressed with the beauty of the country, and its progress in all that makes society blessed. In reply to a welcome from the authorities at Lawrence, he said:

> "Since my first entrance into your free and glorious country, everything I have observed demands my unqualified approbation. It is a country worthy of its great people. Language is incapable of expressing the delightful sensations that throbbed within my bosom as I passed up through the files at each side of youths of both sexes, who are enjoying the blessings of a religious and moral education in your schools, thus giving, at

the cost of the State, free industrial and religious education to the rising generation."

While at Boston he visited the Blind Asylum, and was deeply interested in Laura Bridgman, the deaf, dumb and blind girl. On being told that she was shaking hands with Father Mathew, she expressed great delight. He presented her with a temperance medal, when she wrote: "I thank you for the medal; we are all very glad to see Father Mathew." On leaving Boston an immense body of juveniles were gathered on the Common to bid him farewell. It was a scene of surpassing beauty. He designed visiting Albany, Rochester and the West; but at Worcester he was suddenly disabled by the severity of the cold and some slight paralysis, and it was thought advisable that he should go for the winter to the sunny South. I saw him frequently on his arrival in New York. He was quite changed, especially in his speech. At Philadelphia he remained a week; was presented to the City Authorities in the Old Independence Hall, and administered the pledge in some of the Catholic churches.

In Baltimore he was cordially received by numerous friends. At Washington he was invited to a seat within the bar of the House, but the motion was objected to in the Senate by Southern members. At home, with Mr. O'Connell, he had signed an address to the Irish in America, exhorting them to set their faces against slavery. This was republished in a Georgia paper. Colonel Lumpkin, President of the State Society, addressed him a letter, asking if those were his present sentiments? Receiving no answer, he withdrew his invitation to him to visit the South, and it was thought by many hazardous for him to go; but he was resolved to proceed, and commit himself to Him who judgeth righteously. The opposition to the motion made in the Senate drew out from some of the Senators the most signal tributes to his worth, and to the value of his labors. It was most heart-cheering to the friends of the cause to see it so exalted in the high places of the nation; and these tributes to the cause deserve a place, not only in the notices of Father Mathew, but in every history of temperance. Said the Hon. Henry Clay:

"I think, Sir, that that resolution is an homage to humanity, to philanthropy and to virtue; that it is a merited tribute to a man who has achieved a great social revolution—a revolution in which there has been no blood shed—no desolation inflicted—no tears of widows and orphans extracted; and one of the greatest which have been achieved by any of the benefactors of mankind."

Said General Cass:

"This is but a complimentary notice to a distinguished man just arrived among us, and well does he merit it. He is a stranger to us personally, but he has won a world-wide renown. He comes among us upon a mission of benevolence, not unlike Howard, whose name and deeds rank high in the annals of philanthropy, and who sought to carry hope and comfort into the darkest cells, and to alleviate the moral and physical condition of their unhappy tenants. He comes to break the bonds of the captive, and to set the prisoner free—to redeem the lost—to confirm the wavering, and to aid in saving all from the temptation and dangers of intemperance. It is a noble mission, and nobly is he fulfilling it."

Said General Houston:

"Father Mathew goes not with a torch of discord, but with a bond of peace, reformation, and redemption to an unfortunate class in the community. I, Sir, am a disciple; I needed the discipline of reformation, and I embraced it; and would that I could enforce the example upon every American heart that influences or is influenced by filial affection, conjugal love, or parental tenderness. Yes, Sir, there is a love, purity and fidelity inscribed upon the banner that he bears. It has nothing to do with abolition or with nullification, Sir. Away with your paltry objections to men who come bearing the binnacle above the turbid waters, which unfortunately roll at the foot of this mighty Republic."

At Charleston, S. C., Father Mathew found himself

much improved, and he officiated all the Sabbath at the Catholic Church—a vast crowd in attendance. He administered 1,200 pledges during the day. At New Orleans he occupied St. Patrick's Cathedral, where thousands were assembled. In an admirable discourse, he related what had been done in Ireland, how admirably the pledge had been kept, and called upon his countrymen to come forward and blot out every stain upon their escutcheon. He administered the pledge to large numbers. In gratitude they made him a purse of $700. The authorities of the city gave him a cordial welcome, to which he returned a grateful answer. On his passage up the Mississippi he stopped at all the principal landings for a short time, dropping a few words, and administering pledges; but at times he was quite feeble, and it was often feared he would not see Ireland again. At St. Louis he was received with great attention, and he there administered the pledge to 2,500 of his countrymen.

From St. Louis he designed going East as far as Pittsburg, and then returning South for the winter. Wherever he went, he was urged to make America his home, but he always replied: "It would be violating a promise made to his people, that he would return and die with them."

Father Mathew returned to Ireland in a Collins steamer, November 8, 1850. Crowds welcomed him home, but frequent attacks of palsy drove him to the Madeiras, whence he only came home to die, December 8, 1850, in the 66th year of his age.

The visit of Father Mathew to this country, notwithstanding his bodily weakness, was most happy in its influence. Not a countryman was there of his who did not give him a cordial welcome. Not one, perhaps, who had violated his pledge, who did not feel conscience-smitten and troubled in heart; and not one who had kept his pledge who did not feel rejoiced that he had done so, and become greatly strengthened. In great veneration for his character, and love for his object, temperance societies everywhere sprang up, bearing his name, and based on his pledge. These Father Mathew Societies have not only continued, but greatly increased in number, especially in our large cities, and now, in many, may be considered the chief strength of the cause. May they be handed down in great force to future generations, and his words ever prove a great talisman.

Father Mathew's friends at home were much gratified by the reception which he met with in America. Said the Cork Examiner:

"We have the utmost satisfaction in pointing to the account of the splendid reception given to Father Mathew by the citizens of New York. It was a reception such as the people of that majestic Republic would not have given to a crowned monarch; it reflected honor alike on those who gave, and on him who received it. America recognizes in the humble Irish Friar a man of whom all mankind may be justly proud—a man for whose glories no nation mourns, and no people is in bondage—a man whose victories over sin and evil have been more splendid than it has ever fallen to the lot of mortal save himself to achieve—one whose whole life has been a lesson of universal love—one whose mission is the holiest that could enter into the heart of man to conceive. America beholds in Father Mathew the greatest benefactor of the race of man; one who has conferred more solid advantages and more practical blessings on individuals and masses than any living being.

Lines on Father Mathew's visit to America, by Lady Emeline Stuart Hartley:

"The Hero of Two Worlds," that man of war,
The brave Lafayette, in old times was called;
More hallowed far *thy* deathless titles are,
Friend of mankind—O sainted Theobald!
A peace-apostle 'twixt two worlds of peace,
Thine is the triumph that can never cease!

See! charioted along the hearts of men,
  How that true conqueror reigns where'er he moves,
Blest be the difference wide 'twixt *now* and *then*;
  Then war scowled hate where *now* a nation loves.
Earth round seems one colossal temple made,
Where angels are the only hosts arrayed.

The noble "Hero of Two Worlds" art thou;
  No purer pilgrim ever touched this shore;
Echoes man's voice of praise and reverence now,
  Where raged the battle thunder's deafening roar;
Thrill, softly thrill, thou gracious western air,
With all the meek omnipotence of prayer.

CHAPTER XV.

Temperance Life Insurance Company projected.—Correspondence.—Dr. Nott, E. C. Delavan, S. Chipman, Rev. T. P. Hunt, Dr. J. C. Warren, Gen. Cary, and others—Medical Society at Cincinnati.—Addresses of Dr. Drake and Dr. Mussey.

THE great success and utility of the Temperance Provident Life Insurance Companies in England early attracted my attention, and the attention of friends of temperance in America; and in January 1850, several small meetings were held on the subject in New York. It was manifest to all, that, in the matter of life insurance, temperance men were not on a par with others. Not to speak of drunkards and hard drinkers, many moderation men were not, through a small indulgence in alcoholic drinks, living out their expected days; and life insurance offices were meeting with some of their heaviest losses in the early deaths of drinking men. In England it was found, in an experience of eight years, that the number of deaths in the temperance insurance company were less than half of that insured in all other companies in the kingdom; while they suffered no losses from intemperance. Should a temperance man join in a company with a hard-drinking man, or even a moderate drinker, much more an intemperate man, his money might for years be going to the families of such, while his family, through his long continuance in life from temperance, would have no benefit. The more the subject was contemplated, the more were all impressed with the importance of a company on the abstinence principle.

Much ridicule was elicited from wine and spirit drinkers. We were accused of making invidious distinctions in society, and contending against the natural laws of life; and since the bounds of human life were fixed, we were saying we would break over those bounds, and cause men to live beyond their time. We were also assured that enough of a single class of men could not be found in the country to sustain one institution; but we computed there were a million teetotallers in the country, and one half of these would be sufficient. Besides, so manifest would it soon become, that an advantage would be obtained by having total abstinence in a life insurance company, that it would become an actual means of increasing the number of abstainers. The very existence of such an institution, would be a great temperance lecture. It would lead man everywhere to inquire: Does the use of intoxicating drinks actually shorten human life, and would it be a strengthener of the principles of temperance where adopted? Would it not be a powerful confirmer in all who were insured? Would it not act like the pledge? Knowing that he forfeited his insurance if he was seen to drink, would not the young man be careful how he yielded to temptation? "I have my life insured for $5,000. Shall I now forfeit that for a single glass of wine?"

While we were thus examining and discussing the subject, I sent out a Circular to reflecting minds over the country, asking their opinion; from which were received encouraging replies.

Said Dr. Nott:—"I am, on satisfactory evidence, convinced that entire abstinence from intoxicating liquor, as a beverage, tends to increase the duration of human life. I am therefore pleased to see that a company is about to be formed exclusively for insuring the lives of 'teetotallers,' as it is unreasonable that those who do not drink should be subject to pay for the greater hazard of death in those that do."

E. C. Delavan:—"I cannot hesitate a moment in expressing my most cordial approval of such an undertaking. I doubt not the practical working of a company formed on the principle of *true* temperance (*total abstinence from all that intoxicates*), would bring to the aid of the cause you have so long advocated, overwhelming evidence of its advantages in prolonging life, over even the moderation principle—a principle no one yet has been able to define satisfactorily, and which if it could be defined, few would for any length of time adhere to.

"It is as well known to you as to me, that there is little or no intoxicating drink in this country, whether distilled or fermented, free from base adulterations. So that, in addition to the poison alcohol, other poisons more intense and more fatal to life are consumed by that part of the community which still use *intoxicating liquor.*"

Samuel Chipman, Esq.:—"I must express my gratification at the proposed measure, and wish it a hearty God speed. It is right in principle that temperance men, in getting their lives and those of their relations and friends insured, should enjoy the pecuniary advantages which abstinence from the use of intoxicating drinks may give them.

"There is one way in which the use of liquor, in what is called moderation, greatly increases the dangers to which human life is exposed, that is seldom thought of. It operates directly on the nervous system; and, at one time, the same quantity will produce a greater amount of excitement than at another, owing to different states of the system. And who that has had experience, or has observed in regard to others, does not know that, under such excitement, persons are frequently led to attempt some dangerous exploit, some hazardous experiment—the fording of a swollen stream, the riding of a colt, or a vicious horse, which they never would have attempted but for the unusual stimulus? I have known a person thus excited, in the most reckless manner seize hold of his neighbor, and, in a scuffle, he was crushed down, and his back broken. There was an inconsiderable number of this class that I found on examination in regard to deaths from intemperance, but they were always placed among the temperate in my classification. In that examination of all the towns of four of our Western counties, although I have shown that in one county 40 in a hundred, in another 36, and in two others 39 per cent. of the men over twenty-one years of age who had died in the year, were intemperate—yet that proportion, as large as it is, would have been greatly increased, had I charged to the account of intemperance the cases where the physician told me that, although the individual was considered a temperate drinker, yet he was fully persuaded, had not the system been deranged by the liquor he drank, he would have recovered. But what is still more to the point; at the suggestion of Dr. Nott, in three of the four counties, I ascertained the ages of both classes, and found that, on an average, the temperate had lived ten years longest. Another fact which it appears to me may have great weight in regard to life insurance as connected with temperance, is that, during the visitation of cholera to this city last summer, which took off over 150 of our inhabitants, out *of one thousand Sons of Temperance, not one* fell a victim to that terrible scourge."

Dr. Charles Jewett.—"Why should we who abstain from the use of intoxicating drinks, pay, when we get an insurance of our lives, for the additional risk to which those of the company are exposed who daily pour into their stomachs an intoxicating poison subjecting their physical constitution, either to the necessity of harboring it, which tends to the destruction of vitality or wasting its self-preserving power in one ceaseless struggle to throw off the poison? That human life is thus shortened, no candid and intelligent person will deny. Why then should we, who endeavor to order our lives in conformity with the laws of our Creator, and thus secure to ourselves health and long life, as well as the ability, mentally and morally, to accomplish more for God and humanity, go into a Mutual Life or Health Insurance Company on equal terms? No good reason, I believe, can be given; and if I can do aught toward securing to the friends of temperance an opportunity to effect insurance of their lives on more equitable terms, it will afford me pleasure to do so. The moral influence of such an arrangement cannot but be great.

Rev. Thomas P. Hunt, Pennsylvania:

1. Is moderate drinking a shortener of human life? *Most certainly.* And any man who will take the trouble to examine the effect of any *unneeded stimulant* on the human system, will see at once that it is so.

2. Are temperance men on a par in an Insurance Company, with men who drink? You might just as reasonably ask, are men who have had the small pox, on an equality, as to exemption from that disease, with those who are inoculated with its virus? All men admit that drunkards and teetotallers do not stand on an equality. Drunkenness is a physical disease, produced by moderate drinking. No moderate drinker can prove by a train of philosophical reasoning, that he will not be a drunkard. He may not be; but he may be. While I do not affirm that he will be, he cannot assure me that he will not be. He is using the virus. I look out for the disease. If he has it, it is what philosophy led me to expect. If he escapes, it is what he had no reasonable right to expect. We are not equal in a Life Insurance Company.

Moderate drinking renders men more liable to disease;

and more difficult to be cured. This is not mere assertion. In one of the oldest settlements (Saybrook) in Connecticut, the oldest minister in the State kept a record of all the deaths and their causes, for many long years. He was kind enough to permit me to see it. I was struck with the unusual number of deaths from palsy, epilepsy, &c. On inquiry into the habits of the persons, I was told, that many of them were most exemplary, pious persons—none of them were what would be called drunkards, but all of them *habitual cider drinkers.* About the beginning of the temperance reform, many cut down their orchards. The number of deaths from palsy, &c., decreased from that period. And when they occurred, *cider drinkers* were the victims.

3. "Do we deal unkindly with wine, beer and cider drinkers, because we say, "Gentlemen, your lives lie under a heavy mortgage"? I think not. It may be best sometimes to let some men have their own way. But no man has a right to complain, if another set of men follow out their own rights without interfering with theirs. I would not complain if the moderate drinkers excluded me from their insurance, if they believed that a little liquor drank daily promoted the health of the corporation. They would act consistently in rejecting one who pursued a course that endangered the profits of the company. Moderate drinking has caused more pecuniary and social injury than drunkenness ever did. And I would much sooner insure *some* drunkards, than I would *some* moderate drinkers. They will outlive them. This may sound strange in your ears. But it is true. And more men have died from the result of moderate, than from immoderate drinking. The Physicians of the Union will sustain this declaration. But be it correct or not, I can conceive of no injury done to the character or feelings of any gentlemen, by our refusing to insure on the same grounds

with men who drink. I act according to my best jndgment. I would allow others to do the same.

Most heartily do I approve of the formation of a Company on the principles you suggest.

Doctor J. C. Warren, Boston:—Having received from you this day a communication requesting my opinion on the expediency of forming a Mutual Life Insurance Company, on the ground of abstinence from intoxicating drinks, I would express my opinion as follows: All intoxicating drinks produce an unnatural stimulus to the vital actions, and hurry them on more rapidly than nature designs. In proportion to the strength of the stimulus will be the overplus of action, and the waste of vitality. In other words; life will be shortened in proportion to the power of the artificial stimulants. Hence it must follow, I think, that persons who employ no intoxicating drinks will average a longer life than others, and be entitled to insurance at a lower rate.

General S. F. Cary, Cincinnati:—Dear Brother Marsh: Your excellent journal of February states that several meetings have been held in New York City, by friends of the Temperance Reform, "on the subject of forming an American Temperance Life Insurance Company." Such an association commands my warmest approval, for the following among many reasons:

1. The subject of Life Insurance has not received that attention which its importance demands. It is certainly a matter of great moment that a man of limited resources may, without inconvenience, secure to his rising and dependent family, in case of his death, ample means for their maintenance and education.

2. Such an association making total abstinence a *condition of insurance*, would enable the temperance man who would avail himself of its benefits to do so at a lower premium than could otherwise be afforded. It is mani-

festly unjust to tax him with any portion of the risk incident to the use of intoxicating drinks. That total abstinence men are less liable to disease, casualty, and death than others, cannot be controverted. Let the skeptic on this point examine the journals of the Sons of Temperance for the past three years, and he must be convinced. No association on earth, not incorporating the total abstinence principle, can compare bills of mortality with that Order. There were but 1,260 deaths in 1840 in a membership of 221,478.

3. If such a Company was organized, multitudes of temperance men would avail themselves of its benefits, whose families will otherwise be left to struggle with adversity.

4. Such an association would lead many to inquire into the importance of temperance in prolonging life, who would never think of the destructive influence of intoxicating drinks.

5. Connecting, as this Society would, temperance with length of days, it would serve powerfully to confirm temperance men in their resolutions, and would furnish another and powerful motive to induce the insured to remain true to their pledge.

6. The distinction of the temperate and intemperate classes, which necessarily must be recognized, would give character and respectability to the one, which the other would lose in the same ratio.

While many moderate drinkers may not wish to have their lives insured, it would be no small rebuke to them to be informed that they *could not, if they would.*

7. The general cause of temperance would be promoted, as everything promotes it that brings the subject before the public mind.

Deacon Moses Grant, Boston.—The project is one of vast and incalculable importance, and calls for the profound and deepest attention of those who may be interested in it. That temperance men, who have their lives insured at a mutual office, do not stand upon equitable grounds with the other assured, is a proposition too plain on its face to need defence. I know of but one mutual life insurance company here, that even partially protects itself against intemperate men, and that is the New England Company. In their list of questions, is the following:

No. 13. Is he of temperate habits? Has he always been so?

If the applicant answers Yes, to the first query, and No, to the last, the company require what they call the temperance clause to be inserted in their policy, never minding if the applicant is a pledged man, and has been for years. Well, it being a mutual company, does he stand upon equal ground with the others assured? Certainly not; for, while his policy is forfeited, if he is known to drink, half of all the others, who, though daily in the use of intoxicating drinks, having, on application, answered Yes, to both queries, may increase their potations, become intemperate, and die drunkards, having shortened their lives by their evil habits; and our temperance man is yearly losing something in the way of money, by not receiving any return premium, as provided for in mutual companies, because drinking men and drunkards, assured at the same rates that he is, are dying out, and the policies are to be paid. If my engagements admitted, I could go into statements of facts and principles connected with this business which would show the vast importance of temperance men establishing such a company.

Gen. Cocke, of Virginia.—To the scheme for a life insurance company upon the basis of total abstinence from intoxicating beverages, I hasten to express my entire approbation.

It may well be placed among the felicitous conceptions of this our age, so fertile in the production of enterprises pregnant with future blessings to mankind.

These various opinions strengthened us in our determination to proceed. A constitution was adopted, and capital fixed at $100,000, in 1,000 shares of $100 each, on which were to be paid ten dollars, at commencement; and officers were chosen. But, alas! there was not sufficient advance of public sentiment in the matter for success. Other cities wished for the location; moneyed men in New York were already stockholders in institutions which might be injured by this; a spirit of rivalry and jealousy sprang up; temperance men might be good moral reformers, but no managers of moneyed institutions; and so, from a failure to get the stock taken, it died out, when, it is even now believed, it might have become one of our greatest insurance companies, and been of incalculable importance to the cause of temperance.

About the same time, we were encouraged by the proposed formation of another institution, which promised great and good results to our cause, viz.: A Medical Society by the Professors and Students of the Oldest Medical Institute in Cincinnati, to call out discussions among professors and students which might show how alcoholic stimulants undermine the constitution, and debase the moral sentiments. The first lecture was delivered by Dr. Drake, of Ohio Medical College.

After a few introductory remarks, the Doctor proceeded to define alcohol, and to investigate its effects on the human economy. "It was formed with the same chemical constituents which compose sugar, but in different affinities: alcohol was only from sugar. This substance might be obtained from starch, and alcohol distilled from the sugar, but it could not be made directly from the starch. It was a stimulant and narcotic, and was ranked among the deadliest poisons. Numerous experiments had demonstrated it to be a rapidly fatal poison; but it was unnecessary to make such experiments at this day, in the laboratory; because they were continually being made through the community.

"The influence of alcohol upon the human system was an important matter for the study of the medical man. He was expected to understand it, and he ought to be able to give instructions upon it. Drunkenness was a disease, a disagreeable and dangerous disease; it deranged all the functions. Its injuries were not only physical, but mental and moral." As a general proposition, the Doctor stated that the liquor in common use was about one half alcohol and one half water. "When a person took a glass of spirits, he only felt at first its stimulating influence, and was inclined to doubt that it was a narcotic, but as he repeated the glass, he found that a larger quantity was necessary to produce the first excitement; and after numerous repetitions, without the spirit, he felt dull and inclined to sleep, and was often rendered perfectly stupid. In large doses only was alcohol a narcotic; then its narcotic effect went before, and prevented the action of the stimulating property. It was the narcotic property which made it necessary that the drinker should continually increase the quantity or frequency of his glasses, to keep up the wonted excitement. It stultified the sensation. In the growth of this stupefying influence, the disease of drunkenness was produced; not the derangement particularly of any one organ, but a morbid, unnatural appetite in every part of the system; from the most important to the most insignificant organs and vessels, were mouths craving, crying out, sending an account of their pressing wants, by means of the nerves, to the sensorium, there acting upon the will, and driving the victim to great lengths and desperate means to obtain the bane which has thus deranged the entire economy of his system.

"This would account for the violent, disgraceful, and unfeeling acts intemperate men had committed, when their debased system required ardent spirits. There was, to many persons, a delicious sensation in partial intoxication; but it was a dangerous pleasure. Every repetition led nearer to the dreadful condition of him who was so dreadfully diseased that he could not exist without stimulus. The moderate drinker ran a great risk. In what was he indemnified? Where could he take out a life policy? Only from a teetotal abstinence society."

Before the same Society, Dr. REUBEN H. MUSSEY said:

"So long as alcohol retains a place among sick patients, so long there will be drunkards; and who would undertake to estimate the amount of responsibility assumed by that physican who prescribes to the enfeebled dyspeptic patient the daily internal use of spirits; while, at the same time, he knows that this single prescription may ultimately ruin his health, make him a vagabond, shorten his life, and cut him off from the hope of heaven? Time was, when it was used only as a medicine; and who will dare to offer a guaranty that it shall not again overspread the world with disease and death."

Throughout the country, at this period, the medical faculty, through the influence of Rush, Sewall, Warren, and Mussey, were generally with us. In a great entertainment given at Boston to the National Medical Convention, where more than six hundred physicians were present, not a drop of intoxicating liquor was provided. And, in the annual meeting of the New York Medical Society, at Albany, temperance and total abstinence were fully sustained by the most distinguished physicians. A practical view of the mutual duties, relations, and interests of the medical profession and the community was presented, in a work styled "Physician and Patient," by Worthington Hooker, M. D., Norwich, Connecticut. Few men felt more deeply on the subject of temperance than did Dr. Hooker. He had gratuitously spent much of his time in the Alms House; and, finding the rich and luxurious ignorant of the state of things there and its causes (their own practice and example) he published a series of letters from the Alms House, giving inimitable delineations of the degradation and miseries of the drunken poor; enough to cause every man, how rich soever he might be, to dash the wine cup from his table. Under the influence of his own observation and experience, he said:

"It is difficult to conceive that a physician possessed of the ordinary feelings of humanity should fail to be decided on this subject, either in his opinions or in his influence. No man has had so varied and extensive opportunities of witnessing the ravages of intemperance. It is not occasionally that he has heard from trembling lips the tale of woe, and seen its painful and often hideous signs. It has been with him an almost every-day occurrence. Misery on every hand, has made it appear to him. And if he has suffered his desire for popularity to hinder him from heeding such touching and frequent appeals, it is not too much to say to him that he has been shamefully recreant to the dictates of humanity, and that he will have to render a large account of neglected opportunities of doing good."

CHAPTER XVI.

The Half-century—Retrospect and Prospects—Tribute—Power of the Enemy—Army for Future Conflict—Truth and Love—Ministers—Churches—Temperance Orders—Sons of Temperance—Grand Division at Boston—Recent Publications—Fifteenth Anniversary A. T. U.

When a traveller has been long ascending a great height, and has at length reached the summit and sees all beyond him, below, and witnesses the setting sun going down on distant regions, he naturally pauses, looks back on all the way over which he has travelled, and girds himself with new courage for what lies before him. The middle of the century was such a summit for us temperance men; and if we had not labored full half a century in regular organization, we had for a quarter; and near half was completed since Rush and Porter and Beecher sounded the voice of alarm. As standing officially on the watch tower on the mount, looking behind and before, I felt it incumbent on me to prepare and publish a Half Century Tribute, in which I endeavored to show what we had done, what we had gained; where we were now standing, and what was before us; with an appendix of important documents of forty pages; which was well received, and had a circulation of six thousand. In fact, mighty changes had been effected among almost all classes, and in almost every department of human industry.

Thousands on thousands had been reclaimed, and ten thousand times ten thousand had been prevented from entering into the drunkard's path, and suffering his terrible woes. But many a dark cloud hung over the past. Amid all our exultation, intemperance had been the master-spirit of evil; wasting millions of dollars; breaking up the peace and comfort of happy families; sending procession after procession to the poor house, the jail, the mad house, and the orphans' refuge, and at least a million to the drunkard's eternity. We stood in hope for the future; but oh! what heart would not have been appalled could he have foreseen what already, in the first half of this half century, have been the ravages of the great destroyer. Whether we look forward or backward, the true estimates are beyond human comprehension; yet, in the almost universal disposition—especially among the unreflecting—to think lightly of them, and to inquire, when money is asked to arrest the evil, Why all this waste? it is well to look at it.

Not to speak of our own,—for we cannot get statistics here as they can be obtained in the fatherland—an English writer at that time estimated, from authentic and undisputed data, that, if drunkenness in that country goes on unopposed, to the end of the present century, there will have been consumed from 1801 to 1900, inclusive, fifty-one thousand million gallons of intoxicating liquors; causing eight hundred and fifty thousand million cases of drunkenness, and turning fifteen million seven hundred and fifty thousand sober men into common drunkards; exciting five million persons to commit crime; reducing twenty million individuals to pauperism, and taxing the community seven hundred million pounds sterling for their support; four million individuals will have been deprived by it of their reason; 255 million years of human life will have been cut off and wasted; eleven hundred millions sterling will have been lost to the trade of the country—equal to the foreign trade of 210 years; 5,800 million bushels of grain will have been destroyed for liquor which, made into bread, would feed the present population for twenty-four years; in the manufacture, and trade, and drinking, would be 21,774 million violations of the Sabbath; three million persons, equal to thirty thousand congregations, would have been expelled or departed from Christian churches; and 4,700,000 of the children of the church will have been demoralized, if not ruined. Well did he exclaim, "O COME TO THE RESCUE! GREAT GOD, DO THOU."

The means and the ravages of intemperance were, in our own country, appalling. In the State of New York, there were committed to the prisons, in 1849, 36,610 persons who committed the crimes, for which they were arrested, under the influence of intoxicating liquors; and of the poor in the poor-houses, two thirds, or 69,260 were pronounced, in the Assembly document, from intemperance. In Massachusetts (the most temperate State in the Union), of 2,598 paupers, 1,467, or 56 per cent.—and of 8,760 committed for crime, 3,341, or more than 38 per cent.—were from intemperance. In the city of New York, there were, in 1849, 4,425 licensed houses, 750 selling without license, and 3,896 selling on the Sabbath. In the quarter ending December, 1810, there were arrested in the city, 1,600 for drunkenness, 1,485 for intoxication and disorderly conduct, 744 for vagrancy, 1,214 for assault and battery, 1,006 for disorderly conduct; nearly all, the results of drink—in five years, 111,360 victims of the grog-shop. In Philadelphia, there were admitted to the alms-house, in 1849, 5,119; 2,323 were intoxicated when received. In the Mayor's Court, there were 5,987 cases of drunkenness and disorderly conduct, and only 324 of other descriptions of crime. In his work on Intemperance in Cities, R. M. Hartley, Esq., estimated the annual aggregate expenditure for intoxicating liquors alone, consumed in New York city, at $13,030,000—four times the cost of administering the State government, with the interest on the public debt; twelve times the annual receipts of the Bible, Tract, Missionary, and other public benevolent societies in the United States; twenty times the sum expended for religious works and educational expenses.

What army and what forces had we wherewith to commence the second half-century warfare with this terrible foe, in our own land? Truth and love were the great weapons by which we were still to conquer. The Christian ministry and churches had taken the field more decidedly and boldly than for several years. The American Temperance Union was well holding its own, scattering widely its tracts and papers. Numerous State societies, and county and local organizations, were doing as much as at any former period; though some, alas! had quit the field. Temperance lecturers were still abroad, with their armor bright. The Father Mathew Societies were becoming numerous and powerful. Throughout Canada, the cause was almost equally prosperous as with us. The Rev. W. Chiniquy, a young Roman priest, and powerful speaker, had there, and in the adjoining States, arrested much attention; and, in a short time, administered the pledge to 250,000 persons; 18,000, in four days, in Montreal. The marvellous Washingtonian movement had indeed finished its course, and its fruits were gathered into new organizations. Rechabites, Samaritans, Temples of Honor, were doing their work, in their various departments. But the Order of the Sons of Temperance had now swelled beyond any other single organization, and was spreading widely over the States and British provinces.

To the Fourth Annual Meeting of the National Division, to be held at Boston, June 11, 1850, I repaired, though not a member of the order (not being a reformed man), and still preferring open organizations, as best fitted to the cause and the country—though others, highly esteemed, differed from me. This meeting was the representative of no less than thirty-six grand divisions, 5,894 subordinate divisions, with 245,233 paying members. Its meeting at Boston, with its banners and regalia, was very imposing.

At an early hour, there had been seen rail trains coming from every direction, laden with members of different Divisions, who, at ten o'clock, began to form in different places, and, by twelve o'clock, began to move in one very imposing procession through the various streets of the city. Heading the line, was William A. White, Esq., the Chief Marshal, on a splendid charger. He was followed by the Boston Brigade Band, and thirty-six bright boys, Cadets of Temperance, each bearing a small, but neat flag, having the names of the different States, and British Provinces, representing the thirty-six Grand Divisions of the Order.

The line of procession occupied over an hour in passing a given point, and arrived at the Common at about half-past one o'clock, where a countermarch took place; the divisions were dismissed, and proceeded to their respective head-quarters, with music playing and banners flying.

At half-past three o'clock, a mighty gathering was to be seen on the Common, to hear speaking at the stand from Gen. Cary, Philip S. White, Rev. Thomas P. Hunt, Dr. Charles Jewett, Rev. John Pierpont, William R. Drinkard, and Mr. Copway, the Ojibwa Chief. All these gentlemen were popular orators; and their addresses, chiefly relative to the iniquity, abomination, and ill-deserts of the traffic, were responded to with loud cheering.

On Thursday evening, the 13th, Alderman Grant had, at his house, a Temperance soirée. More than one hundred gentlemen from abroad were present, who were welcomed to Boston by a neat address from Dr. John C. Warren, which was responded to by Gen. Cary and others. The meeting passed off with great sociality, and all felt that, though engaged in different ways in promoting the cause, all were of one brotherhood, and should labor with a kind and friendly spirit, in delivering our land and world from a fearful bondage.

A WELCOME.—BY GEORGE W. BUNGAY.

With the voice of many waters,
Let us sing while echo starts—
Welcome! Welcome! sons and daughters,
To our hearth-stones and our hearts!

With your snow-flakes where our fountains
Fall in showers of golden spray,
Ye have come from snow-flaked mountains,
Like an avalanche, to-day!

Here are banners and devices
Borne aloft with stalwart arm,
From the South-land, where the spices
Kiss the winds with lips of balm!
Onward! upward! bear the banner,
Like an angel's wing, on high;
Whilst your loud and glad hosanna
Shakes, with thunder-shouts, the sky!

From 1846 to 1851 there were continually laid upon my table productions of powerful minds, which showed that the nation was resolved not to sleep under the ravages of Alcohol, and suffer the drinking usages of society to drag thousands down to death, or the manufacturers and venders of strong drinks, for gain, to fill up, unrebuked, our jails and almshouses with wretched victims.

The first that occurs to my recollection, for it made a deep impression at the time, was AN ADDRESS TO THE PEOPLE OF OHIO, by S. F. Cary, Esq. This appeared in 1848. General Cary, though a successful lawyer and a man of wealth, had devoted himself to the temperance cause, and had become the head of his favorite organization, "THE ORDER OF THE SONS." He had visited and spoken in every city and town in the State. No man better knew the ravages of Alcohol; the miseries carried into unnumbered families—the taxes imposed upon a hardy and laborious and honest people, and the impossibility of overcoming and subduing the traffic by mere moral suasion. To no man would the people so listen as to him, and from no one would an address come with equal force. And though many might occasionally hear him in the large places, it was desirable that his words should go, as they might and would in a tract, to every hamlet. It was a subject of rejoicing, therefore, that he had made and published this address. He said: "A crisis had come to the people of Ohio. The question was to be settled by them, whether the land, overshadowed by the wings of the Almighty, should belong to drunkards and be under the dominion of that most heartless of all tyrants, the drunkard maker." In no common language he called their attention to the

Evils of the traffic;
Dishonesty of the traffic;
Their connection with it;
Remedy to be applied. He then called upon the people to
Dissolve the partnership; to
Brand the traffic as criminal; and to
Believe and feel that the Rumseller must be punished.
Moral appliances alone are ineffectual;
Our position is right, and we must
Petition the Legislature at once to abolish all laws regulating the sale of liquor, and to incorporate the traffic among its kindred crimes of theft, arson, robbery and murder.

These were his positions; half a million copies were published; and few were the men in Ohio or elsewhere, who did not see that they were well sustained.

The next that comes to my recollection was: AN APPEAL TO THE PEOPLE for the suppression of the Liquor traffic, by Rev. A. D. Kitchell; a prize essay.

When Mr. Kitchell wrote this, he was a minister in Connecticut. It so brought him to the notice of the public, as a man of power, that he was called to a pulpit in Detroit. The appeal was lengthy; it answered every objection which the rumseller could make to the overthrow of his traffic, and left him without a word in defence. This was published in 1848.

My own sermon upon the Sunday Liquor traffic has

already been alluded to. This was soon followed by another, upon The True Element of Moral Reform, and hope of the temperance enterprise. I knew many leaders in temperance did not sympathize with me, and would keep all religion out of temperance meetings, on the plea that it would keep from the meetings all irreligious, profane, drinking men, whom we most desired to benefit. But my anxieties were to place the cause upon Christian principle, to build it up in Christian love, and in dependence on a higher power than man.

Dr. Charles Jewett's Lectures were first published in 1849. Many were opposed to his publishing them, as it might prevent his delivering them more, which would be a calamity, since the force of what he presented lay much in the delivery. But as he had ceased reading, and as in his extemporaneous lectures he brought forward whatever was appropriate or demanded from all he had written, it was of small consequence. In a printed form they have been read by hundreds, and perhaps by thousands, who would never have had the opportunity to hear him. These lectures, as was the case with most of the Doctor's speaking, were of a scientific and practical character, upon the connection of temperance with the agricultural, commercial, and educational interests of human society, showing that, like Christianity, temperance brings men out of a state of darkness and barbarism, and elevates man into a condition of refinement, purity, and blessedness, which it is beyond the power of language to express. It is to be regretted that they have for a time been out of print; but they will not long be so when the public are deprived of his bodily presence, his expressive countenance and living voice.

The Crisis and the Triumph; a sermon by Doctor Nathan S. S. Beman, appeared in the same period. Dr. Beman was most thoroughly radical whenever he touched the cause of temperance with his pen or voice. He admitted no apology for the vender of intoxicating drinks or the consumer, even if he stood on the highest pinnacle of the church and was most careful not to pass, in the slightest degree, the bounds of moderation. He saw no hope for the community, but in perfect, total abstinence, and in the prohibition of the traffic. His heart was exceedingly cheered by the triumph, in 1846, in the License question before the people, as was his indignation kindled at the subsequent conduct of the New York Legislature.

Scripture View of the Wine Question, by Moses Stuart, Andover, and Reply by Rev. James Lillie, Carlisle, Pa. These discussions, which appeared in 1848, had so long been before the public that most men had lost their interest in them. Mr. Lillie discovered not a little critical acumen in detecting errors into which the learned Professor had fallen, but he showed little disposition for total abstinence.

Temperance Anecdotes, by myself. This was a small work, a collection of 200 anecdotes for the aid of speakers in public meetings to arrest attention where dry abstract truth failed. It commanded at one time a large sale.

Groceries, a Source of Mischief, by G. Magoun, Tennessee. A thoroughly practical exhibit of an enormous evil in every village, where groceries and liquor-selling were under one roof, exposing servants and children to inevitable ruin.

Address on Wine, by Sumner Stebbins, M. D., Chester, Pa.; an address of much power by one who, more than most other men, had made temperance his study.

Zoological Temperance Convention, by Professor Hitchcock, Amherst, 1849; an exceedingly ingenious and amusing work, from one of the most profound minds in America. It was a Pictorial Temperance Convention of birds and beasts, well illustrated; and each made to play his part in temperance or intemperance, in smoking or chewing tobacco, &c., &c.; designed greatly to attract the attention, and impress the minds of children and youth. One of the first publications on temperance was from the pen of this excellent man in 1829, entitled, "An Argument against the Manufacture and Sale of Ardent Spirits." Few men did more in his day for the temperance cause, than did President Hitchcock.

NATIONAL TEMPERANCE OFFERING, SONS' AND DAUGHTERS' TEMPERANCE GIFT BOOK, by S. F. Cary, 1850; a splendid volume of 500 pages, containing the portraits and likenesses of several of the principal officers and speakers of the Sons of Temperance. As a gift book, it had a large circulation.

PUTTING THE BOTTLE TO OUR NEIGHBOR'S LIPS; a sermon by T. L. Cuyler, Trenton, 1850. A spirited and timely attack upon the traffic and drinking usages in Trenton.

Sermon on the DEATH OF THOMAS TEW, agent of the Rhode Island State Temperance Society, by Rev. Dr. Cleveland. Mr. Tew had, by indefatigable labor, almost entirely extricated Rhode Island from Intemperance, and he well deserved the character given of him in this discourse. Dr. Cleveland showed why the course of true reformers appears to men of the world perfectly absurd. 1. Their principles are Christian, opposed to the selfishness of worldly men. 2. Their faith is in things unseen; not in present circumstances, which may be all unfavorable, but in the providence and provision of God.

"Sermon on the State of Morals in New Haven, Conn.," by Dr. Cleveland, 1850; a bold and faithful exhibit of the intemperance of that beautiful city.

Address of the NEW YORK CITY SOCIETY on Christian Principles.

"Responsible Agents of Intemperance," by Rev. J. F. Williams, Eastford, Conn.; a pungent discourse.

Dr. Carpenter's Prize Essay (England). "Should alcoholic liquors form part of the ordinary sustenance of man?" Republished in Boston with a glossary; the most able and convincing work, in the opinion of Dr. Warren, which had been written.

"Intemperance in Cities and large Towns, its causes and cure," by R. M. Hartley, Esq., the long and efficient Secretary of New York City Temperance Society; a most valuable work.

Several tracts. No. 2, for sons of Temperance, by Horace Greely. No. 3, by S. F. Cary. Curse of Meroz; Kingdom of Intemperance; Delirium Tremens; by Rev. J. Marsh.

Pictorial Tales and Anecdotes, Oliver and Brother.

Such were some of our forces in the field, and new weapons in our armory.

Nor had the Muse been backward to come to our help. The last four years had brought out stirring songs.

The last drunkard;
He stood the last—the last of all.

The prairie fire.—*Pierpont.*

The maniac's plea;
There's none can plead, as I can plead.

The drunkard's snare.—*Carter.*
I loathe it, I loathe it, the poisonous wine.

The wine fiend.—*Kimball.*
Away with songs of revelry.

There's a good time coming.

Upward! onward!
This your watchword! glorious one.

Look out while the bell is ringing.—*Bungay.*

Triumphs of the Pledge.—*Tappan.*

The tempter.—*Burleigh.*
If angels in the heavens rejoice.

A song of welcome.—*Bungay.*

The Wife's Appeal.—*Mrs. Rich.*

I stood near his grave.—*Mrs. Richmond.*

The temperance shout is ringing
In triumph through the air.—*Atwood.*

Muster for the battle glorious.—*Rev. P. Clark.*

The Temperance Banner.
Hail thou blest king! to thee we bring.

The temperance "No License" Triumph.
From hill-side and from valley.

Temperance Harvest home.—*Star of Temperance.*
A voice from the mountain, a voice from the plain.

Down with the groggeries, down.—*George Burleigh.*

The Hope of the World.—*Hatfield.*
They come, see they come from the land and the sea.

Widow's Petition to the Rumseller.—*Star of Temperance.*
Have I e'er wronged thee?

Fanny Forrester to the Sons of Temperance.
God bless the Mayor's casting vote.—*Boston.*

Our FIFTEENTH ANNIVERSARY, held in the Broadway Tabernacle, May 8, 1851, was one of much interest, as we were standing between two half centuries. In absence of the President, John Tappan, Esq., of Boston, Vice-President, took the chair. He stated that it was just twenty-five years since the first Anniversary of the American Temperance Society—a quarter of a century of great and glorious labor to rid the world of an insufferable evil. He congratulated the officers and members of the Union at the progress of the cause; and only regretted the absence of our distinguished President on an indispensable and joyful occasion. After the reading of my Report, the Hon. Andrew T. Judson, Judge of the U. S. District Court, who had become a warm supporter of the cause, was announced as a speaker, but a letter from him was handed in, informing us that a sudden illness had prevented his attendance. The letter expressed his ardent wishes for the ultimate success of the good cause and a final conquest over the greatest enemy of mankind.

The meeting was addressed by Rev. H. S. Carpenter, of New York, William H. Burleigh, Rev. Dr. Cleveland, of Providence, P. T. Barnum, on a donation from Jenny Lind, the queen of song, of an hundred dollars, Rev. John Chambers, of Philadelphia, and Rev. Dr. Tyng. Dr. Cleveland, speaking on progress, said:

"When two trains meet, travelling at the rate of twenty-five miles an hour, we seem to be going fifty, when we are going but twenty-five. The croakers say, we are now going backwards. The question is whether the croakers are right, who say we have done nothing, or the temperance workers, who think we have done much for which to be thankful. I think we have mowed a pretty handsome swarth. I am willing to admit, there is as much rum drunk now as there was twenty-five years ago, yet it must be remembered that twenty-five years ago, there were but twelve millions of people in the land, whereas now there are twenty-five. If we have reformed no one, we may have kept our twelve millions from falling into the sin and ruin of drunkenness."

His address was throughout one of great wit and humor. To Rev. Dr. Tyng, of New York, was specially assigned a half-century speech on the following resolution, but his time had been nearly all engrossed by others.

Resolved, That, standing on this interesting point of time, one half century behind and another before—one, a half century of preparation, the other, we trust, of decisive battle and conquest, we pause, grateful for the past—stern and uncompromising for the future. To ministers, to legislators, to magistrates, to judges, to parents, to teachers, to young and old, we appeal for co-operation in labors which, under God, are to remove one of the greatest moral evils afflicting our race, and prepare the world for the reign of the Prince of Peace.

Dr. Tyng remarked, "that it was too late in the evening for him to think of speaking much, but the resolution spoke of pausing; there is no time to pause in the great work that is before us. The Half Century that has passed has been one of stirring effort, and there should be no cessation in the exertions of this Society. A short time since a friend who had been travelling in the West, told him that in his travels he had one day encountered an emigrant journeying with his family to the fertile regions beyond the Mississippi. He had all his worldly goods packed on wagons, and on one load there hung a huge jug with the bottom broken out. He asked him why he carried that with him. Why, he said, that is my Taylor jug. And what is a Taylor jug? asked my friend. Why, said he, I had a son with Gen. Taylor's army in Mexico, and the old General always told him to carry his whiskey-jug with a hole in the bottom; and since that I have carried my jug as you see it, and I find it is the best invention that I ever met with. Now," said Dr. Tyng, "if our Presidents, and Governors, and Legislators would only carry such whiskey-jugs as this Western emigrant carried—if their jug had no bottom to it, we should have much less drunkenness and misery. It is their example that does more mischief than rum-sellers do."

CHAPTER XVII.

Death of General Taylor—Vigor of old Temperance men—Permanent Temperance Documents in School Libraries—Collision between New and Old Organizations—Letter of Gen. Cary—Temperance Hotels—Delavan House—Efforts of Dr. Jewett—Navy—Abolition of Flogging—Evil continuance of spirit-ration—Spirit-ration Abolished.

At the commencement of the second half of our century, the nation was suddenly called to mourning by the death of Gen. Zachariah Taylor, President of the United States. He expired on the 9th of July, 1850, in the sixtieth year of his age. Temperance, religion, and patriotism wept at his tomb. During the Mexican war, he ever showed himself a decided temperance man; and hence, it was conceded, was much of his calmness and power. He was succeeded by Vice-president Fillmore; also a decided temperance man. Not a few of the early friends of the cause were still in the field, to stamp their features on the second half century. Dr. Hewitt was still living, and powerful as he ever had been in the pulpit, at Bridgeport, Connecticut; Dr. Humphrey, by his graphic and energetic pen, was doing great service to the Church; Dr. Lyman Beecher was vigorous at Cincinnati. Visiting Boston, he was pressed for an address, before he left for home, at the Tremont Temple. The New Englander, in an account of it, remarked:

"The fire of the old warrior, in his noble philanthropy, burned as brightly on this evening as in the days of his vigorous youth. Time had possibly impaired his vision and his memory; but there was still manifest the same active vitality of brain, the same force of utterance, the same fitly chosen words, the same hearty vehemence against this giant evil of the land. His illustrations were deduced from a most extended experience; his teachings had all the import of patriarchal words. Though he had preached two sermons the same day, there was no exhaustion of the system manifest, no evidence given that fatigue had come upon him; but clear, rapid, powerful, were his premises and conclusions, his delineations of the cause, and his description of the effect of the vice. It was a thrilling sight—that crowded auditory, hanging with intense interest on the faintest lispings of the aged laborer."

One of the most important and laborious of the operations, of this period and of my life, for the cause, was the reprinting and placing in the school-libraries of the State of New York, the three volumes of the Permanent Temperance Documents. It was believed that, for family reading, consultation by clergymen, teachers, temperance speakers, and young men, who might wish, in every place, to make themselves acquainted with the history of the cause, nothing would be more valuable; and, as there was a public library in every school-district, it would give these Documents a wide circulation, and do much toward securing, in the State, permanency to the cause. The plan was cordially endorsed by the following friends:

SARATOGA SPRINGS, *July* 2, 1851.

REV. J. MARSH:

SIR—In my opinion, the volumes of Permanent Temperance Documents, furnishing a history of the Temperance Reformation from its commencement, would be a valuable acquisition to every school-library in the State.

REUBEN H. WALWORTH.

We fully accord with Chancellor Walworth:

ELIPHALET NOTT, President of Union College,
EDWARD C. DELAVAN, Ballston Centre,
FREDERIC WHITTLESEY, Vice-Chancellor, Rochester,

SAMUEL CHIPMAN, Rochester,
GEORGE PECK, D. D., New York,
STEPHEN H. Tyng, D. D., New York.

ALBANY, *July* 3, 1857.

SIR—The three volumes made up of the Annual Reports of the American Temperance Society and Union, Addresses and Statistics upon the subject of temperance, would, in my opinion, form interesting and instructive books for the district-school libraries.

CHRISTOPHER MORGAN, Secretary of State
and Superintendent of Public Schools.

REV. J. MARSH.

Having secured the approbation of the authorities at Albany; and as the trustees of each school had the privilege of selecting their own books, for which they paid from the public moneys appropriated to the district, I sent a circular, with the above recommendations, to every school-district in the State, agreeing to deliver the three volumes of about five hundred pages, each bound in muslin, and lettered "SCHOOL-DISTRICT LIBRARY," for four dollars. I little knew what I had undertaken; but I earnestly and vigorously engaged in the work, and continued in it successfully, for about three years. I was enabled to supply over eight hundred libraries. But there was a difficulty in obtaining payment, as almost every library was in debt for books previously taken; and new trustees were often unwilling to be held responsible for what past committees had done; so that I was compelled to relinquish the work, though it was generally highly approved of. Five hundred sets, in sheets, were ordered for the school-libraries in Ohio, by the superintendent of common schools at Cincinnati, and were forwarded there, to be bound up in uniformity with other works.

As we were pressing, in every place, our claims upon the community, and endeavoring to draw the entire temperance population into combined action against the retail traffic, and the drinking usages, we were much hindered by continual collisions between the old, open organizations and the new temperance Orders which became exclusive, and whose popularity, and success in securing members, resulted in the extinction of many associations, on whose continuance hung, to a great degree, the sympathy of ministers and churches. Their forms and ceremonies, regalia and exclusiveness, were of little moment, provided it was based on Christian principles, and had the promotion of temperance at heart. To satisfy myself on this subject, I addressed a letter of inquiry to Gen. Cary, of Ohio, who returned me the following answer, which did such honor to his head and heart that I am happy in putting it on record. It showed that, if we walked in different paths, there was no cause of alienation.

TEMPERANCE COTTAGE, Monday, Oct. 8, 1849.

REV. AND DEAR BROTHER—Your valued letter of the 10th July reached me when I was upon a bed of sickness, and for some time subsequent I was unable to answer it. On my recovery, a multiplicity of duties compelled me to defer writing. Your letter afforded me real gratification, not only on account of the continued confidence which you were pleased to repose in me, but more especially for the zeal and devotion manifested in the great cause of temperance. The Order which I have the high honor to lead into the battle against the common foe, is worthy of commendation and confidence only so far as it promotes the *total abstinence* reform. I am glad that you appreciate my position so well, in reference to the great cause to which your energies have been so long and so well devoted.

I am not tenacious of the form of organization, or the means by which the great end shall be attained, provided they are not inconsistent with the word of God. I have ever maintained, that no society or organization, which has for its object the elevation of man's moral condition, can long prosper, or even exist, unless it is based upon eternal truth. The Bible is the only safe rule for faith and practice. Again, I regard it as a fundamental truth, that no standard of reform can be maintained higher than is assumed by the *Christian Church sanctified.* Mind must take the lead in the great warfare against vice and sin of every description, or defeat is certain. I see nothing in our Order that conflicts with the revealed will of God; nor do I believe that there is anything which can hinder its members from making the highest attainment in Christian excellence. But, as I have said, I am not tenacious of forms. I am a Son of Temperance only because I suppose it better adapted than any other *known* form of voluntary association to advance the Temperance Reformation: but I am not an exclusive. I am prepared to labor with any and all who differ with me on this subject. I would abandon this organization in an instant, when another should be formed more likely to succeed. I think there has been some misapprehension, as to the chief object of the temperance reformation, on the part of many of its advocates. They seem to think that its chief glory consists in picking up drunkards and reforming them. However praiseworthy and honorable may be this employment, I think our aim should be higher. We should direct our chief energies to prevent the present and coming generations from becoming drunkards. Those degrade our enterprise who regard it as doomed to be a mere scavenger, generation after generation. We must purify the moral atmosphere by holding up the terrors of intemperance, and the beauties of total abstinence, by way of encouraging the power of resistance within; and another and important part of our work is to remove, by moral and legal means, the temptations from without. But I am taxing your attention too much. I hope to hear again and again from you. While we may differ as to the best means of promoting the cause we love, we, I trust and believe, have but one object in view—the utter extirpation of intemperance from this sin-stricken earth.

May God bless you, my dear brother, in all your efforts to promote the great reform.

Truly yours, &c.,

Rev. JOHN MARSH, N. Y. City. S. F. CARY.

Our friends in Canada were much troubled on the same subject. With a spirit of kindness, they bore with the new organizations, deprecated the divisions, but held firm to the old societies. Said the Canada Advocate, in 1850:

"Sincerely as we rejoice in what has been done by the Sons in the West, the Rechabites in the east, and the Cadets of Temperance, we cannot shut our eyes to the fact, that the old Total Abstinence Societies are the root out of which they have all sprung. We do not desire to see any of them given up, or feebly carried on; on the contrary, we wish to see them push forward with as much energy as ever; they are all important in their place, and all fitted to enlist many on our side who would never join the old societies. Yet these latter are the trunk of the temperance tree; the new organizations are branches that have sprung from it; and, though they spread wider, and look more beautiful and attractive, with their verdant foliage, we should not lose sight of the stem which they both conceal and adorn. There are many who may be expected to join the old society, that would not join any of the newly formed organizations; and many old valued friends will gladly remain in connection with the former, and coöperate with the Sons or the Rechabites. Let, therefore, these old associations be still assiduously kept up, in town and country. Let all the doors be kept open, by which new friends may enter our ranks, and all the machinery be still plied, by which friends, whether new or old, may render us assistance."

TEMPERANCE HOTELS were early forced upon our attention, as absolutely essential to the success of our cause. Temperance men had banished liquor from their houses;

they had resolved never to be seen frequenting a saloon, or supporting a grocery, by purchasing its articles, which sold liquor; and yet, when travelling, they were compelled to make their home, at least for the night, where was the revelry of the rum-fiend; and, as they left in the morning, to leave their money for the support of a public curse. A combination among the friends of temperance throughout the country, never to patronize such houses, would, it was seen, reduce their number; and should their patronage be exclusively given to strictly temperance houses, they might be well sustained.

The Marlboro' Hotel, in Boston, was early placed on strict temperance principles. The Adams and Quincy House soon followed. The Croton was early established in New York; the Delavan, at Albany; and soon there was scarce a large town or city in the country which had not its temperance hotel.

These institutions, how much soever called for and valuable they might be, for the most part soon degenerated. It required too much capital in the proprietors to sustain them, and give the satisfaction to travellers—usually exorbitant in their demands—that other hotels could give, which made great profit on their sales of liquors; so that the contrast was drawn, in the estimation of the public, very much to the disparagement of the temperance house, and it was often forsaken, even by temperance men. In 1850, my friend, Dr. Charles Jewett, took up the subject in earnest, in the Worcester Cataract, and endeavored to gain the confidence of the public in such houses; while he gave all a severe scathing who kept such houses without any principle—merely for gain—giving their patrons the lowest, and often most miserable fare.

"Temperance men cannot be comfortable, where sights and sounds are every moment reminding them of that terrible scourge which is annually dragging down thousands of our countrymen to graves of infamy. There must be houses, where such music and exhibitions are not added to the bill of fare, for the accommodation of temperance men, of whom New England can number her tens of thousands. But why should a friend of temperance go out of his way, or make special efforts to send his friends to a particular hotel, though it holds out a temperance flag, and is called a temperance house, when he knows that its landlord or proprietor has no interest in the cause, and would sell liquor to-morrow, if more money could be made by it, or the public opinion and the laws of the State allowed him to do it? Some seem to have supposed that the word temperance could feed, warm, and lodge men. They have therefore put the word on the sign which swung before, or was placed above the door, and neglected to make provision for the comfort of their guests."

His remonstrances were not without effect, and a better state of things was widely visible.

The SECOND ARM of our National Defence, our gallant Navy, had had, from the commencement of the temperance reform, much of the attention of the friends of temperance. Noble officers, as Foote, Hudson, Stringham, and Jones, themselves abstainers, had long wished and hoped that the spirit ration, *alias* the whiskey tub, the cause of most of the difficulties in the Navy, might be abolished; and, at their instigation, numerous petitions, largely signed, had been sent to Congress for its removal. One member, whose services deserve to be held in lasting remembrance, John N. Rockwell, Esq., of Connecticut, devoted himself for several sessions almost entirely to the work; and often was he sure, such were the impressions he made, that he should be successful. Letters to him from numerous commanders, presenting the ration as a nuisance, the great cause of crime, were laid by him before Congress. One, in a special manner, from Commander Wilkes, on his return from his exploring expedition, came with great power. "There are," said he, "more drunkards made at the grog-tubs of our ships, than in any other place in our country with a hundred times the same population. The best men on our ships do not draw their spirit ration." But the only thing Mr. Rockwell, after years of labor, was able to accomplish was, the procuring a commutation of six cents. Numbers accepted this in lieu of their grog; but the mischief was done to young seamen, before they had time to estimate the value of the exchange. While, however, the Navy seemed destined to suffer under this evil for years to come, a new excitement arose, in 1849–50, on another point, which ultimately was to secure all that was desirable. A Mr. Watson G. Haynes, a bold and fearless seaman of the Navy, visited all the ports and cities, and by his rude and harsh eloquence, endeavored to arouse the public attention to the horrors of the flogging system. Many of his representations were of the most thrilling character. Of a thousand seamen, paid off in Boston, from three ships of war, some had received 2,700 lashes on their cruises. While many might be unwilling to take away his grog from poor Jack, every one would be anxious to spare his back from the cruel stripes. And yet the two were so intimately connected that they could not be separated.

If the spirit ration was continued, there would inevitably be cause for the stripes. The Captain of the Saratoga declared that nearly the whole of the offences for which the punishments were found necessary on his ship might be traced directly or indirectly to the effects of liquor. Captain Wilkes said, "I am satisfied that nine-tenths of the punishments of the Navy may be traced to the spirit rations; certainly, this was the case in my four years' cruise with the exploring expedition." In the great excitement, therefore, relative to the abolition of the flogging system, it seemed almost absolutely certain, that if flogging was abolished, the spirit ration would be also. And yet, strange to say! Congress abolished the flogging system, but left the spirit ration. The punishment for offences was taken away, but the cause of the offences was suffered to remain. This brought the government of the Navy into a bad condition. What punishment could be substituted for flogging? Confinement in the hold? This would be just what the offender would like, especially if he was too lazy to work. But his services were needed, and he could not be spared for this. A man must often be brought instantly to duty, perhaps to save the ship. Some officers threatened to resign, as they saw no way to govern the ship without flogging. A large crew, on coming into port, hearing that flogging was abolished, declared they would not enlist again, for without the summary punishment, they had no protection from thievish and bad men, who might be among them. The more the subject was agitated and discussed, the more did the spirit ration appear as at the bottom of the whole difficulty. Intemperance was the cause of two-thirds of all the disobedience and crime on board ship; and the spirit ration must now be abolished under the new plea, that it was the cause of nearly all offences, while for those offences there was no penalty. I one day said to Captain Hudson, one of the Vice-Presidents of the Union, as he was going on a two years' cruise in the ship Vincennes in the Pacific, " Well, Captain, are you going to deal out the spirit ration?" "Going to?" he replied, with a look of indignation; "I must, I must. It is the abhorrence of my soul, but I must to all who wish it. But I have some fine temperance men with me, and hope to make all so. I want a good supply of books and tracts. Send me some." I sent him to the amount of ten dollars. He was opposed to connecting the abolition of the spirit ration with the discipline of the ship. He would never flog, but in the most extreme cases; but he thought the power to inflict such punishment should be left with the commander to make him respected. So many and great were the difficulties, that it was much feared that the flogging system would be brought back. Nearly all the good seamen were in favor of it, while the vile and disorderly were opposed. Said Captain McIntosh of the U. S. Frigate Congress: "My crew are generally well disposed; and if I had the power, I would not have the law abolishing the lash repealed to-morrow, but should the crew of this ship be mustered, and the question asked, 'Cat, or no cat?' it would almost unanimously be given for the cat." In this state of things there was much trembling for the Navy; and the friends of reform saw there was no hope for the Navy but in the abolition of the spirit ration. At the annual meeting of the Seamen's Fund Society, 1850, Charles Tracy, Esq., of New York, offered and sustained a resolution on the subject. He said:

> "Government had done a good thing in abolishing flogging. There were those who said the time had not come for that, but Congress had to come to it, and do it before the time; and they would have to do the same thing with the grog. They had taken one step. Revolutions never go backward. They had taken one step forward, and thrown the 'cat' overboard, and would they say the grog-tub should remain?
>
> "Lieutenant Jones, of the U. S. N., in seconding the resolution, said 'he had seen men come on board vessels, who were not in the habit of drinking, who had fallen into the habit in consequence of the grog rations. He had visited a great many of the ports where are seamen's chaplains, and bore honorable testimony to their good influence. At Honolulu, at one time, on visiting the chaplaincy, 100 signed the pledge, and many more afterwards.'"

But great bodies move slowly. The public fell again into a strange apathy, and for more then ten years the spirit ration was continued, and Commanders were left to struggle on, punishing disobedience as they best could, with the great cause of disobedience continued. The cause of delay was supposed to lie in depriving the officers as well as the men. At length, as we were thrust into war, and it became necessary to bring our gallant

Navy up to the highest point of discipline, Congress were ready to listen, and did listen, to the long-repeated demand, and banished utterly from all ships of war the ruinous spirit-ration.

In the Senate of 1862 the Hon. Mr. Grimes introduced the following resolution:

Be it enacted, That, from and after the first day of September, 1862, the spirit-ration, in the Navy of the United States, shall cease; and thereafter, no distilled spirituous liquors shall be admitted on board of vessels of war, except as medical stores, and upon the order, and under the control of, the medical officers of such vessels, and to be used only for medical purposes.

To avoid all complaints of injustice to any, five cents a day was allowed to any who had enlisted in the service under the implied promise of the spirit-ration.

Mr. Grimes stated that the resolution was offered in accordance with the wishes of almost every officer with whom he had been brought in contact, and that almost all the difficulties that had grown up during the war, on board our vessels, was traceable to liquor, of which the resolution deprived the officers as well as men. The bill passed the house, and at once received the signature of the President.

Thus was finally accomplished one of the most important projects of reform for our beloved country, after years of much labor in a few individuals, verifying the declaration, "In due season we shall reap, if we faint not." All who now say, "The temperance cause is a failure; you have done and are doing nothing," I ask to look at our gallant navy. See in what condition it was, and in what it now is; what commanders we have under the temperance flag, and what glorious deeds our men with sober minds, and strong heads and hearts, have been able to accomplish!

I had an expression from Rear-Admiral Foote of his high satisfaction at the expulsion of the spirit-ration from the navy, and an assurance that when he should have leisure, he would give some account of his long labor to accomplish the object, and his own happy experience in the cold-water system. He was then on his way to Washington, on his crutches, to take charge of the new bureau. But, alas! he was to remain with his grateful country but a short period. He was soon to be translated to a higher state, where he should receive, not the patriot, but the Christian crown.

Commodore Stringham, too, expressed to me the high joy he had at the passage of the resolution; and he gloried in saying to the Governor of Massachusetts, when asked to take wine, "Sir, I have not known the taste of wine for twenty years." Such men feel their responsibilities; and are the life, too, of their country, in the hour of danger.

So, FARRAGUT. [To Secretary Seward I am indebted for the following.] Everybody admired Farragut's heroism in clinging to the topmast to direct a battle; but there was another particular of that contest that no less forcibly illustrates his heroic character. "Admiral," said one of his officers, the night before the battle, "won't you consent to give Jack a glass of grog in the morning, not enough to make him drunk, but enough to make him fight cheerfully." "Well," replied the Admiral, "I have been to sea considerably, and have seen a battle or two, but I never found that I wanted rum to enable me to do my duty. I will order two cups of coffee to each man, at two o'clock; and, at eight o'clock, I will pipe all hands to breakfast, in Mobile Bay." And he did give Jack the coffee; and then he went up to the mast-head and did it. —*Speech at Auburn.*

Well versified.

"No, I'll give them good coffee, there's no need of rum
To keep up a man's courage, when fighting hours come.
I've been on the ocean, in stormiest nights,
Have seen some hard service, and one or two fights;
But I never yet found that I needed a glass
Of spirits, to help, or the danger to pass.
They'll have two cups of coffee, at two, and then wait
Till I pipe all to breakfast in harbor at eight.

"The men had their coffee, and each seemed a host,
As he manfully stood at his perillous post;
For their leader shrank not from the danger they passed;
They knew he would stand with them, firm to the last,
And many an anxious glance upward was cast
At the heroic Admiral, lashed to the mast."

LINDA MAY.

CHAPTER XVIII.

Great Progress in Foreign Countries, and in British Provinces—Prohibition —Agitation—Wisconsin Law supported by Dr. Hewitt—Maine Law—Rise—Adoption, and Enforcement under Neal Dow—Approvals of.

As we were rallying our forces in America, for a general conflict with our great enemy, at the commencement of the second half of the century, we had the happiness of hearing of great and good progress in other, and even distant parts of the world. More tidings of good were continually laid upon my table than I was able to present in brief to the public, in my small monthly Journal. In England, the Chancellor of the Exchequer had reported an increased consumption of tea, coffee, and cocoa, and a proportional decrease of drinks which intoxicate. The Naval Lord Admiral had reduced the spirit ration one half, and taken it entirely from all under eighteen. Into the Crystal palace, for the great Industrial Exhibition in 1851, no wines, spirits, or beer were to be admitted; and the contractors were to be required to supply glasses of water *gratis* to all visitors;—a temperance lecture for the world. Ireland was in a state of great prosperity. Oscar, King of Sweden, accompanied by his queen, attended personally a grand temperance meeting, held recently at Stockholm, and became himself so impressed with the importance of abolishing intemperance in his dominions, that, besides giving his adhesion, and that of the queen, to the principles and practices of the temper-

11

ance societies, he offered full pecuniary compensation to all distillers of ardent spirits who would cease manufacturing alcoholic drinks; which was accepted by many. Over six thousand persons were enrolled in the Netherlands. Liberia had entirely excluded all spirituous liquors. In South Africa, at Cape Town and Port Natal, were flourishing societies. At the Sandwich Islands, temperance was triumphant; liquors on sale were seized and destroyed. In British America, 220,000 French and Irish Catholics, and 240,000 Protestants were enrolled on the total abstinence pledge; 35,000 were embraced in the Order of Sons. In Nova Scotia, ten counties were without license; and vigorous efforts were making for a prohibitory law, under the action and eloquence of our friend, F. W. Kellogg.

For such a law, the friends of temperance were now earnestly looking, in almost every State. Perhaps unwisely (but it seemed, as human nature is constituted, unable to look at more than one point at a time), turning away from the subject of personal total abstinence—the great basis—and the training of the young in the way they should go, all minds were beginning to be engrossed with the removal of temptation by some strong legislative action. For years, it had been thought sufficient if the license system was abolished, for then common law would shut out the sale; and it was effected in many of the States. Ohio and Michigan had made it forever unconstitutional to grant license, and yet venders would sell without. To meet them, Wisconsin had, it was supposed, completely confronted them however, by holding them responsible for all damages. This, known as the WISCONSIN LAW, was, with many, exceedingly popular, and considered the *ne plus ultra* of legislation. It was taken up and improved, and pressed upon the public, by the old pioneer, Rev. Dr. Hewitt, of Connecticut. "He thought a petition for such a law, carefully prepared, and sent to the legislatures, would at once be attended to. There could be no valid objection to it. The State is bound to provide for the protection of wives and children against the avarice of the rum-seller. As it is, they are left widowed and fatherless; there is no redress. No other such wrongs are left without provision. "We have the liberty of speech, but we are accountable for the use of it; and the liberty of the press, but those who publish a libel are held responsible. Suppose a law cannot be passed prohibiting the sale of liquors, why at least should not the liquor-seller be put on the same footing with us all —held responsible for the use of his liberty?"

To this it was objected, that no court or jury could rightly estimate the damages done, as in the death of a husband, or father, or son—above all, in the loss of the soul. "A minor becomes a drunkard, whereby the father loses his services. What damage can be laid for converting an only son into a sot? And it was forcibly inquired how it could be proved who did the damage? A man gets drunk, and is frozen to death. It is proved that he bought his last glass of A. Was A. the cause of his death, or some one or more of half a dozen other rum-sellers of whom the drunkard had bought liquor shortly before the occurrence?"

But the people seemed to be resolving that no damage should be done; no drunkards should be made; nor, for gain, should venders be continually inflicting upon the community terrible calamities, and then challenging the people to prove that they were criminal. Prohibition of the traffic in intoxicating drinks in opposition to license, and in lieu of free trade as in all animals and useful articles, was slowly taking possession of men's minds; and when it had got possession, no plea of the rum-seller or of the panderer to the appetite of the consumer could ever blot it out.

It was first presented in 1837 in a memorial from the pen of General James Appleton, of Portland, to the Legislature of Maine, demanding an abrogation of all license laws as the support and life of the traffic, and also an entire prohibition of all sale, except for medicine and the arts; for the same reason that the State makes laws to prevent the sale of unwholesome meats, or for the removal of anything which endangers the health and life of the citizen, or which threatens to subvert our civil rights or overthrow the government. That document, surpassed for clearness and force by none since written, made an impression on a few minds, though it was considered by the mass of political and commercial men as too impracticable for human society in its present state, and especially, in its republican character. Yet it formed a school who were ultimately to have the mastery, at least in all New England.

The Washingtonian movement soon cast in the shade all projects of law. It was believed, especially by the reformed men, that nothing was needed to effect an overthrow of the traffic, but appeals from the sufferers to those who unintentionally caused the suffering; and it was only through sympathy with the reformed men, as they became sufferers from the liquor dealers, and were often drawn back to drunkenness and woe, that the indignation of the community was once more roused against the traffic.

Neal Dow, a citizen of Portland, whose family were Friends, took a deep interest in the reformed and their families. He mingled much with them, and rejoiced to see them made comfortable by the thousands of dollars which had before gone to the rum-seller, and he now resolved that it should not go in that channel again; and if venders would not be persuaded to give up their traffic by moral suasion, they must and should by the law of the State. His first effort was to have the question of license or no license referred to a vote of the people. This was in 1839. But here he was defeated. That only roused his energies and gathered around him the reformed men; and in the year 1842 he carried his position by a majority of four hundred. But it was of little avail while he had none but the city authorities, many of whom were in league with the venders, to enforce the law on such as sold without license, and brought ruin and desolation upon the reformed. He now resolved to go to the Legislature, and get the power of the State to put a stop to the traffic, which he stamped as "an infamous crime." He succeeded with the House but not with the Senate; and at once resolved ona Legislature which should favor his views. In 1846 he travelled over four thousand miles in the State, everywhere holding meetings for discussion, and securing a prohibitory Senate as well as House. In that he succeeded; and, in July, 1846, he appeared before the Legislature with the names of forty thousand petitioners for a prohibitory statute. A bill was introduced and passed in the House, 81 to 42, and in the Senate, 23 to 5. In a letter addressed to me, he said:

> "This is the first instance, I believe, in which the government of a civilized and Christian State has declared by statute, that there shall not be within its borders any traffic in intoxicating liquors to be used as a drink; and that if any such liquors shall be sold for such purpose, under any circumstances, it shall be against law, and equity, and a good conscience. It was enacted in answer to the petition of more than forty thousand of the good people of the State, and constitutes the first blow only which the friends of temperance here propose striking at the traffic in strong drinks."

But the bill was an inefficient one; the penalties struck no terror into the hearts of the liquor-dealers and the victory was lost. The dealers and consumers of the infuriating poison made a desperate effort for its repeal, but utterly failed. Intemperance rolled in like a flood, for the law was void. One was resolved on, however, which should be efficient, and a Legislature was secured which would not fail to pass it—the Legislature of 1849. But it was vetoed by Governor Dana, to his political death. In August, 1850, he appeared before the Legislature with what is known as the Maine law, but it was lost by a tie vote in the Senate. This produced the greatest excitement throughout the State, and true members were returned in the fall election, so that on the 26th of May Mr. Dow appeared before the Legislature with his law perfected, and he had the great happiness of seeing it become the law of the State by a vote of 86 to 40 in the House, and 18 to 10 in the Senate. It was approved by the Governor on the 2d of June. Mr. Dow assured the members that, if they enacted that bill, in six months the State would be cleared of every grog-shop.

Foreseeing the absolute necessity, if the bill should pass, of an efficient magistracy; its friends, in the spring election, had elevated Mr. Dow to the mayoralty of Portland; thus throwing upon him the responsibility of executing the law.

All eyes were at once turned upon Maine, to see if she would execute her law. Will the Mayor of Portland stand firm at his post, and do his duty, or will he shrink in fear of mobs and riots? Almost at once he issued his proclamation, declaring that he should promptly enforce the law; first giving all venders sixty days to ship their liquors to States whose governments would admit their introduction and sale. The Mayors of other cities did the same; some giving a longer, and some a shorter term.

The Mayor of Bangor resolved on a prompt execution; and on the morning of the fourth of July rolled out of the basement of the City Hall ten casks of liquor, seized and confiscated, and destroyed the whole. At the expiration of the term allowed, the Mayor of Portland issued his search warrant, seized two thousand dollars worth of liquor, and had it openly destroyed. No resistance was made. The people stood quietly by, and witnessed the whole in respectful silence. The smaller cities and towns followed on; and throughout Maine, with some exceptions, prohibition was established. The world were taken by surprise and filled with amazement. The predictions of opponents were all proved to be without foundation. Tippling-shops and bar-rooms were everywhere closed; temptations removed; no more drunkards were seen in the streets. Old inebriates were of necessity reformed, and their families comfortable. "Oh," said one tenant of the almshouse, as she saw the liquor poured out, "that this had been done twenty years ago; my husband would not have died a drunkard, and I should not have been here with my children." Pauperism and crime were reduced 50 and 75 per cent.; and jails and poorhouses were scarce needed. The immense sums everywhere expended before for strong drink, now being expended for clothing, fuel and bread, made hundreds of families, once subjects of charity, comfortable and happy. In his first quarterly report, after the enforcement of the law, the Mayor of Portland said:

"At the time of its passage, there were supposed to be in the city from two hundred to three hundred shops and other places where intoxicating liquors were openly sold to all comers. At the present time there are no places where such liquors are sold openly, and only a very few where they are sold at all, and that with great caution and secrecy, and only to those who are personally known to the keepers, and who can be relied upon not to betray them to the authorities.

"The results of the law so far have been more salutary and decisive than its most ardent friends had reason to anticipate."

The marshal of the city of Augusta, the capital of the State, reported:

"Augusta had four wholesale stores, business worth $200,000 a year; retail shops, twenty-five. The city was exempted from the new law for sixty days by a dispensation of the mayor. During the sixty days, one dealer made a profit of about $900. As soon as the sixty days were out, three of the wholesale dealers sent off their liquors to New York, and ultimately to California. The remaining firm persisted in selling, until about $1,000 worth of their liquors were seized. Liquor may be sold at the principal hotels, but stealthily. The police used to be called up a hundred nights in a year. Since the passage of this law they have not been summoned once."

The Mayor of Bangor, in his message to the Council of that city, on its organization the 22d of April, bore full testimony to its benign operations. The occupants of the almshouse and house of correction in the year anterior to the creation of the law were 12,206; in the year subsequent, 9,192; the prosecutions varied from 101 to 58. "On the 1st of July," he said, "when I gave notice that I should enforce the liquor law, 108 persons were selling liquors here openly; twenty of them have left the city, and are carrying on their trade in Massachusetts. Of the remaining eighty-eight, not one sells here openly."

Unable to remain a listener to all that was reported, I made a tour through Maine, that I might be an eye witness of the wondrous spectacle. Patriotic, philanthropic, and Christian men, throughout the nation, were filled with admiration of the law, and its operation. Said the venerable Professor Moses Stuart of Andover, Mass.:

"I thank and praise my God, that, by his holy providence, there is one people on the face of this wicked world who dare to do their duty boldly, faithfully, and thoroughly. People of Maine, the God of heaven bless you for achieving such a victory! Many triumphs have been achieved in the good cause, but none like yours. Others have, more or less, fought with the drunkards and the liquor-sellers, in the way of arguments and moral suasion, and indirect, and inefficient, and temporizing legislation. You have followed the most adroit conqueror the world has ever seen, in your scheme of policy or struggle. You have steered for the capitol itself, with all its magazines and material of war; and these once in your hands, you know the contest cannot long continue. Whence are the arms and ammunition, and rations, to come, when all the depots are seized? You have the unspeakable advantage of making war upon all the supplies of war, and not directly upon the men who take the field against you. You combat with the body of sin and death itself, and not with those who are deceived and misled. You do not purpose to destroy those who are misled and drawn to ruin, but to cripple and annihilate the power that misleads them. It is an elevated and noble purpose. When mighty conquerors and crafty politicians will be forgotten, the laurels on your brows will be freshening and blooming with a beauty and glory that will be immortal."

Said the Hon. Lucius M. Sargent, of Boston, author of the Temperance Tales:

"Maine has most worthily extended her legislative arm for the protection of her children. How long she will be enabled to retain it in its present position, is a question of the deepest interest to the inhabitants of that commonwealth, and of no ordinary solicitude to the citizens of other States, who, equally in the event of ultimate failure or success, will accord to her all the merit of her noble example, and yet more warily contemplate the course of her experiment, and abide their time. I have read—I may say studied—the several provisions of this law, with considerable care; and I have not been able to raise a doubt of its constitutionality."

Said General John H. Cocke, of Virginia:

"I am grateful, indescribably grateful, that my life has been spared to see the day when a sovereign State has outlawed the master evil of our day and generation."

Said the Rev. John Pierpont, of Boston:

"My private opinion is, that the liquor-law of Maine is a new era in the Temperance Reformation."

Said the Rev. Justin Edwards, D. D., of Andover, Mass.:

"If the people prevail, and permanently defend themselves and their children as they have a right, and it is their duty, to do, from the evils of the liquor-traffic, they will be benefactors, not only of the present generation, but of all future generations of men; not only in Maine, but in every State in the Union, and throughout the Christian world."

Said the Hon. Gerritt Smith, of Peterboro', N. Y.:

"That law has laid the foundation for an unrivalled progress in respectability and knowledge and happiness. If no other State should follow her example, in this respect, Maine will very soon be able to boast—if, indeed, she cannot thus boast now—that her people surpass every other, physically, mentally, and morally."

Said the Hon. Thomas S. Williams, Chief Justice of Connecticut:

"Honor to the men by whose energy this mighty victory has been won! Honor to the legislature who yielded to the wishes of a virtuous community! Honor to those who have so faithfully executed it; and honor to those who, being originally opposed to the law, have now become its strenuous supporters!

"As a matter of political economy, the value of this law can hardly be overestimated; but, in its moral bearings, it is beyond all price."

Said Governor Briggs, of Massachusetts:

"This law, so far as I understand it, is above all laws that I have ever seen. It is clear; it deals with vice just as all laws should deal with it. It puts in the plough to the beam: aye, it puts in the *sub-soil* plough, and lets in the pure air of heaven on this infamous, this polluting traffic."

Said Dr. R. D. Mussey, head of the medical profession at Cincinnati:

"We, temperance men, all pray for the Maine Law, that it may be sustained, and ultimately overspread the land and the world."

CHAPTER XIX.

Fourth National Convention—Great Rejoicings—Thankful Resolution—Maine Men heard—Workings of the Law—United and Decided Action agreed upon—Speech of Dr. Edwards—Action in Massachusetts—126,000 Petitioners—Adoption of Maine Law—Adoption in Rhode Island—In Connecticut—In Vermont—Action in New York—300,000 Petitions at Albany—Adoption of Maine Law—Governor Seymour's Veto—Maine Law Record—Workings.

So excited were the friends of temperance throughout the country at the passage and enforcement of the Maine law, that a great desire was expressed for a general gathering, that they might take each other by the hand, and unitedly bow before the Sovereign of the universe in thankfulness and praise. Accordingly, on consultation with several individuals of enlarged views, the Executive Committee of the American Temperance Union issued a call for a National Temperance Convention, to be held on the 20th of August, 1851, at Saratoga Springs. The call was well responded to;—more than 300 delegates were enrolled from seventeen States, and the Canadas. Chancellor Walworth was elected President. Letters were read from Father Mathew, Judge O'Neal, of South Carolina, Hon. Neal Dow, and Christian Keener, expressing regrets at unavoidable absence. Mr. Dow was unable to leave his post as Mayor of Portland. The Convention, on gathering, manifested the greatest exhilaration and joy at the progress in legislation against the traffic, and early unanimously adopted a resolution, declaring:

"That the recent discussion and action in the Legislatures of New Hampshire, Massachusetts, Rhode Island, Connecticut, Vermont, and Indiana, on the legal suspension of the traffic—the constitutional exclusion of all license in Michigan and Ohio, and the entire outlaw of the traffic in spirituous and intoxicating liquors as a beverage in Iowa and Maine are gratifying tokens of advance in public sentiment, and give reason to hope that, with the Divine blessing on judicious and persevering efforts, the immoral and pernicious traffic will, ere long, be done away."

Dr. Edwards remarked that the State upon which the sun first shines in the morning in its upward course is making an experiment which no legislative body is called to make more than once in a thousand years. If their way is the best way, they are setting the world an example it will be wise to follow.

Dr. Jewett thought the resolution was defective, inasmuch as it did not allude to that feature in the Maine law which destroys the liquor in possession for sale. It was, therefore, judged proper that the delegates from Maine be heard fully in relation to the law and its workings. Rev. Mr. Peck, of Portland, then took the stand, and at length addressed the Convention. He was followed by Rev. Freeman Yates. Their developments were intensely interesting. They were followed by speeches from General Cary, of Ohio; Mr. Kilbourn, of Iowa; Rev. Mr. Thurston, of Maine; Deacon Grant, of Boston; John A. Foot, Esq., of Cleveland, in warm congratulatory speeches. In the evening an enthusiastic meeting was held in the Presbyterian Church. On the ensuing day a series of resolutions, adapted to the times, were introduced, discussed and adopted. General Cary, and Mr. Godfrey, of Maine, and myself, were appointed a Committee to prepare an address from the Convention to the friends of temperance throughout the United States; which, on being read at the close of the Convention, was unanimously adopted, with great cheering. A desire existed to embody in one resolution, more explicitly than any which had been offered, the full views of the Convention on the character and correctness of the Maine Law, to be put on record, and spread abroad over the world. After several vain attempts, as if guided from above, I presented the following, which seemed fully to satisfy all parties, and was declared to be the great resolution of the Convention. I felt grateful in my heart for such an inspiration, though so unworthy an individual.

"*Resolved*, That the principle assumed and carried out in the Maine Law, that spirituous and intoxicating liquors, kept for sale as a beverage, should be destroyed by the State, as a public evil, meets the approbation of this Convention, as consonant with the destruction of the implements of gambling and counterfeiting, of poisonous food, infectious hides, and weapons of war in the hands of an enemy; that if the liquor destroyed is private property, it is only so as are the implements of the counterfeiter, dangerous and deadly to the best interests of the community; that its destruction is no waste of the bounties of Providence, more than the destruction of noxious weeds, while its very destruction enriches the State exceeding the amount for which it could have been sold. It tends to put an end to all subterfuges, frauds, and secret sales, and to the demand for it in the community. It makes the State a perfect Asylum for the inebriate. It is a solemn manifestation to the world of the vile and worthless nature of the article destroyed; and an unmistakable token to the vender of the end to which a righteous public sentiment will ultimately bring his business. For these and other reasons the Convention give it their hearty approbation; and they do strongly recommend to all the friends of temperance to cherish it as the sure, and the only sure triumph of their cause, and continually to urge its adoption upon every Legislature."

At the conclusion of all business, Dr. Justin Edwards addressed the Convention in an able, dignified and impressive manner; which, however, seemed to be the close of his long and able services, through threatening ailments. He said:

"As to the future, we take it for granted in this delightful Convention—delightful as to union and results—if we do not displease Him from whom all blessings come, we shall be prospered. The Convention is only a development of what has been done for fifty years. Every town will have such a temperance meeting as was never held before, to hear what has been done at Saratoga. The press will be employed. Every paper will speak. The pulpit will speak; and patriots and philanthropists will unite their efforts, until the evil shall all be done away; and all the glory will be given to Him from whom all good cometh, and to whom it is the happiness of all to live forever and ever.

All retired from the Convention with clear and decided views, relating to the falseness in principle of all license laws or efforts to regulate the traffic in intoxicating drinks, and with the determination to take the earliest practicable measures to establish a prohibitory law in every State. Where Legislatures were in existence who would enact no such law, all felt that appeals must be made at once to the people, with whom was the "hiding of the power," and who must, if possible, be induced to elect such Executive and Legislative officers as would give the people the protection demanded.

In Massachusetts, a petition for the law was at once circulated among the people, for signature; and on the first of January, 1842, a large meeting, for its presentation, was held in Boston, at the Tremont Temple; Hon. A. Huntington, of Salem, presiding. After a few remarks from him, the petition, containing one hundred and twenty-six thousand names, of whom fifty thousand were legal voters, was brought in, and placed upon the platform. It was then borne to a double sleigh, containing the committee, with the venerable Dr. Lyman Beecher, Chairman. Before it was borne a banner, on which was inscribed, "THE VOICE OF MASSACHUSETTS; 130,000 PETITIONERS IN FAVOR OF THE MAINE TEMPERANCE LAW." A procession, preceded by the police and a band of music, passed through several streets, to the State House, where it was duly presented. On return of the procession, a series of spirited and decided resolutions were adopted, and sent over the State.

In the Legislature, the petition was referred to a select committee, who gave its friends a public hearing, where it was ably sustained by Rev. E. Othman, Hon. Neal Dow, Dr. Beecher, Rev. John Pierpont, and others. A bill was reported, containing the great features of the Maine Law, with modifications adapting it to Massachusetts. In the debates, facts were brought to light most appalling: 8,394 persons were committed, in 1851, to the jails and houses of correction, 29 per cent. of which were for intemperance; 1,200 idiots were in the State (children of drunken parents.) The retail traffic of the State was annually $8,400,000. Opponents denied the right and expediency of the measure. But the Hon. Mr. Pomeroy, of Southampton, ably supported the bill, and it finally passed both Houses, by handsome majorities, with a submission to the people, in open ballot. It was, however, vetoed by the Governor, he preferring the secret to the open ballot. The Legislature then passed the bill, without submission, to go into operation in sixty days. It was approved by the Governor; and thus the LAW OF THE DAUGHTER BECAME THE LAW OF THE MOTHER.

In Rhode Island, the then existing Legislature rejected the law on its first presentation; but the people at once returned a new one, which passed the law, almost by acclamation; while the city of Providence elected a Mayor who would secure its immediate and perfect enforcement.

In Connecticut, a State Temperance Convention for revising the tickets for State officers, was held at New Haven. Eight hundred and forty delegates were enrolled from all parts of the State. Replies were read to inquiries whether candidates for office would vote for the Maine Law. Such as said Aye, were to receive the votes of temperance men at the next election. A Legislature was returned which, on the 14th of June, 1854, adopted the Maine Law, by a vote of 148 to 61 in the House, and 19 to 2 in the Senate, to go into operation on the first day of August. It was immediately signed by the Governor, and, on the 22d, a large congratulatory meeting was held in New Haven.

At Albany, N. Y., an exciting scene was witnessed, on the 28th of January, in a large gathering of the friends of temperance, at the Delavan House, whence they moved in procession, led by the Albany Artillery Company, through the principal streets, to the Capitol, where they entered, by permission, the Assembly-Chamber, with an immense roll of 300,000 petitioners for a Maine Law. There they were addressed by Dr. Jewett, W. H. Burleigh, and myself. On the following morning, the petition was presented to the Legislature, and was referred to committees of the Senate and House, which shortly reported acceptable bills, with reasons for their adoption. From this time until early in March, there was great excitement among the friends and foes of the law. Whenever the subject was before the Senate or Assembly, floods of eloquence were poured forth for its adoption or rejection; until, at length, on the 9th of March, 1854, the bill, complete, was passed in the Senate, 21 to 11; and in the House by the decided vote of 78 to 42—absent 7. As the two bodies differed on the time of execution, by compromise, the 1st of December was agreed upon.

This was viewed, excepting by the trade, as a day of great glory for the Empire State. All eyes were now upon Governor Seymour, for his signature. But, alas! they were destined to sad disappointment. The Governor VETOED the bill. Overlooking entirely the great question on which a constitutional question could properly be raised, viz.: the right of a State wholly to prohibit the sale of an article pronounced to be destructive of the public good, which had been settled by the Supreme Court of the United States affirmatively, Governor Seymour confined himself to the mere machinery, or workings of the law. In this, he found some constitutional difficulties; some interference with the practices of the courts; much that would be oppressive to the people, and injurious to the cause of temperance. An immense meeting of the friends of temperance was at once called, at the City Hall, to express their indignation. The Maine-Law members of the Legislature held a meeting in which they agreed to issue a document reviewing the Governor's veto, and scattering it broadcast over the State; and to seek out a man for the high office of Governor, at the next election, who would give the people the protection they demanded.

The essential features of the Maine Law were, that alcohol was necessary for medicine and the arts, and must be sold; but that the unrestricted sale was ruinous to the community. When sold for medicine and the arts, it was to be by agents appointed for that purpose. All other sales were outlawed. Wherever found, it might be destroyed. Officers might search stores, vessels, and all public conveyances, and destroy, without compunction. No action for damages could be brought. If any one was found unlawfully selling, the fine, for the first offence, was $20; for the second, $30; and for the third, a fine and three months' imprisonment.

What Maine had accomplished for the protection of her citizens, other States were anxious to do; and soon, many were found coming up with vigor and power—some in one form, and some in another, but all sustaining the great principle of prohibition of all sales of intoxicating liquors as a beverage, on pains and penalties.

The first Legislature which moved in the matter was Minnesota, in the year 1852; submitting the law to the people, who decided favorably; but the act of submission was pronounced unconstitutional by the Supreme Court of the State. In the same year, the Maine Law was adopted by Massachusetts, Rhode Island, and Vermont. In 1853, by Michigan, and ratified by the people. In 1854, by Ohio and Connecticut. In 1855, by Indiana, Illinois, Iowa, and Delaware. In 1855, by Wisconsin—and twice vetoed; also, in New Hampshire.

The workings of the law at first, in every State, were almost equally as surprising and gratifying to its friends, astonishing to its enemies, as it had been in Maine.

In Rhode Island, both at Newport and Providence, there was a general acquiescence in the law. Hon. Mr. Barstow, Mayor of Providence, issued his proclamation, calling on good citizens for acquiescence, assuring them that he should do his duty. In some places, the law was openly trampled upon; but the people were determined upon its enforcement, and the refractory were compelled to yield.

In Massachusetts, with the exception of Boston, and some other large cities, there was a good observance. Said the Minority Report against its repeal, in 1864: "The same public sentiment that spoke this law into being still rallies around it, and is making it effective throughout the Commonwealth. Its prospects for efficiency and success were never better than at the present time."

From New Hampshire, the most cheering tidings reached us of the enforcement of the law, even beyond any other State in the Union. The expectations of the friends of the law were more than realized.

In Vermont. In answer to an inquiry, relative to the working of the law, ex-Governor Eaton said:

"The law has exerted an immense influence, and accomplished great good; yet, I would not overstate the amount of what it has accomplished. Enacted as it was, and executed as it has been, in defiance of the strong and bitter opposition of a portion of the community, no one would suppose that, in the short space of a few months, it could have exerted, in full, its beneficent influences. And, besides, so vast is the magnitude and extent of the evil to be removed, no reasonable man could expect to see the whole work accomplished in a single year, even under the most favorable auspices."

In CONNECTICUT, the Governor of the State declared, after six months' trial of the law:

"The Maine liquor-law, in its operation, has been decidedly successful. Not a grog-shop, so called, is to be found in the State, since the law came into force. I do not mean that there are not a few dark spots, where, by falsehood and secrecy, evasion may not be managed; but, in a word, the traffic is suspended. I have not seen a drunkard in the streets since the first of August. Crimes which directly result from rum have fallen away half. The opposition predicted to the enforcement of the law, is not realized. Its enemies cannot get up an opposition to it, because it commends itself to all men's judgments; another reason is, the incentive to violence is taken away—riot is always preceded by rum. Take away the rum, and you cannot have the riot. At the late State Agricultural Fair, from 26,000 to 30,000 people, of all conditions, were assembled, and not a solitary drunkard was seen, and not the slightest disturbance made. Some jails are almost tenantless. The home of the peaceable citizen was never more secure."

At the meeting of the State Temperance Society, at Hartford, November 14, 1854, it was unanimously

Resolved, That the universal experience of the people, under the operation of our excellent prohibitory law, fully confirms our most sanguine expectations, and establishes, on a firm and sure basis, its wisdom, efficiency, and power. With the poor people, many of them say, "the law must have come from heaven; it is too good to be from man."—*City Missionary*.

Amid all this excitement, and advance of the Temperance community, the vast hosts of distillers, brewers, importers, venders and consumers, were not in a state of indifference, much less of acquiescence. They held numerous meetings, wherever they could find sympathy. In New

York, a call for a meeting, signed by from two to three thousand names, was sent out. The Maine Law was denounced as an outrageous attempt to destroy the interests of the city; to rob respectable men of their capital; to disfranchise many of their inherited rights, guaranteed by the Constitution. All temperance men were called upon to put down these fanatical movements, which must ultimately destroy temperance itself. Thirty thousand names were sent to Albany, remonstrating against any Maine-Law action.

A similar, and even more violent meeting was held in Detroit.

The brewers and maltsters of Philadephia city and county issued an address to the Farmers of Pennsylvania revealing the astounding fact that to supply the demands for brewing, 600,000 bushels of barley had been obtained from the State of New York; that Pennsylvania was better adapted to the raising of barley, and that, therefore, the farmers of Pennsylvania should be on the watch against a Maine law, which would make valueless their beautiful soil.

False-hearted politicians were continually active to thwart the Maine-Law men in their attempts to secure prohibition; often drafting bills of a special character, bearing the appearance of friendship, and getting the Maine-Law men in their web, from which there was no extrication.

Scientific gentlemen were found ready to come forward and declare that Alcohol, the good creature of God, was useful and essential to the constitution of man; that to a Maine law none could be obedient, more than to a law which should deprive them of bread and meat; and such, connected with the rich and luxurious, declared in their merriment, that it was unconstitutional, or against the interests of their constitution, more ready to consult the appetite, and make their God their belly, than to read the lectures of Professor Youmans on Alcohol and the constitution of men, giving the chemical history and properties of Alcohol, and its leading effects upon the healthy human constitution, illustrated by a beautiful colored chart, which appeared about this period, and in the midst of these discussions. Said Professor Youmans:

"ALCOHOL IS A BRAIN POISON. It is so to all intents and purposes. It seizes with its disorganizing energy upon that mysterious part whose steady and undisturbed action holds man in true and responsible relations with his family, with society and with God, and it is this fearful part, that gives to government and society their tremendous interests on this question." In other cases of insanity, the criminal is not held responsible. Here it is voluntarily brought on, and is, therefore, crime, and the drunken murderer is hung upon the gallows. But, inquires Professor Youmans, "Is not society, is not every individual who makes, sells or patronizes the use of Alcohol, and leads the wretch to temptation and death, responsible also? Must not Alcohol be a subject of law? Surely it must. There has always been a jurisprudence of Alcohol; there is still, and the necessity for it will continue. But the demand of the age is for a new, a higher and juster legislation, for more thorough and potential law, through which the most ubiquitous and omnipotent energy of government shall be expressed for the protection of society."

With Professor Youmans I was on terms of great intimacy; and from him I derived my most decided confirmation of the correctness of total abstinence, for the human constitution; and of prohibitory law, for human society.

CHAPTER XX.

World's Temperance Convention in New York, September 6, 1853—Neal Dow, President—Slight Disturbance—Lady on the Platform—Introduction of Foreign Delegation—Wendell Phillips—Great Tumult—House cleared by Police—Soirée abandoned—Peaceable Progress—Children's Meeting—Speech of Dr. Lees—Address to all Nations—Dr. Pierpont's Speech and Poem—Tribute to Dr. Edwards—Meeting of Sons of Temperance—Adulterations—Frauds in the Liquor Traffic—Rum Maniac.

On the 6th of May, 1853, at a meeting of the friends of temperance, in New York, it was resolved, that it was expedient and desirable to hold a World's Temperance Convention, in the city of New York, in September next. A committee of forty gentlemen from every State, Territory, and the British provinces, were appointed to issue the call, inviting all temperance organizations and associations, based on the principle of total abstinence, to appear by their delegates, for mutual congratulation, but more especially for the enactment of a prohibitory law, like the Maine Law, in every State and nation; and extending the invitation to friends of temperance in all parts of the world, assuring them of a cordial welcome, and of an opportunity to present the full progress of the cause in their own district or country. The day appointed for the Convention was the 6th of September, and its continuance to be at least four days. Large preparations were at once made, and several gentlemen were requested to prepare dissertations on important topics, to be read at the Convention.

On the day designated, a very large body of men, from all parts of the country, were gathered, by ten o'clock, A. M., at the Metropolitan Hall—the largest and most magnificent room in the city. They were called to order by John W. Oliver, Chairman of the Committee of Arrangements, who invited Gen. S. F. Cary to the Chair. Gen. C. made a few eloquent remarks, appropriate to the occasion. A committee on organization reported, for President of the Convention, Hon. Neal Dow, of Maine; twenty vice-presidents, six secretaries, and a Business Committee, of which the Hon. J. Belton O'Neal, of South Carolina, was chairman. Mr. Dow was conducted to the chair by Gen. Cocke, of Virginia, and Judge O'Neal of South Carolina, amid loud acclamations. Mr. Dow returned thanks for the honor done him. He said:

"They had assembled to take counsel on the cause of temperance. He regretted there were men hostile to it; but it was not surprising. All great enterprises, which had for their object the amelioration of society, were destined to opposition. On passing through the Park, he had just noticed the statue of one of our great men (De Witt Clinton), who, when he proposed to join the waters of the Great Lakes and the Atlantic, met with nothing but scorn and opposition. And yet, they had all lived to see that mighty work accomplished, and contributing more to the wealth and power of the State than anything else. The cause of temperance was no exception, either in reproach or blessedness. They had gone steadily on against opposition, and were now about at the termination of their labors.

A female from Western New York presented herself on the platform, expressing much interest in the cause, and asking to be received as a delegate from two societies —admitted. A motion was made that the platform be occupied only by officers of the Convention. Gen. Cary moved that the platform was not the appropriate sphere of woman. Some confusion ensued, and the Convention adjourned.

An immense meeting was held in the evening, which was addressed by Rev. Rufus W. Clark, of Boston, and Gen. Cary. He said, "We are in the midst of a great moral revolution; so let us buckle on our armor, and go into the conflict undaunted; and we may rest assured that a grateful posterity will ever bless our memory." A splendid song was sung by M. Colburn, Esq.:

"From hall and from hamlet, from mountain and plain,
The songs and the prayers of the just are ascending;
The armies of Truth, and the Revellers' train,
In the tumult of conflict and battle are blending.
Then on! while the ranks of the foe shall unfold;
Press forward, for victory smiles on the bold.

After a collection, Rev. Dr. Patton introduced the foreign delegation, viz.: John Cassell, of London; Dr. Lees, of Leeds (England); Mr. Jeffries, of Scotland; John Dougal, of Montreal; and E. N. Harris, of New Brunswick. Mr. Cassell addressed the audience, giving an account of the rise and progress of the cause in England; the miseries inflicted on that country by strong drink; the opposition they met with from the higher classes and the clergy; and the hope they indulged that the day was not far distant when England and America would both be blessed with a Maine law.

On Wednesday morning, prayer was offered by Rev. T. L. Cuyler. Letters were read from a number of distinguished gentlemen in America, England and Scotland. A large number of committees were appointed; when Wendell Phillips, of Boston, reporting himself as a delegate from a New York society, made several reflections upon the action of the day previous relating to speeches from the platform, causing, for an hour, great confusion. When order was restored, at the request of Judge O'Neal, I read, from the Business Committee, fifteen resolutions, expressive of the sentiments, purposes, and designs of the friends of temperance in the United States and the world, to be discussed and adopted. To these, another was added, viz.:

That, while we do not design to disturb political parties, we do intend to have, and enforce, a law prohibiting the liquor manufacture and traffic as a beverage, whatever may be the consequences to political parties, and we will vote accordingly.

John Dougal of Montreal was heard in an able speech on the first resolution; when all was thrown into confusion by the lady's taking the platform in opposition to the resolution passed. The Chair decided that she had a right to the floor; and invited her to the platform. The Chair was sustained, on an appeal. As it was supposed that many were in the hall who were not delegates and had voted, it was moved that the hall be cleared, and none readmitted but regular members. The police at once cleared the hall. The process of reconstruction engrossed all of the morning.

A most magnificent soirée had been for days in preparation, for which the sum of $1,100 had been subscribed. Expensive articles of furniture had been procured, and insured against damage. The committee, filled with fears of disorder, or fire, concluded to abandon it, to the great regret of all; especially from other cities and county towns. The afternoon meeting was one of great beauty and loveliness. More than five thousand children filled the hall, and were addressed by Dr. Edward Beecher, of Boston; the Mayor of Providence; Christian Keener, of Baltimore; and Hon. Neal Dow. Mr. Dow was welcomed by the waving of a thousand handkerchiefs. He put it to vote whether the children wanted any grog-shops; when all shouted, No! and all sang, "Some Wine to Drink, from the Foamy Brink;" and also, "The Noble Law of Maine."

The evening was occupied by a masterly speech from Dr. F. R. Lees, of Leeds (England), new, in its chemical developments, to most of his hearers; and acceptable to all in his moral applications:

"It is necessary," said he, "that the body should be pure, in order to the soul being pure. This must be the appropriate temple for the Spirit of the living God; and if you defile that temple, in which the Spirit dwells, you defile and grieve the Spirit itself. We borrowed this doctrine from you, and we return it to you, with our hearty commendations. (Loud applause.) We will adhere to it forever. Intemperance interferes with the health, the temper, the social prosperities; with the laws, the political economy; with the courage, the advancement, the education, the religion, and virtue, of the human race; and the highest sanctions of earth and heaven, of the past and the future, demand that we should, as far as we can, exterminate the destroyer. You dwell in a wonderful age. To you, the nations of the earth are now looking—to you, in whose bosom burns the love of liberty exhibited by the old Puritan Fathers—to you we are looking, for the future steps in this great work. (Applause.) Finish the work so nobly commenced; and the magnificent destiny, and glorious opportunity before you, will make you the future glory of the world, and the wonder of all ages.

Dr. Lees was followed by Rev. Mr. Wolcott, of Providence, and Rev. Thomas P. Hunt.

On Thursday, none but delegates were admitted to the body of the House. Strangers occupied the galleries. Wendell Phillips would amend the minutes. Honorable Judge Hoar, of Massachusetts, rose to a point of order. He said: That gentleman, learned, eloquent, and powerful, whose aid was desired in every cause in which his heart was concerned, was not a member of this body. He moved that the credentials he had presented be recommitted. It was done. Mr. Phillips asked whether he was a member of the Convention. The President said his rights were suspended. Gen. Cary offered a resolution that the common usages of society had excluded women from the platform · and, whether right or wrong, we will in this Convention conform to this usage. This was carried and restored quietness to the Convention. Reports of Committees were received and adopted. The Report on obstruction to progress, ended with the following resolution, which was adopted:—

"Resolved, That the cause of Temperance is a question altogether separate and apart from the question of Woman's Rights, Land Reforms, or any other, and that it must stand or fall upon its own merits."

On the case of Mr. Phillips, the Committee reported that he was not a delegate from any regular organization, but from a Society which was a new creation, formed after the Convention had assembled, for the purpose of sending delegates to this Convention, and that he was not entitled to a seat.

Rev. R. W. Clarke read an able address from the Convention to the governments of the world, and recommended the adoption of the following sentiment, "Sink or swim, live or die, survive or perish, I give my heart and hand to the enactment and execution of the principles of the Maine Law throughout the world." Adopted by a unanimous vote.

The regular resolutions were discussed and adopted. On an objection to mingling temperance and politics, Rev. John Pierpont, of Boston, rose and said:—

"We ask at the hand of our civil legislatures a prohibitory law which we cannot get except at the hands of political action. It is, therefore, to me absurd to renounce or reject all pretensions to mingling in politics. We mean to carry it to the polls and to carry the polls in our favor. We do it upon the principle that it is a moral question, paramount in God's eye to questions of office holding, of finance and of policy. We have up to this time been timid before politicians. We have said, 'We did not mean you.' We say now, 'We do mean you, and will put you down, if you do not give us what we ask.' These are our sentiments."

A long debate ensued on temperance and politics, when

Mr. Carson had leave to unfold to the Convention the entire system of THE CARSON LEAGUE.

The social gathering and soirée having been given up, Thursday evening was devoted to a speech from Judge O'Neal, of Charleston, S. C., a splendid poem by Rev. John Pierpont, and an auction of a barrel of Wisconsin flour. (This had been sent from Wisconsin to be sold in the Convention, and its avails to be returned to that State in Maine-Law tracts.) Rev. Thomas P. Hunt was appointed auctioneer, and bid it off, in great sport, to Bowen & McNamee, for $100. Addresses were then made by Rev. Mr. Hatfield, of New York, and Gen. Cary.

Friday was devoted to hearing reports from foreign delegates: Dr. Lees and Mr. Cassell from England, and Rev. Mr. Scott, from Montreal.

Mr. Cox, of Georgia, then offered a glowing tribute to the memory of Dr. Justin Edwards, deceased, in the following resolution :—

"Resolved, That the Convention hereby expresses its high and grateful appreciation of the distinguished services rendered the cause of Temperance by the late Justin Edwards, D. D., and that while they bow with resignation to the decrees of that unerring Will which has removed him from his position of earthly usefulness and toil, we cannot too deeply mourn the loss from our ranks of so efficient and useful a laborer."

The motion was responded to in impressive speeches from Christian Keener, Mr. Cassell, Rev. Dr. Kennedy, and Gen. Cary. Gen. Cary said:

"I desire to say, as Chairman of this Convention, that the name now mentioned in the resolution was a dear one to me. I learned my first temperance lessons from Justin Edwards twenty years ago in his meetings. His virtues are recorded in the living tablets of my heart. Posterity will honor him; succeeding generations will sigh over his ashes, and the children of the future will drop tears of gratitude and plant perennial flowers on his tomb."

On an unanimous vote of thanks to Mr. Dow, for so ably presiding, the Convention adjourned *sine die.*

Well might my recollections of this Convention be fresh, for its preparations, its arrangements, its correspondence, its resolutions, an attendance upon it night and day, and finally its summing up, publishing and sending abroad the report of its proceedings, cost no small amount of labor; but it was a noble Convention, never to be forgotten by those who mingled in it. Could the soirée have been carried out, it would have surpassed in beauty anything our country had witnessed; but the owner of the building was unwilling to incur the risk of fire in case of a disturbance like the morning meeting; which, for temperance men, was truly intemperate.

The National Division of the Sons of Temperance held an adjourned meeting during the sitting of the Convention, and closed the meeting by a great demonstration at the Metropolitan Hall, on Friday evening, Judge O'Neal, of S. C., M. W. P., presiding.

The exposure of Frauds in the liquor traffic, by Rev. Thomas P. Hunt, in 1838, by means of the Brewers' Guides and Receipt Books which he had procured from London, produced no small sensation through the country. The authentic statements which were also made relative to the vast manufacture of Port wines, out of Oporto, and of Champagne wines which were never on the ocean, but made in New York and elsewhere, troubled their consumers with the thought that they were taking logwood, sulphuric acid, arsenic, nux vomica, gypsum, cocculus indicus, into their stomachs, not for their own good, only for the good of the manufacturers and venders, who, by these means, often increased their profits an hundred fold; and it greatly advanced the temperance reformation. Men who gloried in their old wine, finding that it was manufactured within six weeks; and who drank pure, wholesome ale and beer, learning that it had little or nothing of the hop, but some cheap, venomous drug, said, "If this is so, we will have none of it,"—took to the pure beverage of heaven, and found themselves and families in better health and spirits, besides saving much of their money, which had gone to enrich the trade. The Beer Trials in Albany, showing that the choice beer was made of the filthiest water—water into which were thrown dead animals of every description—increased the disrelish for the products of the brewery. A tract published by Mr. Delavan on adulterations had a wide circulation; and, coming from so creditable a gentleman, made a great impression upon the masses. Dr. Nott in his lectures said: "I had a friend who had been once a wine-dealer, and having read the startling statements made public, in relation to the brewing of wines, and the adulterations of other liquors generally, I inquired of that friend as to the verity of those statements. His reply was, 'GOD FORGIVE *what has passed in* MY OWN cellar, *but the statements* MADE are true, and ALL TRUE, I assure you.'" And yet, such were the fascinations of the drink, that thousands of intelligent, discerning men would persist in its use, always flattering themselves that, if others were imposed upon, they were not. Unbelief here proved the damning sin to many a man who prided himself on his good judgment.

Hearing of the appalling statements of Dr. Cox, of Cincinnati, that he had been analyzing liquors for five years, and, during that time, had tested 2,279 samples, alcoholic and malt, and had found only 350 that were really pure; two hundred and fifty were mixed liquors; all the remainder were adulterated with prussic acid, sulphuric acid, stramonium, strychnine, etc., I sent for him to come to New York, give a course of lectures, and perform his experiments in presence of an intelligent audience. He came, in the spring of 1860, and commenced his lectures in the Cooper Institute. I procured for him wines and brandies from the first-class venders, but without stating the object. Notices were given by the press of the lectures, and much excitement was created for the movement. His lecture was well attended. But, unfortunately, the Doctor was advanced and feeble; slow of speech, and slow of movement—the result of much nice operation in his chemical laboratory. The consequence was, the audience got wearied and retired disappointed; and the Doctor proceeded no farther. The correctness of his examinations and developments were not called in question, though many liquor-dealers were present, and witnessed his tests. The press, the next morning, gave to their ten thousand readers full information, with striking comments. Said the New York Express:

"Every man, with a grain of common sense, knows very well, that it is not the pure juice of the grape that fills the almshouse with paupers, and digs a drunkard's grave in Pottersfield, almost every hour in the day, but poison—*poison*—POISON! Twenty-four thousand dollars' worth of these villainous substances, we are assured, is consumed every day in New York; but who can calculate, with anything like a certainty, the awful cost to the bodies and souls of the drinkers? Who, indeed!"

In the year 1857, the Legislature of Ohio passed a law prohibiting the use of strychnine, or other active poisons, in the manufacture and sale of intoxicating or alcoholic liquors; the penalty prescribed was, imprisonment in the penitentiary, at hard labor, not more than five, or less than one year; showing the indignation roused in the public mind at the developments. Yet few results were visible. The works of darkness continued, and men drank on. Pure alcohol itself is a subtle and dangerous poison, against which men should be warned, were there no adulteration. The millionnaire, glorying in his old and pure wines and best of brandy, is as miserable an object, when groaning with the gout, or raving with delirium tremens, as the wretched pauper lying drunk in the gutter—drunk on the liquor sold by law in the filthy dram-shop. What the brain-fever is, produced by the brain-poison by which many are swept awfully into eternity, all our young men should know, before they experience it, as they are most likely to, if they will madly indulge in these intoxicating drinks. A much-esteemed friend of mine, in Bordentown, New Jersey, Joseph Allison, wrote a description of the delirium, which he gave me, and which I published in the Journal, January, 1842. I afterwards published it in tract form, with a striking engraving, entitled the Rum Maniac. It was as follows:

THE RUM MANIAC.

(A SOLILOQUY.)

"Say, Doctor, may I not have rum,
To quench this burning thirst within?
Here on this cursed bed I lie,
And cannot get one drop of gin.
I ask not for health, nor even life—
Life! what a curse it's been to me!
I'd rather sleep in deepest hell
Than drink again its misery.

"But, Doctor, may I not have rum?
One drop alone is all I crave.
Grant this small boon—I ask no more—
Then I'll defy—yes, e'en the grave;
Then, without fear, I'll fold my arms,
And bid the monster strike his dart,
To haste me from this world of woe,
And claim his own—*this* ruined heart.

"A thousand curses on his head
Who gave me first the poisoned bowl,
Who taught me first this bane to drink,—
Drink—death and ruin to my soul.
My soul! oh, cruel, horrid thought!
Full well I know thy certain fate,
With what instinctive horror shrinks
The spirit from that awful state!

"Lost—lost—I know, forever lost!
To me no ray of hope can come;
My fate is sealed; my doom is—
But give me rum; I will have rum.
But, Doctor, don't you see *him* there?
In that dark corner, low, he sits;
See! how he sports his fiery tongue,
And at me burning brimstone spits!

"Go, chase him out! Look! here he comes!
Now, on my bed he wants to stay;
He shan't be there. O God! O God!
Go 'way, I say! go 'way! go 'way!
Quick! chain me fast, and tie me down;
There, now; he clasps me in his arms;
Down—down the window! close it tight;
Say, don't you hear my wild alarms?

"Say, don't you see this demon fierce?
Does no one hear? Will no one come?
Oh, save me—save me! I will give—
But, rum! I must have—will have rum.
* * * * * * *
Ah! Now he's gone; once more I'm free:
He—the boasting knave and liar—
He said that he would take me off
Down to—but there! my bed's on fire!

Fire! water! help! come, haste—I'll die;
Come, take me from this burning bed!
The smoke—I'm choking—cannot cry;
There, now—it's catching at my head!

But see! again that demon's come;
  Look,! there, he peeps through yonder glass;
Mark how his burning eyeballs flash!
  How fierce he grins! what brought him back?

"There stands his burning coach of fire;
  He smiles, and beckons me to come.
What are those words he's written there?
  '*In hell, we'll never want for rum!*'"
One loud, one piercing shriek was heard;
  One yell rang out upon the air;
One sound, and one alone, came forth—
  The victim's cry of wild despair.

"Why longer wait? I'm ripe for hell;
  A spirit's sent to bear me down.
There, in the regions of the lost,
  I sure will wear a fiery crown.
Damned, I know, without a hope!
  (One moment more, and then I'll come!)
And there I'll quench my awful thirst
  With boiling, burning, fiery rum."

CHAPTER XXI.

Campaign in New York for the Maine Law—Publications issued—New York State Society—"Prohibitionist" established—Frequent Meetings—Methodist Fire—Congregational Convention—Address of Senators—Anniversary A. T. U. of State Temperance Society—Convention at Auburn—Nomination for Governor—Election of Governor Clark—Congratulatory Meeting—Meeting of Opposition—Adoption of the Law in New York—Hesitancy of Mayor Wood to its Execution—Success in the State—Opposition—Pronounced Unconstitutional by the Court of Appeals—Results and Opinions.

The full and decided opinion of a large number of the most intellectual, patriotic, and Christian men of the country, on the wisdom, justice, and necessity of prohibitory law, in opposition to a license system, and the action of several State legislatures strengthened the friends of temperance in the Empire State, in their resolution to make another bold and powerful effort to secure it at the ballot-box, though they had been sadly thwarted by the Veto of Governor Seymour. It might cost them much labor; but what was labor, in view of the poverty, crime, and drunkenness, to be prevented? It might cost them money; but what, compared with the amounts levied for poor-taxes, prisons, alms houses, and courts of justice? It would bring upon them reproach and hostility; but it would be the reproach and hostility of men who would make no sacrifice of luxurious indulgence, to save thousands from death; and who, for gain, would persevere in a traffic which was, as Chancellor Walworth expressed it, a traffic in the bodies and souls of men.

From the adoption of prohibition by Maine, an immense amount of labor had been performed in the State of New York, by the State Temperance Society and other organizations, to prepare the public mind for the reception and adoption of the same principle. Col. Herman Camp, the President, and William H. Burleigh, Corresponding Secretary, and Messrs. Gregg and Crampton, lecturers, were men of power, and caused their influence to be widely felt. At their first meeting, held at Syracuse, their Executive Committee were directed to confer with me on the subject of preparing and publishing a series of short and impressive tracts, such as the exigencies of the times might require.

As the result of this conference, I speedily prepared and published, in pamphlet form, SIX REASONS WHY THE STATE OF NEW YORK SHOULD ADOPT THE MAINE LAW. These reasons approved themselves to all reflecting men; were widely circulated by the agents of the Society, and were inserted in several of the public papers of the State. Subsequently, I prepared and published about twenty Maine-Law Tracts, of four pages: THREE CHEERS FOR MAINE! SHALL WE HAVE THE MAINE LAW? TWENTY-FIVE OBJECTIONS ANSWERED. TRIUMPH OF HUMANITY. FEMALE INFLUENCE FOR THE LAW, &c., of which there were sent out from the office of the American Temperance Union over a million. I also prepared a life of NEAL DOW; Review of Gov. Seymour's Veto; and published Dr. Spear's and Albert Barnes' sermons on the Law These, for a time were our ammunition for the great battle.

In 1853, Mr. Delavan entered into the work, became president of the State Society, and instituted at Albany the PROHIBITIONIST, of which W. H. Burleigh, first, and Amasa McCoy, next, became editor; and for which he secured throughout the country, a great circulation. He also caused to be prepared for the State Society, a series of twelve MAINE-LAW TRACTS, suited to all the leading topics, and printed in cheap style. Of these, an immense amount were sent forth. The State Society early resolved on the most active and determined measures; and they spared no effort or expense to create a right public sentiment. Throughout the State, frequent Maine-Law meetings were held, for discussion, and to answer the objections which were continually made to the Maine Law, as unconstitutional, and depriving men of their natural rights. The pulpit was prompt to perform good service; and the religious press spoke with energy for the great object. Said the Christian Advocate and Journal (Methodist):

"We bespeak a little of our characteristic denominational element, *fire*, for the cause out of Maine. Every man should be up and doing. Petitions should be circulated, signed, and loaded upon the tables of the Legislature of every State. None of these memorials should stop short of asking the total abolition of the traffic. Let Methodists be in the van of this mighty movement."

A mammoth Congregational Convention was held at Albany during the conflict. On my offering a resolution approving of the Maine Law, it was moved that it be referred to the committee. "No, No!" uttered a dozen voices; "pass it at once." "It must be referred," said the moderator, "by rule." "No matter; no matter," it was replied. "Will you suspend the rule?" asked the moderator. "AYE," came like a thunder-clap from the whole house. "Will you adopt the resolution?" "AYE," was swelled up by the voice of every member of that august body. "Old men, with whitened locks; young men, in the full vigor of their prime, vied with each other in throwing into that response all the energy, the determination, the fire, of their souls."

The Address of the Senators and Members of Assembly, who had voted for the suppression of intemperance, to the people of the State of New York, was an able production; and put all the supporters of Governor Seymour's veto beyond a word of defence. They said: "A single man has stood between the will of the people, clearly expressed, and the accomplishment of their purpose. That will, founded, as it is, on the principles of eternal truth, on the profoundest wisdom, and looking to the greatest possible good of the people, will not change." Nothing was wanting more, but that time should roll on, and the State of New York would surely wheel into line. The fall election of 1854 was to give a new Assembly and a new Governor, who would not veto a bill.

The American Temperance Union held its Eighteenth Anniversary on the 11th of May, 1854, all in sympathy with the State in its present struggle. The Report detailed the extraordinary progress of the cause; the adoption of a prohibitory law in five States, and its marked results in the improved condition of the people of those States—especially of the industrial working classes. The meeting was ably addressed by Hon. Mr. Powers, of Vermont; Rev. Henry Ward Beecher, of Brooklyn; Rev. Dr. Cleveland, of Northampton; Rev. R. M. Hatfield, and Rev. T. L. Cuyler, all on much the same topic. Mr. Cuyler said he had but one short speech to make; it was, "Go home, ye men of New York, and make up your minds to vote, at the next election, for the passage of the Maine Law, as Henry Ward Beecher has told you; and go home, you men and women, and pray, that you may know the truth, to that same God from whom he has received all that he has."

On the 22d of June, the State Society held its annual meeting at Albany; Mr. Delavan presiding. Resolutions were unanimously adopted, denouncing Governor Seymour's Veto, and appointing a committee of five to confer with committees of other denominations, on calling a State Convention. The Society resolved that, if they would succeed in their great work, they must closely adhere to the one great idea, PROHIBITION; suffering no love of gain, no desire for popularity, no attachment to partisan organization, no longing for political success, to keep it out of view. The 27th of September was fixed upon, by a committee at large—a committee of the State Society of the Sons of Temperance—as the day for a State Convention, at Auburn, for the prosecution of measures to procure the Legislation that was now demanded.

That Convention consisted of over three hundred of the self-sacrificing and energetic temperance men of the State. Coming in a late train, I found it difficult gaining admission to the Hall. E. C. Delavan was appointed President, but he declining, David Wright, of Cayuga, was substituted in his place. Amid such a multitude, processes of organization were slow; some proposed one thing, and some another. Early in the afternoon session, a venerable gentleman from Oneida moved that Myron H. Clark, of Canandaigua, be put in nomination for Governor; but he was premature, and the nomination was withdrawn. He, however, was the man toward whom the eyes of the temperance men were turned for the high office; and when business had assumed its regular shape, and a series of strong resolutions by Mr. Burleigh were adopted, he was again nominated by the same gentleman, Mr. Leonard Moore, of Oneida, and the nomination was approved by acclamation. Mr. Clark had for some time been State Senator from Onondaga County, and had been most prominent and active in preparing and supporting a prohibitory law. Seldom has a nomination to high office been made with more harmony and enthusiasm, by a large body of most intellectual and patriotic men. The harmony, however, was broken, upon the nomination of the second officer of the State government, as a portion of the Convention wished it to fall upon some gentleman of an opposite political party, inasmuch as in that party were many of the friends of temperance and of prohibition. Such desired Bradford R. Wood, of Albany, of the Democratic party, and one of the earliest and most devoted friends of the temperance cause; but Mr. Wood withdrew his name, and Henry J. Raymond, of the Whig party, who had sent in his adherence to the Maine Law, obtained the nomination for Lieut. Governor. The Convention adjourned in great confidence of success.

Great efforts were now made to secure the election. Four candidates were in the field. Mr. Clark, Gov. Seymour, Mr. Ullman, the Know Nothing candidate, and Judge Bronson, the Conservative Whig. A plurality vote secured the office. While the friends of the opposing candidates were not lacking in efforts, the friends of Mr. Clark held a most enthusiastic meeting at the Broadway Tabernacle on the 4th of November. It was my province to read the proceedings at Auburn, the nominations and resolutions; when the meeting was powerfully addressed by Rev. T. L. Cuyler, Mr. Greeley, and R. M. Hatfield. The day of election was one of intense excitement, as the returns brought the opposing candidates so near together, that it was exceedingly doubtful which would prevail. At length it was manifest that Mr. Clark had the lead, and was to be Governor of the State of New York. Mr. Clark had 158,795 votes, Gov. Seymour, 156,501, Mr. Ullman, 122,274, and Judge Bronson, 33,820. We felt it to be a great moral as well as political triumph, inasmuch as there were involved in it vast moral interests, as well as humane, and we felt disposed to give God the glory.

A card issued by twenty citizens, headed by W. E. Dodge, invited the temperance community to set apart the twentieth, as a day of rejoicing. It was honored by a display of flags and banners, and in the evening, a large meeting was held in the Broadway Tabernacle. On each of the main pillars which supported the roof, were suspended banners, with the names of the States which had adopted the Maine Law, *viz.*, Maine, Minnesota, Massachusetts, Rhode Island, Vermont, Connecticut, and Michigan, with the dates of adoption; and hanging over the organ, was a banner of muslin, on which was inscribed, MYRON H. CLARK. NEW YORK IS COMING. NO RUM AT ALL. Mr. Dodge was elected President, and the meeting opened with prayer and thanksgiving, by Dr. Cox. It was my province to read several congratulatory letters from friends abroad, to read the resolutions, and to welcome the good ship Maine Law into port, with Commodore Clark hoisting his Broad Pennant. Governor Dutton, of Connecticut, warmly expressed his congratulations in an able speech, showing the condition of things in Connecticut, followed by the Hon. E. D. Culver, and others, with soul-stirring addresses. Chancellor Walworth said in his letter, which was read:—

"If the result of the recent election shall be the passage of a law to prohibit the sale of intoxicating drinks, to be used as a beverage, all the friends of humanity may well rejoice and congratulate each other. One thing is certain, the election of Gov. Clark will prevent the vetoing of a law, if a proper law should be passed by the Legislature, and submitted to him for approval. And from what I can learn of the Legislature, a clear majority of temperance men have been elected to the Assembly."

Said the Hon. Neal Dow:—

"I rejoice with all my heart, in the glorious triumph of our friends in New York, at the recent election. It is right and fitting that you should hold a Jubilee to thank God that the right has triumphed."

The inauguration of Governor Clark, on the first of January, was a proud day for temperance, though few knew with what trials he and his friends were to meet; but all were in the hands of a righteous Providence. His messages was very decisive and satisfactory. The Senate of the last year held over, and the new Assembly was one in which the friends of prohibition had confidence. When the Prohibitory Liquor Bill came before the Legislature, every possible obstacle to its passage was thrown in its way; but all in vain. On the 21st of February, it came to a final vote in the Assembly, when it was adopted: 80 for its passage and 45 against it; absent or not voting, 3. In the Senate every possible obstruction was thrown too in its path, but on the 3d of April, at a quarter before twelve, it was passed by the overwhelming vote of 21 to 11, to take effect on the 4th of July. The Assembly concurred, and on the ninth of April, the bill was signed by the Governor, and became the law of the State of New York.

Through the State were great sensations of joy and gladness, excepting among the manufacturers and venders of intoxicating drinks. On the 26th, a congratulatory meeting was held in New York, in the Metropolitan Theatre, quite unsurpassed by any before held. Here again, I was permitted to read many timely and important documents, especially a letter giving great satisfaction, from the new Governor of the State. The resolutions were modest but firm; congratulatory; inviting the most searching scrutiny; expressive of a determination to persevere; for, sink or swim, live or die, we shall not again quietly submit to alcoholic dominion.

Mr. Dodge, on taking the Chair, warmly congratulated the meeting on the occasion. He had just returned from a four weeks' tour, in the course of which he had passed through most of our cities and towns at the West and South, and had been astonished and gratified at finding the cause of temperance widely spreading. He introduced the Hutchinson songsters, who greatly delighted the audience, after which, spirited speeches were made by Prof. Mattison, Rev. Henry Ward Beecher, W. H. Burleigh, Dr. Peck and

Rev. Dr. Tyng. Seldom was a meeting known of such enthusiasm and power.

H. W. Beecher said:

"This was the most important meeting that had been gathered in New York for many a day. The whole State would be looking towards it. They would ask, what does the city of New York think about that Maine Law? What is the pulse there? and what do they intend to do about it? We had, at last, procured common and statutory law to this effect, that making and selling intoxicating drinks, for purposes of diet, was now declared, by the voice of the people (what he regarded as common law), and by the voices of their representatives (which was statutory law), to be a crime. We might be baffled and baulked a great while, before we could make all the teeth of this law meet, with a good subject between them; we might have to deal with men who could come, and disappear, as spirits do; but there was one thing they could not reverse; after years of discussion, the people in this empire State had declared, that the making and selling of intoxicating drinks, for such purposes, was a crime. The principle was born; and there was nothing born on the face of this earth that carried such joy as the birth of a moral principle. They could never get that back again; they might as well try to crowd the last year's chicken into the shell. (Loud cheers.) Till now, we had been working zig-zag before this Sebastopol; but we would not be long taking it. Efforts would be made to destroy the law in the courts; but what the courts decided to be wrong, could be rectified; we were in for the battle, and would have perseverance and ingenuity, until the law succeeded. (Applause.) The voice which the State sent up to the city to-night was, 'Will you abide by the prohibitory law?' The response he would send back was this: 'We are watching and waiting; we are like the men at Waterloo, lying close to the ground, until they should hear the old hero cry, 'Up! Guards! and at them.'"

Mr. Burleigh said:

"For two hundred years, the license laws had been undergoing amendments; and those engaged in the traffic looked on with perfect complacency. The liquor-dealers were in no degree annoyed by the speeches of the temperance men, so far as those speeches reached the newspapers, and were confined to moral suasion. But from all of them—from our gin-princes down to the very democracy of our rot-gut—there came up a demonical howl against the law of prohibition. We now stood front to front with the enemy. It was for this that we had labored, and we had prayed. It was for this that we had sent up our supplications to the throne of God, that he might give us a fair word in open fight; that in the arrangements of his Providence, He would bring us face to face with the foe, where foot might be planted against foot, where eye might meet glowing eye, where hand might clutch with hand in the contest. We asked for no odds, we required no favor; we had but one prayer, 'God, defend the right.'"

Following our great congratulatory meeting, as might have been anticipated, was one of the liquor-dealers, and their defenders, at the Tammany Hall, where the law was violently denounced as unconstitutional and fanatical; but the meeting was reported as one of great confusion. The very distinguished lawyers said to have been feed for needed service, by the Liquor-dealers' Association, and whose presence was promised, were none of them there; nor was the stand graced by any distinguished orators.

But, in fact, throughout the city and State, there was silence, for half an hour. Men of all parties were impressed with the vastness of the change which would come over the community, and of the sacrifices which many heavy dealers must be called to make. The general feeling in the city and throughout the State was, that the law would become the governing rule of the State. Scarce any were to be found among the venders themselves, who were of a contrary opinion. In the city of New York, its enforcement would lie much with Mr. Wood, the Mayor of the city. It was supposed he would be very decided and very efficient. He had, a little before, acquired the confidence of the people, by a surprising and efficient enforcement of the Sunday liquor law. In his inaugural speech, he had declared that the laws must be respected and obeyed. On the first Sunday after his assumption of office, two hundred and eighty liquor shops were open; on the second, one hundred and thirty; on the third, but twenty-six. Such a

Mayor was raised up for the crisis; and Mr. Wood received many compliments from the temperance men, and the religious community. At an early period, his minister, Rev. Dr. Tyng, preached, before his Honor, a plain and powerful sermon on the responsibilities of rulers in great exigencies, and the duty and encouragement of sustaining, in firmness, law and government; and seemed confident of a response in the judgment and heart which would lead to no disappointment. But, as an evil spirit came upon Saul, so his Honor consulted his district and corporation attorneys, as to what would be the operation of existing laws; and received as reply that, as there would be no license given, after the first of May, free trade should be given to all people, till the Fourth of July; and that, even then, and after, it would be so continued in all foreign liquors. By these opinions he concluded to abide, and thus opened for the season the floodgates of rum.

In a short time, questions were rising relative to the constitutionality of the law; and some judges of inferior courts had given opinions on the subject adverse to the law, which were at once seized upon by its enemies. Some distinguished men in the city, also, eminent lawyers, had expressed themselves strongly and adversely on some points of the law, the result of which was that the Mayor not only refused to exert any positive influence for the enforcement of the law, until its constitutionality was settled in the courts, but warned his police of the penalties which would be visited upon them, should any of them make mistakes in arresting any, in the performance of duty, for violation of the law. The entire power of the city government was at once neutralized. So was it, also, at Albany; but not so in other cities.

In the city of Brooklyn, the Hon. George Hall, then Mayor, took bold and decided measures for the enforcement of the law. On being asked if he would not let the subject rest until there had been a decision of the courts, in the autumn, he said, "No; the law is a law now; he wanted no decisions of courts. Wherever the law was violated it was his duty to take cognizance of the violation; and he should do so." The same was the case with the mayors of other cities. In Utica, Syracuse, Oswego, Rochester, and in most of the towns, and in some entire counties, the law met with acquiescence and support. In his message, at the opening of the Legislature, January, 1856, Governor Clark said:

"The Act for the Suppression of Intemperance, Pauperism, and Crime, passed by the Legislature, in accordance with the clearly expressed demand of the people, went into operation on the Fourth of July last, notwithstanding it has been subjected to an opposition more persistent, unscrupulous, and defiant, than is often incurred by an act of legislation; and though legal and magisterial influence, often acting unofficially and extra-judicially, have combined to render it imperative to forestall the decision of courts, wrest the statute from its obvious meaning, and create a general distrust in, if not hostility to, all legislative restrictions of the traffic in intoxicating liquors, it has still, outside of our large cities, been generally obeyed. The influence is visible, in a marked diminution of the evils which it sought to remedy."

The autumnal elections in the State were favorable to the law. But little could be expected by its opponents from the new Legislature. Two judges of one judicial district had pronounced it unconstitutional and void. Some distinguished lawyers, in New York, had given their private opinion on the same side. This had drawn out some of the best talent of the State: Judge Edmunds, Chief Justice Savage, Judge Shankland, Judge Conklyn, and others, in its support. As it was known that the whole subject would be brought before the Court of Appeals, in March, all eyes were upon that, to see what its decision on the constitutionality of the law would be. That Court was composed of eight judges. By that Court, on the 29th of March, the law was pronounced unconstitutional; five of the judges uniting in the decision, viz.: Denio, A. S. Johnson, Comstock, Selden, Hubbard; and three dissenting: Mitchell, Wright, and T. A. Johnston. The Court was of opinion, that the various provisions, prohibitions, and penalties contained in the act, substantially destroyed the property in intoxicating liquors already possessed, in violation of the terms and spirit of the constitutional provisions; and also, that no discrimination was made between liquors possessed, and those which might hereafter come into possession. But it was remarkable that the five did not unite on one and the same reason. Hon. Mr. Bradford, of the Senate, introduced a bill for a prohibitory law like the present, but conformed to the Court of Appeals. The same was introduced to the Assembly, but was rejected. And, after various struggles for a new law, the Legislature adjourned, leaving the State without any law touching the sale of intoxicating liquors. Thus were all the hopes of temperance men in the State of New York, of legislative aid, baffled, and scattered to the winds. But they had an experience of what prohibitory law would do, which justified them in the course they had pursued, and led them to feel that the welfare of the State could only be secured by a return, at some future day, to the same, or similar action.

In the short period between July, 1855, and the first of December (as compared with the same number committed during the same time in the year 1854), to nine jails out of New York, there was a diminution of 2,062. More than equal to this, was the result in the diminution of pauperism; while visible drunkenness was almost swept away.

Even in the city of New York, though the traffic was unimpeded, there were good results of the liquor law. The arrest of every drunkard abroad, and fining him $10, and committing him in case of default, had a surprising effect.

It both made the vice infamous and diminished it. The commitments, in the month of July, were nine hundred and twenty-six; for August, five hundred and twenty-six. Of these, none were of respectable or young men. In Suffolk county, where there were more than one hundred and fifty licensed houses, scarce one place of sale could be found. In the city of Rochester, the number of arrests, thirty days previous to the law taking effect there, were three hundred and four; arrests in thirty days subsequent, ninety-one. E. B. Day, Esq., wrote me from Greene county:

> "Instead of noise, and the tumult of rum-revelries, daily and nightly in our streets—instead of pinching want and brutal treatment—in place of deep and hopeless sorrow, depicted in the countenances of drunkards' wives and children; and the dark and sombre forebodings of the father, who knows that, except in the law, there is no hope for his son—we have quietness, peace, competency, and domestic happiness. In Rome, was a general surrender; the police expressing surprise. In Courtlandt county, there was a general observance. In Livingston, many opposers, seeing its blessedness, became afraid of the law."

But the suppression of the traffic could not be borne.

> "Man's inhumanity to man,
> Makes countless thousands mourn."

While we were in the midst of all this excitement in the State of New York, tidings of riot and blood came to us from Maine. Indeed, how was it to be expected that the Dragon, bound with a great chain, should do otherwise than rave and gnash his teeth, and seek universal destruction. By vote of the Board of Aldermen of the City of Portland, the Mayor and two of their number were appointed to purchase liquor for the City Agency. $1,600 worth were purchased. Inflammatory papers declared that that they were purchased by Mr. Dow, for himself, without any authority. The liquors were in the custody of an officer; but this did not satisfy a mob who were resolute to have them seized and destroyed. They rushed to the building where they were stored, broke the windows and attempted to force the door. They were repeatedly warned to desist. The riot act was read to them. The military were called out, and the mob assaulted them with stones and brickbats. To quiet them was impossible, and they were ordered to fire. One man was killed, and several were wounded. A great hue and cry was at once raised by the enemies of the Maine Law throughout the land, as a law to be maintained by the military and bloodshed. But the riot was not occasioned by the execution of the law at all. The Court which sat upon the case decided that the liquors were ordered by a Committee chosen by the Board of Aldermen, that they were ordered for the City Agency, and for lawful sale; that they were marked and invoiced to the City Agency. The Mayor was found not guilty of a charge of manslaughter and was discharged, and the liquor restored to the City Agent. A large Committee of highly respectable gentlemen also acquitted Mr. Dow of all error, mistake, rashness, and misjudgment in the matter. Mr. Dow, by his firmness, it was believed, saved the city from being set on fire and burned up. There was reason to believe that the plan of riot was concocted at a distance. The man killed was a profane and riotous sailor from the eastward.

For five years the law stood well in this, the Dirigo State, without any political change. Mr. Dow acquitted himself well, in the high and responsible office to which he had been called. Not a brewery or distillery was left in the State, and but little drunkenness, excepting on the borders of other States. But no State can be expected to continue long without changes. Men die; political leaders remove. New interests come in play. In the election of '55–6, a new political party came into power. Financial questions and strong personal antipathies were mingled in the conflict, and old political organizations were involved. The Republican or Maine-Law ticket mustered 51,000, the Democratic, 48,000, and the Whig, 11,000. The result, however, was not seriously threatening to the Maine Law, as many of the Whig and Democratic voters were decided Maine Law men, but the day for great union and harmony was passing away.

In other States the great principle of prohibition was steadfast and increasing. In Massachusetts, the friends of the law continued in earnest in giving the law fair trial. In 1855, they prosecuted the keeper of the Revere House, the principal hotel, for violations of the law, and obtained judgment; but appeals were made, in expectation of escape from the penalty, under flaws in the statute. On trials, no jury could be found to agree. A powerful address was sent out to all the ministers of the Gospel, September 20th, 1855, rejoicing in the wonderful success of the prohibitory movement, and asking their co-operation, signed by Lyman Beecher, D.D., and fifteen others.

In Connecticut, at the expiration of a year from the introduction of the law, a public meeting was held at New Haven, which was addressed by W. H. Burleigh, Governor Dutton, and Dr. Bacon. Dr. Bacon said:—

"The operation of the prohibitory law of Connecticut for one year, is a matter of observation to the people of the State. It is so to the citizens of New Haven. Its effect in promoting peace, order, quiet, and general prosperity, no man can deny. Here, we owe it in part to the good faith with which most of our merchants, who had previously dealt in liquor, proposed to relinquish the traffic, and did relinquish it in August, 1854. They gave it up. There was no such banded defiance to our law, as there is to the present law in the city of New York. Never, for twenty years, has our city been so quiet and peaceful, as under its action. If it is not equally so for a year to come, I warn those at the head of our government, that the next election will give a sorry account of them. The people must rule. Let them rule. For law is the expression of the moral sense of the people. The enactment which expresses this sense is law; that which does not, is not law, but oppression."

CHAPTER XXII.

Reception of the decision of the Court of Appeals—Death of B. F. Harwood—Twenty-first Anniversary of A. T. U.—Governor Briggs elected President—Meeting one of darkness—State Society—Letters to Daniel Lord, Jr.—Fall Elections—Prohibitory Law giving way to Anti-Slavery—State Society at Albany—N. Y. City Alliance—Peter Sinclair—Gough Festival.

THE decision of the Court of Appeals was received with great exultation by distillers and venders, and with approbation by many highly respectable gentlemen, strong political partisans, (for prohibition was viewed as a child of the republican party,) and many men of wealth who "drank wine in bowls and cared not for the affliction of Joseph," but it filled with anxiety and concern nearly all the patriotic, philanthropic, self-denying and religious men of the State, and drew tears from many a victim of the cup, who daily prayed LEAD ME NOT INTO TEMPTATION.*

* A most tragic event followed the decision of the Court, in the death of Benjamin F. Harwood, the long-beloved and honored clerk of the Court. The prohibitory law was his only hope of escape from that terrible death which followed the cup. On the morning of the decision, he entreated one of the judges to spare the law. Said he, "Sir, you know I am addicted to drinking; but you do not know—no living person can know—how I have struggled to break off this habit. Sometimes I have succeeded; and then, these accursed liquor-bars, like so many man-traps, have effected my fall. For this reason, I have labored for the prohibitory law. Your decision is, with me, a matter of life and death." When the decision was handed him to record, he felt it to be like signing his own death warrant. Hope failed him; despair seized him; amid the horrors of delirium tremens, when four men could not hold him, he sunk away; and in less than four days was no more. All Sunday and Monday, it was the topic of conversation in Albany, DEATH BY THE TRAFFIC, IN THE COURT OF APPEALS.—*Prohibitionist.*

Never, it was almost unanimously conceded, was a law passed by a legislature of whose constitutionality there had been so little question. In the decision, no great point of law was established, only some trivial positions of little value were objected to, which the friends of the law could and would abandon. Judge T. A. Johnston, Judge Mitchell and Judge Wright, men of equal strength with any on the bench, gave elaborate opinions on the constitutionality of the law, and the unrighteousness of the decision ; so that, though the law was killed, yet its principles remained uninjured ; its friends by no means felt disheartened, but were resolved to stand before the world in defence of what they had established, and to support the public sentiment until, at some future day, it should command the ballot-box and the government. Said Judge Johnston:—

> "The whole controversy, so far as it involves any question of principle, is narrowed down to a struggle for the right of the individual to traffic in whatever the law adjudges to be property at his discretion, irrespective of consequences, over the right of government to control and restrict it within limits compatible with the public welfare and security. Everything beyond this is merged in considerations of expediency. As there is nothing in the Constitution either of the State or United States, which takes away or limits the right of the Legislature to make such regulations in regard to the traffic in property among the citizens of the State, and to impose such restriction and prohibitions upon it, as it shall deem necessary for the public good, so far as it restrains and prohibits the sale of intoxicating drinks it must be pronounced a valid, constitutional act, and entitled to obedience from every citizen of the State."

The prohibitory law of the State of New York was indeed dead and buried. No thought would exist on its being revived, but the same great principles might be put into another law, and therefore, with such support, its friends fell into no depression, but girded themselves to some future and successful conflict. But the State was not wholly without protection. The existing law was against the whole retail traffic in intoxicating liquors. No liquor licenses could be granted, and any man selling under five gallons, could be prosecuted for misdemeanor; the penalty being a fine of not more than $250 and imprisonment not to exceed one year.

The twenty-first anniversary of the A. T. U. was held at the Academy of Music, on the fourteenth of May, 1856. In October, 1855, Chancellor Walworth, long its distinguished President, had resigned the office, and Chief Justice John Savage, of Utica, one of the ablest Jurists as well as most decided temperance men and prohibitionists, was chosen in his place. But being advanced in years and going but little from home, he had consented to serve only to Anniversary week, when the Hon. George N. Briggs, late Governor of Massachusetts, and a most devoted friend of the cause, was elected in his place. A letter of acceptance was received from him on the morning of the Anniversary, in which he manifested his readiness of acceptance, but his regret at not being able to attend on that occasion.

The meeting was in some respects one of darkness and gloom. After indefatigable labor to gain the law, it had been wrested from us, not by the whole people, not by a State or National Convention, but by five individuals clothed with power. Maine also, after sustaining and enjoying the prohibitory law for five years, becoming a perfect asylum for reformed men, (where in their walks and labors they would meet with no temptations,) and the admiration of all nations, had experienced a political reverse, and Mr. Dow had been permitted to retire from an office which he had filled with honor to himself and great usefulness to his country. But other States were standing in their integrity, and their people were enjoying a deliverance from casualties and sufferings which no other enemy but Intemperance was capable of inflicting.

Dr. Tyng presided on the occasion, and opened one of the largest meetings we had ever held, in an admirable address. "We are here assembled," he said, "in this noble edifice, to congratulate ourselves upon the attainments of the past and to express our hopes for the future, and we meet with the solemn determination never to give up the ship; never will we give up this work till the whole American Union shall become the American Temperance Union."

After singing to the tune of Old Hundred, led by George Andrews, Esq.,

> "We praise Thee, God, our fathers' God,
> For ceaseless mercies from Thy hand:
> Still spread the temperance cause abroad
> Till it extends to every land,"

The immense audience were addressed by Benjamin Joy, Esq., and John B. Gough, once more on his adopted soil. Mr. Gough said his first appearance was in New York, at the anniversary of the American Temperance Union in 1844. He remembered that he was clad on that occasion in a brown coat and gray trowsers, and that he was very shaky and very thin, and that he came forward to say his say and then sit down. He was rejoiced to be present at another Anniversary, and to hear a report read that contained enough to cheer the heart. He was never discouraged by apparent temporary or real defeat. It was to be expected in such a cause as this. He felt like the little Scotch drummer, who, when a captive in the hands of his enemies, beat at their bidding the reveille, the advance, the charge, but said he had never learned to beat a retreat.

The semi-annual meeting of the N. Y. State Society was held at Albany, on June 18th, Mr. Delavan presiding, and adopted a series of resolutions expressing fully the views of the Committee relative to the repeal of the prohibitory law. They encouraged no relaxation, but a renewed and vigorous effort to create throughout the State a right public sentiment, and to secure a Governor and Legislature which would enact another temperance law, in the belief that no Court of Appeals would ever again pronounce it unconstitutional. Much sensation was felt on the power of the Court of Appeals; five men could there override the Governor and Legislature of the State, and back all the wheels of government; while those five were but men, and as subject to party influences and not unfrequently as servile and weak judgment, as other men. But it was the Constitution of the State.

At this time, I took the liberty to address, through the Journal, a series of letters to Daniel Lord, jr., Esq., the head of the bar in New York, and a professor of religion, but the leading gentleman in hostility to the prohibitory law, inquiring of him, if the victory was not too dearly won? I asked him to look back at the condition of things in the Empire State, with her teeming millions, when, by request of thousands on thousands of her best citizens, a Legislature, not surpassed by any in wisdom and intelligence, had extended protection over the State, by suspending a traffic which was, by friends and foes, acknowledged to be the source of the greater part of the pauperism, and crime, and insanity, and personal and domestic sorrow in the State; an act which was fully approved by the Executive, and hailed with joy throughout the State by multitudes of the wisest and best, and bringing deliverance to almost numberless suffering families; enabling wives to look upon husbands reformed, and no longer to be led into temptation, and fathers to look upon this as the land where they should now delight to rear their children, and the Church to send up her thanksgivings to God, that the greatest obstacle to her growth and prosperity was removed; and now see that, through his counsel and influence, all this defence was swept away, and the flood-gates of drunkenness and vice were to be set open, and the hopes of the good and the suffering were all to be blasted, and our children, and children's children, might be left to go in crowds to the drunkard's grave, and the drunkard's eternity. I could but ask him, if his victory was not too dearly purchased. He might indeed say that, in matters of constitutional law, the cries of humanity were not to be regarded. Perish, man! perish, domestic peace! perish, public virtue!—property is sacred, and must be preserved. Let it be that, "like a kennel of ferocious bloodhounds, the whole pack of alcoholic stuffs is let loose, to worry and destroy innocent women and children;" let it be that "drunken orgies again break the solemn stillness of the midnight hour; that again, does the sigh of the heart-broken drunkard's wife or mother, the low wail of agony from the drunkard's widow, the bitter, burning tears of the drunkard's orphan children," give evidence that the reign of sorrow has recommenced—property is sacred, and the rights of the liquor-dealer in what he has on hand must be respected and maintained; yet could he, and would he and others, professing humanity and patriotism, rejoice and be thankful that they were permitted to be the instruments of this great ruin? I asked him to say if protection from evil was not the constitutional right of the people, as much as the protection of property—and property that was a curse, and not a blessing? I asked him to listen to the laments and appeals of the suffering throughout the land; if he could glory in the honor and plaudits he would receive, and if his shoulders were sufficient to bear all the responsibility?

As the seasons rolled onward, and the fall elections approached, the temperance men were resolved on doing their duty at the polls. But here, we were to be thwarted on the very plea of humanity. The slavery question was now the great question before the nation. Temperance men, for humanity's sake, must yield to that. Thousands of men, we were told, there were in the State, who would vote for an anti-slavery Governor, who would not vote for prohibition. "Now, you must stand aside; give us your vote, or New York goes for slavery." So I found it, in my attendance on the nominating convention, at Syracuse. Our excellent Chief Magistrate, Gov. Clark, I believed to be right. In a letter to me he said:

"Let us not, however, lose sight of the great and glorious cause of Temperance. Whiskey, after all, is of greater consequence to us than even the slavery question. If everybody would abstain, entirely, from the use of intoxicating liquors, none of the atrocious scenes we have witnessed and heard of would occur again. It is while men are intoxicated, in some degree, that these outrageous scenes in Washington, and in Kansas, and elsewhere, occur. The question of temperance is more important to-day, than ever before in the State; therefore, I trust we shall not allow any other question to overshadow it."

The temperance men might have controlled the nominations; but, such was the pressure upon them, and such the solemn assurance that, by an anti-slavery government, though not prohibition, a better law would be given to the State than that which had been declared unconstitutional by the Court of Appeals, that a large portion gave way, and further effort ceased. The Empire State again wheeled into the old license system; under, indeed, better regulations than ever before made, and which, if thoroughly enforced, would greatly suppress intemperance. But the State legalized and protected the traffic, greatly to the relief and comfort of liquor-dealers and consumers; and how much to the ruin of thousands on thousands, the judgment only will reveal.

The State Society held a special meeting at Albany,

January, 1857, relative to the state of the cause. It was numerously attended, but was a meeting of doubt and difficulty. It was reported that Intemperance had been greatly augmented by the annulling of the Prohibitory Law, and that the excitement attending the election had led many back into Intemperance. But the records of the Police Courts and Jails showed a great good from the law during its continuance. The Society however resolved that they could not assent to the decision of the Court of Appeals as either just or right; and that they would relax no efforts until they should see its principles re-established as the governing law of the State. Exhausted by his labors, Mr. Delavan threatened to resign the presidency of the Society, much to the regret of the members. The Society resolved on raising the sum of $25,000 to pay their debts and prosecute the cause to its legitimate end, if he would remain.

Some were disposed to reflect severely upon the Judges nullifying the law; others opposed that course. After a compromise, they adjourned in harmony. But before that, they adopted a remonstrance to the Legislature against a return to the license system. But as it was done at the next meeting in June, it was the subject of debate whether the friends of prohibition should aid in enforcing it on all who sold without license and give the licensed men the monopoly; or leave the law and the State to take care of itself, under a law legalizing and licensing the traffic. I used what powers I had to induce to the latter course. We had tried a license system for two hundred years, and under it, had grown up all our drunkenness. The Maine Law had in six months suppressed Intemperance more than any license law, had or could do in a century. "Acquiesce in a license law, and it will stand in the statute book another century. Stand off from it and show your abhorrence of it, and it may be repealed in a year." Hon. Horace Greeley regarded the new Excise Law as educational. He regarded it as a bad law, but containing much that was good, which we should at once accept and adopt, leaving the State responsible for all its evil. Dr. H. Corliss considered the course recommended by Mr. Greeley as dangerous and in opposition to all the sentiments of the Society. The Society resolved on a good Prohibitory law as the only sure remedy to close up the liquor traffic, and renewed their pledge to vote for such candidates only, at the next election, as would sustain that principle. Mr. Delavan resigned the presidency, pledging the sum of $4,000 to liquidate the debts for Albany County, to pay it if they would not; and Gen. Joseph S. Smith, of Ulster, was chosen in his place. With Mr. Delavan's resignation the Executive Committee relinquished the further publication of the PROHIBITIONIST as a distinct paper, merging it in the JOURNAL OF THE AMERICAN TEMPERANCE UNION; a paper which they said met their entire approbation and which so nearly expressed the views of the Society, that such union seemed most highly desirable. This, a second time, threw a heavy responsibility upon me. The Prohibitionist had been ably conducted, first by W. H. Burleigh, Esq., and then by Mr. M'Coy, with the daily superintendence of Mr. Delavan; but I was ready to do what I could to sustain the burden, trusting to a kind Providence and to friends of the cause to uphold me. On retiring from office, Mr. Delavan wrote a very able and interesting letter to Gov. King, stating what the cause had done.

On the 25th of May, the N. Y. City Alliance held a public meeting in the Assembly rooms, on the duties of the hour. Numerous speeches were made in favor of energetically enforcing those parts of the New Excise Law which were of a prohibitory character, though none were in favor of a license system. My own mind was clear on these points, viz.: that we never could make any substantial gain under a license law; that if we could suppress all sales but the licensed, about the same amount of drinking and drunkenness would continue, for the licensed dealers would furnish all the community would desire, and have the monopoly; that the consciences of the venders would be quieted, as their sales were legal; and the consciences of temperance men and the community at large would be satisfied with legal sales, whatever might be the mischief done; that it would be no easier stopping the illegal traffic under a li cense law than under a prohibitory law, and that soon the friends of temperance would be weary of the effort; that all compromises with venders should be done away with; that the traffic, whether licensed or not, should be held up as a moral wrong and a nuisance; that if venders would sell, they should sell without permission or legal warrant, and the whole temperance community should stand as a united phalanx against the traffic in all its forms, and expend their time and money in enforcing on the minds and hearts of the people the great subject of prohibition; trusting in God for results, on these principles I should conduct the Journal, if continued in my position.

After a long neglect, from our attention to prohibitory law, of the children and youth of the State and nation, our attention was once more turned to them by the arrival in New York, January 28th, 1857, of Peter Sinclair, from Scotland, a gentleman who had most successfully for years devoted himself to Bands of Hope, in England and Scotland. Mr. Sinclair came to us with the commendations of many distinguished gentlemen, friends of temperance, as a man of ardent piety, great philanthropy, and strikingly adapting himself to children and youth. The Lord Provost of Edinburgh, Rev. Dr. Guthrie, and Dr. Brown, of Dalkeith, all spoke of him in the highest terms as worthy of countenance and support in the temperance cause among children and youth. Of course he had our confidence, and I at once introduced him to Sabbath Schools, and called the attention of the people to him as a great god-send. He at once prepared and published in all our papers a letter to the children of America, which in itself inspired confidence; and, in a short time, few were the schools and youth in the vicinity, who had not heard the pleasant voice and been amused and instructed by the addresses of Mr. Sinclair. Invitations were sent him from all parts of the country to visit and lecture, with a promise of suitable remuneration; and a general revival of temperance among the children and youth of America was confidently and gladly looked forward to.

In March, I accompanied Mr. Sinclair to Portland, Me., to visit the battle-ground where had occurred the far-famed riot; and to see Mr. Dow, who was, with him, more of an object than the President of the United States. We found him at home on a Saturday evening, surrounded by his body-guard, a few chosen friends, who came together on that evening to take counsel and report progress. On Sunday morning, all the Sabbath Schools, by previous notice, were gathered at the Union Church to welcome him, and in the afternoon a second meeting was held in the Rev. Dr. Dwight's church, which was entirely filled with juveniles and their teachers; and in the evening a large and general meeting of citizens was held to hear of the progress of temperance in Scotland and England. In Boston also, large gatherings of juveniles were made for him. At the Tremont Temple in an afternoon, some 3,000 children with 500 adults, were assembled; and a beautiful choir of some 300 children gave him a sweet welcome. The meeting was too large for any profitable address, but the occasion was one of hallowed inspirations. While in Boston, we visited at the State House the Legislative Temperance Society, and both made addresses which drew forth much interest for the youth of the country, hereafter to be the legislators of the land. Mr. Sinclair, after this good introduction, returned to New York, and entered on that field of labor in which he will long be remembered.

After Mr. GOUGH's return from England, where he did much good service, and previous to his going again, I proposed to his friends in New York that we should honor him by a public festival, which was cheerfully acceded to. He was addressed by thirty citizens, headed by W. E. Dodge, to which he returned a favorable reply; and the evening of the 14th of February, 1856, was fixed upon for a festival at Niblo's Saloon. Tables were set for 500 ladies and gentlemen. Single tickets $3 ; lady and gentleman, $5. The scheme was as popular as was Mr. Gough; and in a short time I made sale of all the tickets. The evening was fine, and the company as beautiful and splendid as any which could have been gathered from the votaries of King Alcohol. Indeed, it gave the temperance men and women of New York a fine opportunity to gather together, look at each other and show their strength. Mr. Dodge presided, assisted by twenty Vice-Presidents. Dodworth's Band was in attendance. Dr. De Witt implored the Divine benediction, and I announced the answers which had been given from abroad, but read only that from Governor Clark. After supper a large number of choice sentiments were offered, and splendid speeches made by Rev. Dr. Tyng, Dr. Cox, Henry Ward Beecher, B. W. Tompkins, Rev. T. L. Cuyler, A. C. Barstow and Mr. Gough. It was a beautiful and most appropriate tribute.

The STATE OF MAINE, in which such triumphs had been achieved, was not destined long to be under a cloud. A new prohibitory law was enacted in the winter of 1858, and submitted to the people on the first Monday of June. It received their approbation, and the prohibitionists were not only put in the same position they were in before the repeal of the law of 1853, but their moral position was greatly in advance. The public mind had been well train-ed to appreciate the law and to understand the power and intent of the enemy. The temperance men were no longer attached to and standing in fear of some political party; their position was now an independent one. They had learned their strength, and were able to keep clear of all political entanglements.

The friends of prohibitory law in England had been exceedingly anxious to see and hear Mr. Dow, and they gave him many pressing invitations to come over and let his voice be heard. Accordingly, he left home in April, 1847, for that country, amid the prayers and good wishes of thousands in his city and State. His friends were prepared to give him a magnificent reception, and had carved out for him a great field of labor, designing that he should speak and give an account of the Maine Law and its operations, in all the principal cities of the United Kingdom.

CHAPTER XXIII.

North American Temperance Convention at Chicago—Made President—Action of the Convention—Noble body of men—Cause at the West—Home Missionary Work—Maine Law in Illinois, Michigan, Indiana, Iowa and Nebraska—Cause in California and Oregon—Order of Good Templars—Inebriate Asylums—Binghamton—Boston—Letter of John Tappan—Temperance Battle not man's, but God's—Publications.

On the 10th of November, 1857, there was gathered at the Metropolitan Hall, Chicago, the North American Temperance Convention. It was designed to embrace a delegation from all the States, Canada, and the British Provinces. Only about eighty delegates were assembled from twelve different States, but among them were several eminent clergymen, jurists, and medical gentlemen. With the delegation I went with from New York, I was happy to meet our brethren on their own ground beyond the mountains. In compliment to my office, and perhaps to my age and services, I was made President of the Convention; and found myself well supported by eight Vice-Presidents from as many Western States, and a good business Committee, of which Rev. Dr. Peck, of New York, was chairman. Soon as we commenced hearing reports it was manifest that we were among Western men. Wherever the cause had been taken hold of at all, it was taken hold of strongly and pressed earnestly. Total abstinence from all intoxicating liquor as a beverage, was considered too much as an old, worn-out doctrine, and an early motion was made to strike out the words "as a beverage," and discard all use of alcoholic drinks for any purpose, but the Convention were not prepared for that, yet they unanimously—

> "Resolved, That the principle of unconditional legal prohibition should be the ultimate aim of Temperance organizations and Temperance men."

In the evening, a large assembly was convened in the Hall, to listen to public speaking. I was put forward to make a general statement of the condition of the cause in the world, and to urge the Western States to come up to the aid of the old guard who had labored at the East for near half a century. The Rev. Dr. Peck, of New York, followed in a speech of much eloquence and power.

On the second day, the Business Committee, through Dr. Peck, reported a platform of principles based on Total Abstinence from all intoxicating liquors as a beverage; no license of the traffic, but prohibition of the manufacture and sale by the will of the people, expressed in forms of law; a plan of action by correspondence between all organizations; support of temperance journals and temperance lectures; forming no political parties, but everywhere securing temperance men for civil office to as great an extent as possible. They said:

> "We recognize all the essential principles and measures of temperance as belonging to the purest forms of the Christian religion, as having existence and organic life in the different churches, and depending largely upon their official and individual action for success. We rely most confidently upon the efficient labors of the members and upon the guidance and blessings of the great Ruler of the Universe, which, as we solemnly believe, can, under no circumstances, harmonize with the forms of flagrant vice we are seeking to destroy."

As many pious and good men at the West were engaged in the manufacture of intoxicating drinks, the subject drew out a very spirited and scourging debate. In answer to the plea that moral suasion was better than law,

Rev. Mr. Brooks, of Chicago, showed that there was more moral power in law than in anything else; that God always led men to do right by law; that law was the great educator of the people, and that we never should extirpate an evil from society but by saying—It shall be done. The Rev. Mr. Patton eloquently summoned the ministry and the churches to the work. Much of the day was spent in discussing the subject of organization: some were for having the West unite with the American Temperance Union, and some for having an independent organization at the West. As the debate became somewhat personal, I left the chair for a season. The independent scheme was finally agreed upon and a constitution adopted. Rev. A. Kenyon was chosen Agent for the new Board of action.

During the session, a large union meeting of the Temperance and Sabbath School Juvenile Societies was held in the Metropolitan Hall, which was addressed by Dr. Peck, Rev. Mr. Curtis and Mr. Hewlet.

I was gratified with the appearance and action of the Convention; though there was a great want of plan and harmony. It was composed of men of mind. A large number of ministers were present, who seemed bent on advancing. The cause of Prohibition was popular with all, but with ignorant and corrupt judges, little could be effected; they had overridden popular majorities. The general feeling was that there must be a reform in the courts. A thorough temperance discussion was demanded all over the West. In the same week a Western Sabbath School Convention was in session in Chicago, so that I had an opportunity of seeing many excellent men not only from Illinois, but from Michigan, Wisconsin and Iowa.

Chicago, like all our cities, was sadly abandoned to the liquor traffic, and there was a vast amount of drinking among the Irish and German population. The Eastern men were too much engaged in business, to stop to drink. On the Sabbath evening after the Convention, I preached, by request, to a large congregation in Rev. Mr. Curtis' (Presb.) church, on the importance of an immediate temperance movement among the young in that city. My feelings had been much moved by a procession of five thousand children on Friday, and the sight of many large Sabbath Schools on that day.

A most faithful body of men for the great West, in the cause of temperance, had been the Home Missionaries. Wherever they had been planted, they had come at once in collision with the terrible evil, and they hesitated not to wage a good warfare. Their infant churches were nearly all based on the total abstinence principle, which they fully sustained by example and in the pulpit.

The Maine Law agitation was not a stranger at the West; sometimes it had been successful and sometimes not. In ILLINOIS the popular vote was taken on the prohibitory law, enacted by the Legislature on the first Monday of June, 1855, with a majority of 1,460 against it. The total vote was 167,336. In the northern part of the State, every county gave a large majority for the law, but in the southern, which is Egypt, it was the reverse.

In MICHIGAN, the State Central Committee said, a year after the law was enacted:—

"In the city of Detroit, the supremacy of the law is fully asserted, and we are gratified in being able to state that our good city deserves the credit of a quiet and entirely peaceable submission to legal process. About fifty cases have been commenced in this city. No difficulty has been experienced in convicting in any of the Courts. The friends of the cause have never had any thoughts of obtaining any decision of the Supreme Court."

The INDIANA Prohibitory law took effect on the 12th of June, 1855. At Brockport, Spencer County, the citizens assembled in large numbers in the morning, and about noon, marched to a grove, where they were entertained by addresses and music. In the evening a splendid party was given by the Sisters of the Social Degree of the Temple of Honor. Everything passed off quietly. Two or three drunken men were on the side-walks, but they suddenly found themselves in jail. And all over the State, the liquor-dealers honorably shut up their shops. Indianapolis was as quiet as a Sabbath. The Mayor had for a time no commitments for violation of the law.

In IOWA the prohibitory law went into operation July 1, 1855. A very general disposition prevailed throughout the State in favor of its enforcement. In Iowa City, means were at once raised to carry the violations of the statute to the utmost limits of legal conviction.

In NEBRASKA, the Legislature of 1855 adopted the prohibitory law. In the House there were but two dissentients.

Still farther West, in California and Oregon, temperance even then was gaining foothold, and since has become a living power. The Dashaways at San Francisco, have been a powerful set of reformers. The Pacific, and other temperance papers, have been powerful advocates of the cause. With many respectable individuals, pastors and schools have I corresponded in furnishing them with Journals, Youth's Advocates and Tracts.

In MISSOURI, especially in St. Louis, where the Washington movement and the Father Mathew Societies were once so effective, there was much activity in the cause. In MINNESOTA, the second State that adopted the Maine Law, the principle took deep root and brought forth much fruit. All through the West the Sons of Temperance were once forming divisions; but now they were supplanted much by the Good Templars; an order which originated in Pennsylvania, in 1851, and which now is supposed to number over a hundred thousand. This Order devotes itself much to holding public meetings, scattering tracts and other publications, and inducing men to enlist on their distinctive principles. James Black, Esq., of Lancaster, Pa., is one of its principal leaders, and the Good Templar, at Alton, and the Good Templar Offering, at Chicago, are its principal organs. Before them is a vast work, as the West rolls up its millions.

The subject of INEBRIATE ASYLUMS, already referred to, was renewed in September, 1858, by the laying of the corner-stone of the noble building at Binghamton, N. Y. The inhabitants of the place had given a beautiful site for it, on an eminence about two miles from the village. The Legislature had granted it a charter, in 1854, and some endowment, and Dr. Turner, the founder, had gathered handsome donations. About a thousand persons were present. After the ceremony was performed, eloquent addresses were made by the Hon. B. F. Butler, President of the board; Rev. Dr. Bellows of New York; Hon. D. S. Dickinson, and Professor Edward Everett. A poem was recited by A. B. Street of Albany. It was anticipated that it would become a very large and useful institution. Hon. Mr. Dickinson said, on the occasion:

> The great army of intemperance, those who are wasting and dying of intemperance, if they should march together in solid column, and roll, and heave, and beat, and shout, as though by the convulsive throes of a volcano, what a spectacle it would present! And the cause of philanthropy is marching forward to arrest this foul destroyer. I would gladly speak, did time permit, at length, upon the benefits of the Inebriate Asylum—this great fountain, that is destined to send forth its streams of philanthropy throughout our extended dominions. I can merely say, that this is to be an institution that shall bring back the prodigal son; that shall take him who is insane, and clothe him in his right mind again. How many fathers, how many wives and mothers, will reverently kneel and pray to their Father in heaven for its success!

In Boston, an asylum for inebriates, called the Washingtonian Home (because originating among the Washingtonians, in their desire to reform and save all drunken men), was inaugurated at No. 1 Franklin Place, in 1854; and Mr. Albert Day was elected and installed secretary and superintendent. It was chartered by the State, and soon received aid from the State Treasury. This early attracted attention, and received patronage; and in four years had been the instrument of reclaiming, and making blessings to their families, many most wretched and hopeless inebriates. Whenever I visited Boston, I was sure to visit this institution—removed to 887 Washington street—and found myself richly repaid in all I witnessed. Moral means were more relied upon than medical, and much dependence was placed on the blessing of heaven. In this institution, one of the most wretched inebriates, a Mr. Brown, who had been separated from his family ten years, was, in a short time restored to self-control, and became one of the most eloquent and effective temperance lecturers in the United States. Many had it been my happiness to recommend to that institution, as their relatives and friends came to my office, with tearful eyes and broken hearts, inquiring what they could do with a ruined father, son, or brother.

In one case, I felt deeply interested. A lady and her daughter, from New Jersey, called at my office, impressing me that they were persons of wealth, intelligence, and refinement, and made inquiries for an inebriate asylum, or some private institution. I said, "Surely, madam, you cannot have need of one?" "Indeed I have, sir;" she replied, "we have come to it; we cannot go on any longer as we have gone. My husband is one of the best of men in his family, when he is sober; but when he has been at a drinking party, for two and three weeks we are often in peril of our lives. He has once been in the insane hospital, but the law would not allow them to keep him; and now he is willing to go from home, if a good place can be found for him." I told her of the Asylum at Boston, and advised her to take or send him there.

She inquired of the expense; and I asked her of his ability to defray it. "Oh, abundant," she said; "that was his ruin. He was constantly enticed to card and drinking parties, because it was known he had wealth, and was of a generous nature, and would foot the bills; and we could not keep him from them." I advised her to take him immediately to Boston. The next day he went, a friend accompanying him, and remained for some time. There he was treated with all the kindness and attention due to his standing. The best moral and religious means were used with him. There, among some thirty or forty, he witnessed what he had never seen before in others, though his family had seen it in him—what were the horrible effects of liquor-drinking; and there he was so horror-stricken with the vice of drunkenness, that he publicly renounced the practice, and earnestly entreated that he might be enabled to keep from it forever. A letter from him, to the superintendent, after his return to his happy family, evinced the wondrous change in him—showing what a change of place and companions, and good moral influence, may accomplish.

May 27, 1858.

Mr. Day:—

My Dear Sir,—You must not conclude, because I have not written before this, that I had forgotten you, and the many kind friends I became acquainted with in Boston. I try often to remember the institution over which you preside in my prayers to the throne of grace; that the Lord will continue to bless it, and to raise up to its aid many good and substantial friends. I there learned a lesson which, I hope, I shall never forget, viz.: that a number, who have been very intemperate for many years, and who have broken off, and then drank again, perhaps worse than ever, and so continued a number of years, now have come out decided in the temperance cause, and are now respectable men and good Christian citizens, happy in their fanilies, and among their friends, and are again pursuing a good and profitable business. So there is hope for me; and I mean and intend, looking to the Lord for his help and blessing, to live, while life lasts, a temperate, and I hope a Christian life, and perhaps yet see many and pleasant days.

Few had more interested themselves in Asylums for inebriates than my friend and kinsman, John Tappan, of Boston. I had expressed to him my feelings of revolt at the appropriation, by the New York Legislature, of a portion of the money paid for license to the Binghampton Institution—first establishing drinking houses by law, to create revenue, and then appropriating public money to cure the drunkards there made. It seemed to be, and, in fact, was so used, as an argument for continuing the license. But he viewed it in a different light, and said to me, in a letter, November 19, 1859:

"I hope you will immediately advocate the appropriation of one half, instead of one-tenth of the revenue derived from licenses, to the building up of the Asylum at Binghamton, and kindred institutions through your State, so as to have, at least, as many as you have State prisons; for surely there is crying need of them. So long as your State will license, and your judges support the law, it is the duty of temperance men to obtain, by all lawful means, the revenue derived from the infamous business, for the purpose of taking care of the unhappy victims, who are murdering wives and debasing their children, as well as, by daily drinking, supporting the saloons, hotels and grog-shops, not one of which would continue their business, if none but those temperate and intemperate drinkers, who disdain to enter such places, were to go at large. We must do what we can, by abolishing licenses, and by the strong arm of the law, as well as moral suasion; but, as long as the customs of society remain, and the appetite is not under religious restraint, drunkards will be made, in high places and in low. To meet this, we must labor, and pray for prohibitory legislation; build asylums; arouse parents, and, if possible, persuade them to banish all alcoholic drinks from their families, and to avoid all parties where they are introduced. My belief is, that every man who goes to Binghamton, and all his friends, will be your most powerful aids, in abolishing licenses."

On Mr. Dow's return from England, where he was

most cordially received, and where he accomplished much good, in speaking in numerous large meetings, and explaining the Maine Law, and cheering the hearts and strengthening the hands of prohibitionists, he was honored with many testimonials of respect and affection. At a meeting, at the Academy of Music, in New York, he received a noble tribute from Dr. Tyng, as a man who would be honored and remembered with gratitude when thousands of lecturers, and men who draw admiring crowds, would be forgotten forever. Mr. Dow spoke for an hour, giving an account of his labors in England, and the hopeful progress of the cause in that country; though seventy-five millions sterling were there expended for strong drink, and sixty thousand persons annually perished from its effects.

It was highly gratifying to Mr. Dow and to all the friends of the cause, to see prohibition restored in Maine, after a few years' subjection to a license law, under which the State was flooded with intoxicating liquors. By a vote of the Legislature, the question was submitted to the people, when 28,864 voted for the restoration of prohibition, and 5,912 for the continuance of license. The new law went into operation on the 15th July, 1858. At this time, grog-shops had increased in Portland, doing their work of death, to five hundred; but they were then generally closed; and Maine became once more an Asylum for the inebriate.

In 1858 I published a discourse entitled The Temperance Battle not Man's, but God's, from 2d Chronicles xx. 15. *The battle is not yours, but God's*; 8vo, 24 pp. The object I had in view was not to prove that God was in conflict with Intemperance: I should as soon think of proving that God existed; but to illustrate, draw out and improve this great truth, and derive such instruction from it as would encourage, animate and lead the temperance hosts on to battle. I desired to elevate the temperance cause; to place it on much higher ground than it had been as man's work, and to place it where no professed friend of God could find an excuse for opposition or indifference. I said, "If the battle is God's battle, then the advocates of the cause have no reason to be ashamed; they may leave all their adversaries to settle their controversies with him; they need fear no opposition nor results; they may well look to all the friends of God to be foremost in the fight; they may look too to civil government to sustain the cause and not license the traffic; they may rest assured the battle will go on though they die; it will last while God lives, unless Intemperance be first exterminated by Jesus Christ, who shall have dominion from sea to sea. As the silver and the gold is the Lord's, men of wealth should come to the help; and as there is a certainty of success, they who are fighting this battle should be ashamed of all despondency, doubt or fear."

I desired a wide circulation of the discourse, and was gratified with several contributions, especially the following:

"SOUTH BALLSTON, April 23, 1858.

Rev. J. MARSH:

Dear Sir:—I have perused with great pleasure your discourse: THE TEMPERANCE BATTLE NOT MAN'S, BUT GOD'S. I am glad to perceive that your confidence in the final triumph of our principles, which we have now for near thirty years endeavored to fasten upon the public mind, is unabated. I wish I could send you the means for printing and circulating 100,000; it would do great good at the present time; but as the payment of the debt of the State Temperance Society has fallen upon me, I am, in duty to other claims, constrained to hold up my contributions for temperance at present. I am truly yours,

E. C. DELAVAN."

—

"SOUTH BALSTON, April 28.

Dear Sir:—I cannot feel it to be right to praise a work, and not aid in its circulation; you may therefore draw on me for $100 to send 1,000 copies, post-paid, where you think it will do the most good in the country.

Yours, E. C. D."

From Hon. T. S. Williams, Chief Justice of Connecticut:

"Your address to the friends of Temperance on God's Battle, is a word in season. I hope it will be the means of awakening a new interest in the cause. I enclose a draft of ten dollars for its circulation in this State."

Said General Cary, of Ohio:

"Liquor-sellers should read it, that they may learn that they are fighting against their Maker and Judge. Lukewarm temperance men should read it, and learn that the Almighty is on our side. The professed people of God should read it, that they may know to whom they owe allegiance. We are fighting God's battle, and if kings, rulers and judges, and all the powers of darkness are allied against us, in due time victory is certain."

A large number of valuable publications had been issued in support of the Maine Law, besides those which have been already alluded to. A strong discourse in its vindication was published by Rev. Wm. A. Brown, pastor of the Free Church, in Andover, Massachusetts, from Ex. xxi., 29. "A Good Law," by Rev. Isaac P. Lang, worthy of Chelsea, Mass; "The law of God and the Law of Man," an admirable discourse, by a Massachusetts clergyman; Dr. Spear's "Sermon on the Maine Law," Brooklyn, N. Y.; "An Appeal to the Citizens of the Commonwealth of Maryland, on the Necessity of Prohibition;" "An Argument on Prohibition," before the Temperance Mass Convention at Winchester, Va.; W. Andrews' "Review of Rev. M. Lovejoy's Lecture against the Laws in Maine;" "Alcohol and the Commonwealth; Shall we Legislate," Rev. W. Barrows; "Sermon" by Professor Shepherd, of Bangor; "My Sister Margaret," a temperance story; "Methodist Book-Room, N. Y.;" "Tracts," in variety, by Rev. George Trask, Fitchburg, Massachusetts. Mr. Trask had engaged in combating "Tobacco," a kindred spirit with intemperance, almost its equal in fascination, power, and ruin. By many it had been supposed that the use of tobacco, especially by the young, was a great cause of intemperance; and it was contended that, if parents would lead their children to all disuse of tobacco, they seldom, if ever, would see them in the paths of intemperance. Some lecturers on temperance were great users of tobacco, which was a great offence to the friends of the cause. Bands of Hope were therefore widely pledging themselves to also disuse tobacco, as well as intoxicating drink. The numerous productions of Dr. Trask were powerful and widely spread. Some he wrote and published specifically on temperance, and on prohibitory law, which were very useful. "Life of J. H. W. Hawkins," by his son; Rev. Mr. Crampton, on "The Wine of the Bible;" "Alcohol, its Place and Power," by Dr. Miller, Edinburgh.

CHAPTER XXIV.

Ministerial Fidelity—Boldness of Puritans—Difficulties in Reproof—Dr. Justin Edwards on Sabbath Temperance Preaching—Hewitt, Fisk, Clarke, Edwards—Origin of Washingtonians—Elder Knapp—Twenty-third Anniversary A. T. U.—Speech of Governor Briggs—Death of Anson G. Phelps—Encouraging Report—Mr. Delavan in England—Letter from—English Clergy Address—Massachusetts Alliance—N. Y. State League—Western Pennsylvania Convention.

When Paul stood pleading before King Agrippa, Festus, astounded at his fidelity and boldness, exclaimed, "Paul! thou art beside thyself! much learning doth make thee mad." And when Luther said he would go to Worms, if there were as many devils there as there were tiles on the roofs of the houses, no doubt he, too, was thought to be a madman. And when John Knox stood before Queen Mary, and rebuked her for her sins, he had no claim to the character of a courtier. The puritan ministers were characterized for their boldness. They feared not man; and when there was sin among the people, they hesitated not to rebuke it; and when they did rebuke, none could say to them, "Thou which teachest another, teachest thou not thyself? thou that sayest, a man should not steal, dost thou steal? thou who sayest, a man should not commit adultery, dost thou commit adultery?" It was their holiness and purity that gave them boldness. But as New England increased in population, and luxury abounded, and ministers mingled freely in pleasures and usages, not thought to be decidedly wrong, yet whose tendencies were bad, and unbecoming the ministerial character, they were, in these matters, shorn of their strength.

When the temperance reformation broke out, few were the ministers who did not partake with their people in that which was condemned by the reformers; and how could any, from their pulpits, reprove their parishioners who had furnished them a dangerous article which they had gracefully received. And when they were right, even then, how difficult fidelity and boldness were in the early stages of the work, few now have any conceptions of. The loss of the friendship and support of some of the best families; of a wealthy distiller or brewer, or wholesale dealer; would, perhaps, be the result of a single sermon. Fresh are my recollections of several ministers who were driven from their pulpits, for their boldness in this matter. It was no subject, said many, for the pulpit. "Talk temperance as much as you please, in your temperance meetings, but bring it not into the pulpit, on the Sabbath." So had Satan barred the doors of the sanctuary against the temperance preacher on God's holy day, that Dr. Justin Edwards, who feared not man, felt bound to come out, and boldly remonstrate against a sentiment so absurd and awful. Said he: "Shall the fires which make this poison burn on the Sabbath? Shall Jehovah be insulted by the appearance in the sanctuary of men who use it; and yet the Sabbath not be occupied by light and love to abolish the use? Shall it cause the word of the Lord, even from the pulpit, to fall as upon a rock, and yet the pulpit be dumb? or speak only on week-days, when those who traffic in it have so much to do in furnishing the poison, that they have no time, and less inclination, to hear? If Satan can cause this to be believed, and those who manufacture, sell, and use the weapons of his warfare, and multiply the trophies of his victory, not hear of their sins on the Sabbath, when God speaks to the conscience; or be instructed from the pulpit, his mercy's seat, by the tears and blood of a Saviour, to flee from coming damnation, the adversary will keep his stronghold; church-members will garrison it, and provision it, and fight for him. From the communion-table, he will muster recruits, and find officers in those who distribute the elements, to fight his battles, and people, with increasing numbers, his dark domains to the end of time. If we may not, in this warfare, on the Lord's day, when He Himself goes forth to the battle, and commands upon the field; if we may not use his weapons, forged in heaven, and, from the high places of his erection, pour them down thick, heavy, and hot, upon the enemy, we may fight till we die, and he will esteem our iron as straw, and our brass as rotten wood; our darts he will count as stubble, and laugh at the glittering of our spear."

These solemn warnings brought out many ministers to speak boldly against the traffic, and the drinking usages of their people, as they ought to speak, and not unfrequently so disturbing the conscience, and agitating the souls of their people, that great revivals ensued.

I recall one minister who was greatly distressed on the point of duty; his church-members were selling rum; and his church-members were using strong drink in their families; and there was no rain nor dew; all seemed given over to the evil one. He knew it was most hazardous to allude to the evil on the Sabbath; he expected, if he did, some of his best people would leave the house; but he said, "Sink or swim, live or die, I cannot go on so; I must do my duty, and leave the event to God." He did it; and boldly called the selling of ardent spirit as a beverage, a crime, and the using of intoxicating drink a sin against the body and against the soul. Men felt that they were in a house on fire, and there was no escape into the open air; women felt there was no religion in it, and they would not hear such preaching. The next morning, some wholesale dealers and consumers, heavy tax-payers, met on the side-walk, and said one to another, "We will bear this no longer; let us drive him off." A dry wag, listening to their complaints and threats, said, "That's right, brothers; go and get J. B., and W. T., and R. S. (notorious infidels and Sabbath-breakers, and profane men), and a few more of the same sort, and get a vote to drive him out." They started back, for they were professors of religion and good men; they saw where they were, and where their minister stood, and how he had done his duty. Some gave up their traffic; all were quiet; and never more had that minister any difficulty in doing his duty.

When I first heard Dr. Nathaniel Hewitt on this subject, I was amazed at his boldness. Every stone was the weight of a talent, and it was of no consequence with him who was hit. The first sermon he preached in New York, was in Dr. Spring's pulpit, and it was like the rolling of a ball among ten-pins. Several of the first men of the city went home and emptied their bottles.

A man of great boldness in the Methodist Church, whom I well knew—almost equal in fidelity to John Wesley, was Wilbur Fisk. "I believe," said he, "the time is coming when not only the drunkard, but the drinker will be excluded from the church of our God; when the gambler and the slave-dealer and the rum-dealer will be classed together. And I care not how soon that time arrives." A hard speech forty years ago. And another was Dr. Lyman Beecher. "Oh! were the sky over our heads one great whispering-gallery, bringing down about us all the lamentations and woe which intemperance creates, and the firm earth one sonorous medium of sound, bringing up around us from beneath the wailings of the damned whom the dealer in ardent spirits had sent there, tremendous realities assailing our senses would invigorate our counsels and give decision of conscience to our purposes of reformation." Another was Rev. Daniel A. Clark. Wherever he went he thrust a sharp spear through the bull's hide of the rum-seller, and there were howlings and curses and threatenings, which either drove him off, or arrayed all God's people against the ungodly traffic and its supporters. His two sermons "Am I my brother's keeper," and "His blood be upon us," are sermons of tremendous power. Every minister should read them and resolve that, God helping him, he would preach like them. Others I might mention, as Rev. John Pierpont, of Boston, and Rev. Thomas P. Hunt, of N. C.

Before I go farther, I must speak a word of that admirable man, and dear personal friend, Dr. Justin Edwards. He seemed raised up by a kind Providence just for this great work of moral reform. Possessed of a clear, discerning mind; a strong, commanding utterance, without the smoothness and polish of an Addison; few men ever so commanded the attention of a large assembly, either in the pulpit or in public conventions. Men saw clearly, as uttered from his lips, that "He that soweth to the wind shall reap the whirlwind;" that life and death, blessing and cursing, were set before them; and that it was altogether wisest and best for them, as individuals, as members of families, and as communities, to choose life. His language was the purest Saxon; short sentences, weighty, powerful. His first nine Reports of the American Temperance Society, constituting the first volume of Permanent Temperance Documents, can now be read with more profit by temperance lecturers than any other production. His subsequent labors in the Sabbath cause were almost equally valuable with his labors for temperance; but they consisted rather in collections of facts than of appeals to the heart and conscience. He died at the Sweet Springs, in Virginia, of affections of the liver, July 23, 1853, at the age of sixty-six, and was buried at his home in Andover, Massachusetts, in the Seminary cemetery, where a monument has been erected to his memory.

To the close of life, he was in favor of legislative defence. To Mr. Delavan he wrote, September, 1851: "If we can keep at work all hands, we shall, in due time, secure effectual legislative defence; but, in order to this, there must be a steady, regular, and long course of wise, patient continuance in well-doing, by the old, substantial, and long-tried friends of temperance who, in all their ways, acknowledge God, and act in the spirit, and under the influence of the Gospel, and for the purpose of honoring God in the salvation of men."

Another of the early reformers, and most valuable laborers, who passed away April 20, 1861, at the advanced age of eighty, was the Rev. Dr. Humphrey, of Pittsfield, Massachusetts, formerly President of Amherst College. Dr. Humphrey commenced his temperance labors as early as 1812, when, with Mr. Swan, of Norwalk, he wrote an address to the churches of Fairfield County, Connecticut. It was an able production, and made a great impression through the State. He afterwards drew a comparison between intemperance and slavery, showing that slavery to the bottle was the worst slavery to which man could be subjected. Ever was he ready, to the last day of his life, by his pen, his example, and his speech, whether at home or abroad, to sustain our great cause, and rejoice in its progress. In a letter to me, a little before his death, he said, speaking of the reformation:

"Although so much remains to be done, it is one of the most remarkable reformations that can be found on the page of history. If we could contrast what we everywhere witness with the drinking habits of half a century ago, and count the multitudes who have been saved from falling into the snare of the devil, we should be constrained to exclaim, 'What hath God wrought!' I hope that years are still before you, to labor in the temperance vineyard."

Some ministers did not preach on temperance, because they used tobacco. They felt the inconsistency; and, for that vile weed, let Satan draw their young men down to death. Some, because they occasionally, only occasionally, took wine at parties and festivals. And they were doubtless right; for their hearts would not be in the work and God would not bless them. Some, because they had no drunkards in their congregations. That was more than they knew. But it would not be surprising if it was so; for what was there in their preaching that attracted drunkards? What would drunkards care for their beautiful figures of speech, and splendid rhetoric, and fine-spun morality, and anticipated heaven? Drunkards would go and hear preaching that concerned them; and so would all classes of wicked men. Gamblers would go and hear about gambling; Sabbath breakers about Sabbath breaking, and Thieves about thieving, and feel that the preacher meant them, when he warned them to flee from the wrath to come.

In the eleventh annual report of the Maryland State Temperance Society, the wonderful Washingtonian movement was traced to the fidelity of a Christian preacher, who had given notice that he would preach on temperance. The six founders of this movement were in a tavern, drinking, when their conversation turned on this sermon; whereupon it was determined that four of them should go and hear this Elder Knapp and make a report. After sermon, they returned and discoursed on its merits for some time; when one of the company remarked that "after all temperance is a good thing." "Oh," said the host, "they are all a parcel of hypocrites." "Oh yes," replied one, "I'll be bound for you, it is for your interest to cry them down any how." "I'll tell you what," said another, "let's form a Temperance Society, and make Mitchell president." "Agreed!" they cried, and soon they organized and signed their pledge.

This statement was afterward denied by some who preferred that the movement should be considered an immediate impulse from Heaven, without any human instrumentality. But whether true or not, the same preacher was a well-known instrument of turning many of this misable class to righteousness. That remarkable man, Abel Bishop, in New Haven, said in his account of himself: "I heard that Elder Knapp was preaching on temperance. I took three drinks, then went and heard him. I came home and went slyly to bed, that no one should know how I felt. The next night, I went again; when I came home, my wife and children looked strangely at me, I was so quiet; I walked the room but said nothing; I went to the shelf and got the Bible, and tried to read, but could not; my wife burst into tears. The next day, I heard of the meeting of the reformed drunkards; I went to it and signed the pledge." This man, raised from the very lowest degradation, was restored to his church and became one of the most powerful temperance lecturers, and died in the triumph of Christian faith. Truly the Word, when properly preached, is quick and powerful, sharper than any two-edged sword. Thankful we may be, that we now have so many who handle it skilfully. But oh! what would be the state of our country if all were faithful.

The ravages of Intemperance and its hindrance to the prosperity of the Churches was exciting much alarm in Connecticut, and a large meeting of ministers in Litchfield County was called to consider the subject of Home Evangelization. I received an invitation to deliver an address on the subject. I replied, that I was not as well acquainted with that as I was with Home Demoralization, and agreed to prepare an address on that, which I did—showing that, more than anything else, it was Intemperance, the dram-shop and the constant use by many of intoxicating drinks. It was listened to with attention, and published and sent abroad.

Many ministers and laymen manifested in their districts an earnest and persevering attention to the cause. None more so than those of Suffolk County, N. Y. Through many years they had nobly sustained monthly meetings of two days, passing around the county, until they had attained to the 142d. John Sherry, Esq., had been from the commencement its President, and was ever at his post. All the ministers of the county made it a point to attend. With them, it was frequently my happiness to mingle.

The Twenty-third Anniversary of the American Temperance Union was held at the Cooper Institute, May 11, 1859; Governor Briggs, the President, in the Chair. The Governor, in an address, showed his attachment to the cause, and the happiness he had in being permitted to attend the Anniversary of the Union. He said:

"The object of this, and all other temperance organizations, was the social, physical, and intellectual improvement of men. If he was asked, why it was wrong to use intoxicating drinks? He should reply, 'because the natural tendency of their use is to injure the physical, mental, and moral powers, and to pull man down from his high position to something below a man. Because a vast proportion of those who use such drinks become drunkards, it is wrong.' If the drunkards in this city to-night could be arranged in a single procession, no argument would be needed to show the wrong in the use of intoxicating drinks. For more than thirty years I have abstained; but, oh! how many of my companions who started in life with me, have I seen go to destruction! I have never seen the time nor the occasion to regret that, in 1836, I resolved never to drink any intoxicating liquor. But there have been many times when I thanked God for the advantages of that resolution to me. Who can realize what it is for a man to become a drunkard? From being the hope of parents, the pride of friends, it is to be brought down, in disgrace, to a horrible death; and to be carried to the grave unattended."

The Union were called to lament the death of Anson G. Phelps, Esq., at the advanced age of eighty-one, Chairman of the Executive Committee, who had long, by his excellent character, his inflexible principles, and munificence, been a great support. The annual Report spoke of discouragements, but also of much that was encouraging. The formation of numerous Bands of Hope, under Mr. Sinclair, operating both in the United States and Canada, awoke deep feelings of gratitude and praise. The extensive outpourings of the Spirit of God, in the last two years, had led large numbers of young men to adopt the principles of temperance in their daily practice. Nothing had ever proved such a hindrance to revivals and the advance of the Redeemer's kingdom, as the use of intoxicating drinks. The ministers, and churches, and friends of temperance, were now, therefore, joyfully coalescing. In these seasons of religious awakening, Christian laymen were inspired with unusual boldness and zeal, in breaking up the strongholds of wickedness, in our large cities; and with good success. The restoration of the prohibitory law in Maine, after a two years' trial of a license law, was another subject of congratulation; and an unexpected and extraordinary decision of the Chief Justice of Massachusetts (Shaw) that all intoxicating liquors kept unlawfully for sale, with implements and vessels, were to be considered as nuisances, and to be treated as such, sent alarm among those engaged in the traffic.

The Reports from abroad were of an encouraging character. Immense and enthusiastic meetings were being held throughout Great Britain, at which distinguished gentlemen presided, and liberal contributions were made. In the death of Joseph Eaton, at Bristol, in May, 1858, at the age of sixty-eight, the cause lost one of its greatest supporters. He was of the Society of Friends. At the World's Convention, I much enjoyed his friendship and great decision. He toiled much for the cause; gave liberally on occasions; and, at his death, made large provision for its future support. In Russia, a great revolt from drinking customs had been caused by a heavy tax laid upon brandies. In Australia, the temperance cause had been prosperous, through the patronage and efforts of Chief Justice A. Becket. In the Sandwich Islands, the immense Christian churches held fast their integrity. Able addresses were made by several gentlemen.

In the summer of this year, Mr. Delavan again visited Europe, and mingled freely with the friends of the cause. In his correspondence with me, he gave many interesting and encouraging relations. In a letter dated, London, October 31st, he said:

"On my arrival at Liverpool, I found letters from distinguished friends of temperance from various parts waiting my arrival, and extending to me the kindest hospitalities. At a meeting of friends there, I endeavored to give as faithful a statement of the condition of things in our country as was in my power. What we want, is to show to this country, the practical workings of a prohibitory law, carried out in a single State. I think we must rely upon Maine for this. From what I can learn, there has been great and wonderful progress since I was here twenty years ago. The evils are universally acknowledged. The term as "drunk as a lord" cannot now be applied to the higher classes. Still, they cling to the moderation doctrine. The clergy for the most part occupy this position."

But soon after this I received a most gratifying address, which I inserted in the Journal of November, 1859, to the Clergy of the Church of England, from 130 members of their own body, headed by Francis Close, D. D., Dean of Carlisle. This noble man had, in becoming himself a total abstainer, induced a great change among the clergy of the established Church, until several hundreds of them had come out on the true principle. He had also established The Church of England Temperance Magazine. The address assumed, that total abstinence was the only security against drunkenness; that moderate drinking supports drunkenness; that it is the duty of ministers to oppose the evil by all lawful means; that were they generally to adopt the principle of total abstinence, it would be a great death-blow to the traffic, and exert a mighty influence over the habits and practices of all classes.

In Massachusetts, Dr. Jewett inaugurated, in June, 1859, a new organization on a pecuniary basis, called THE STATE TEMPERANCE ALLIANCE. Every member to pay one dollar a year. Dr. Jewett was principal agent, and entered on his labors with great earnestness. He had long viewed the cause as suffering for want of a pecuniary basis. In the first year of the Alliance the one dollar subscription amounted to $24,844.

In 1859, The State League was organized in Central New York, avowedly to control the Legislative and Executive action of New York State. A strong platform of principles was adopted, but having no distinctive characteristic, excepting in the resolution to vote for no civil officer who was not committed to Prohibitory law. The Organ of the State League had a wide circulation. Connected in some measure with the Carson League, it successfully prosecuted many engaged illegally in the traffic.

Western Pennsylvania was strong for prohibition. On the 25th of May, 1859, a large Convention was held, denouncing all license and upholding prohibition as the only true principle. A reverend gentleman from Harrisburg, the seat of government, strongly depicted the efforts of the liquor-dealers in that place; the immense sums of money spent by them in the Legislative Halls to accomplish their ends, and the contempt with which they treated the friends of temperance. Prof. Barrow considered the only way to strike at the root of the evil was by Prohibition. He deprecated the discouragements among temperance men, and in stirring tones urged them to press onward. Strong and united action was taken by the Convention.

In Pennsylvania, there was a strong support given to their prohibitory law, which was of a peculiar character, but well adapted to the State.

In 1861–'2, a vigorous effort was made in the State and Legislature of New York to incorporate the principle of prohibition in the organic law of the State, by making it an article in the revised Constitution: "That the sale of intoxicating liquors as a beverage be prohibited; that no law authorizing its sale shall be enacted; and that the Legislature shall, by law, prescribe the necessary fines and penalties for any violation of the provisions—as the prohibition of lotteries was inserted in the Constitution of 1832 and 1836." A resolution to this effect passed, both in the Senate and Assembly of 1861, but failed in the Legislature of 1862. Had it passed, it would have been referred to the people, and would have produced the greatest excitement.

CHAPTER XXV.

Death of Governor Briggs, President A. T. U.—Hon. W. A. Buckingham elected to fill his place—Death of Mr. Frelinghuysen—Chief Justice Williams—President Lincoln's Temperance—War—Dangers to the Cause—Visit Washington—Army Tracts—How Supplied and Appreciated—Twenty-fifth Anniversary A. T. U.—Governor Buckingham's Speech—Speech of Senator Pomroy—Deaths of Dr. Beecher, Dr. Baird, Admiral Foote—Navy—Army—Progress of Temperance—War Ending—Assassination of President Lincoln.

On September 13, 1861, the community were greatly shocked at hearing of a wound, by the accidental discharge of a gun in his house, of the Hon. George N. Briggs, of Pittsfield, Massachusetts, President of the American Temperance Union. He survived, in great anguish, for a few days; and then, in Christian faith and hope, resigned his spirit into the hands of his Maker, in the sixty-sixth year of his age.

Governor Briggs was ever accounted one of the noblest specimens of humanity. Though self-educated, he rose to the highest office and honors of his State; and was a man of great influence in the Congress of the United States. Possessed of sound piety, he admirably controlled his appetites and passions; and, being of great benevolence, he deeply interested himself in the temperance cause, and in doing good to all as he had opportunity. Early in his profession as a lawyer, he adopted the principle of total abstinence. On returning from court and stopping to dine, as he sat at the table there was a call in his stomach for something. He quietly dropped his head, and asked, "What is wanting there?" The reply was, "brandy and water." He was startled at the thought that it was demanded; and he said to his stomach, "You never get any more;" and from that hour to the day of his death, he never drank intoxicating liquor. He was first publicly known by his controversy with moderationists in the Saratoga Convention of 1836. He was most active for Temperance in Congress; became President of the Congressional Temperance Society, and afterwards of the Legislative Society, in his own State. Wherever he went, he was true to the cause, and filled the stations to which he was called with great ability and Christian meekness. I was delegated to attend his funeral, and took part in the public meeting which was held at Pittsfield to speak of his worth. At his grave, I could truly say, "The Chariot of Israel, and the Horsemen thereof."

At a meeting of the Committee, in April, '62, William A. Buckingham, Governor of Connecticut, was elected to fill his place. In accepting the office, he said, "While I am conscious of my inability to fill properly the position so honorably occupied by your former distinguished President, yet, feeling a deep interest in the cause, and especially the importance of pressing its saving influence into our army, composed as it is of many of our best and most promising young men; I fear I may neglect a duty if I decline; I therefore accept the honorable position." At its Anniversary, in May, all hoped for the presence of Governor Buckingham; but duties in the Legislature prevented his attendance; he, however, sent a letter regretting his absence, with his cheque of $200 to aid the cause.

Besides Governor Briggs, the Union was called to lament the deaths of distinguished Vice-Presidents, Hon. Thomas S. Williams, a former chief justice of Connecticut; and Hon. Theodore Frelinghuysen, President of Rutgers

College, N. J. Judge Williams lived to the age of eighty-four, in the full possession of all his faculties. He was ever the firm supporter of true temperance principles; was President of the State Temperance Society; an entire abstainer, and decided prohibitionist. His legal opinions gave weight in favor of the Maine Law. In his death, though at an advanced age, the temperance cause met with a great loss. Mr. Frelinghuysen was one of the most accomplished Christian gentlemen the world had seen. Of fine person and manners; a sweet voice and earnest tones; with a large grasp of thought, and unmistakable reasoning, Mr. Frelinghuysen was ever a favorite orator, on all temperance and religious occasions. He was decided for total abstinence, as the only safe principle, when it was not generally received; and for prohibitory law against all license for the sale of liquors as a beverage. His temperance speeches, of which a number are well reported, should be collected in a single volume, as models for all good temperance speaking. For some years, he was Chairman of our Executive Committee, which brought me into intimate relations with him; and he was as devoted and happy there, as in the Chair as President of the American Bible Society, or American Board of Missions. He died in the Presidency of the Rutgers College, at the age of seventy-five.

The Anniversary meeting was ably addressed by James A. Briggs, a nephew of Governor Briggs; Rev. H. W. Beecher, and J. B. Merwin of the United States army. It was a time of great excitement and interest for the cause—when, in fact, it seemed in danger of being forgotten and trampled in the dust, but when its importance to all reflecting minds was never greater. Our nation had received a new President. Nine States had seceded from the Union, and with them we were involved in a terrific war. It was a subject of rejoicing and hopefulness for the cause of temperance, that ABRAHAM LINCOLN, who had been called to lead the nation, was a strict temperance man. No disturbance ever had been, or ever would be effected by Alcohol in that mighty brain; and whatever the friends of temperance would consider desirable in the Government, the army, or the navy, they might ask from him, without a repulse. His example in the high places of power would always be right, and his consequent good influence great. When the Committee of the Nominating Convention came to him, at Springfield, Illinois, to inform him of his nomination, some of his neighbors, acquainted with his temperance habits—his unpreparedness to give a political committee the usual treats,—sent to his house some bottles of Champagne; but he said, "It won't do here," and ordered it back where the Committee might be assembled. When offered wine, at Cincinnati, on his way to take the reins of Government, he said, "For thirty years I have been a temperance man, and I am too old to change." When asked by a friend, after his inauguration, if he was not overawed in addressing that immense audience of intellectual men, "Not half so much," he replied, "as he had been in addressing a temperance meeting." To this he had often been accustomed. Thanks to God! we exclaimed, for such a gift.

But war was upon us, and war and intemperance were kindred spirits, dragging thousands down to untimely graves. My mind woke up to the solemn inquiry: What is to be done? What can be done in this momentous hour to save our army, to save our nation from the ravages of intemperance; hitherto the invariable accompaniment of war. Vast numbers of our noble young men, members of churches and members of temperance societies, were enlisting for the fight. Shall they be sacrificed? Are they not a reliable basis for some temperance action? At the suggestion of a member of the Sanitary Commission, I visited Washington to see if I could not prevail on that Commission to institute a Temperance department, through which tracts and papers should be distributed in the forts, shipping, and every branch of the army. I sent in my proposals. I consulted with the Medical Bureau and other officers of the Government, but no apprehension of danger seemed to arise; and though general approbation was expressed of some temperance action, I found it must be from private, individual, and not governmental, or even Sanitary Commission action. Clean beds, good food, comfortable tents and efficient discipline, were all, in the opinion of many, that was needed to secure from intemperance. Alas! little was then known of its serpentine power and its awful delusions. I returned and devoted myself to preparing short but stirring tracts with striking captions for the soldiers and officers. Ten were prepared, with the design of sending one thousand to each regiment. In the first year there were supplied 270 regiments, besides several forts and hospitals. The President of the United States expressed his high approval of them. Gen. Fremont and other officers of rank gave their approval. One said in a letter to the office:

"You cannot possibly do so much good for our country's cause in any other way, as in circulating among the soldiers of our army your admirable temperance tracts. If our men of wealth could only see the eagerness with which they are read, and the salutary influence that they exert in our camps, they would furnish means to place them in any desired quantity in the hands of all our men. For be assured you may, intemperance is a terrible enemy to soldiers, and kills far more of them than fall on the battle-field, and it is a great interest to the country to save them from the foul abomination."

The hopeful expectation of many, that efficient military discipline would keep out all intemperance from the army, was soon disappointed. The men themselves, who should effect the discipline and protect and guard the soldiers, were often found drunk, and severe orders were issued against the officers leaving their posts and visiting Washington, where they might get the means of indulgence. So impressed was the Commander-in-Chief (Gen. McClellan) with the greatness of the evil, that in a review of a Court-Martial decision, when an officer had been on trial for drunkenness, he declared: "Would all the officers unite in setting the soldiers an example of total abstinence from intoxicating drinks, it would be equal to an addition of 50,000 MEN to the armies of the United States."

Several distinguished officers, naval and military, were decided temperance men. Foote and Stringham and Dupont, in the Navy, and McClellan and Mitchel and Butler, in the Army, all deprecated the ravages of intemperance; but to Gen. Butler belonged the honor of first interdicting the presence in camp of any intoxicating liquor whatever, and renouncing all use of it in his own quarters. In his general order he declared that, "As he desires never to ask either officers or men to undergo any privations which he will not share with them, he will not exempt himself from the operation of this order; but will not use it (liquor) in his own quarters, as he would discourage its use in the quarters of any officer." Similar orders followed in other posts, and a resolution passed both houses of Congress, that any officer guilty of habitual drunkenness should be immediately dismissed from the service. The notorious drunkenness of an officer high in command in the first great and afflictive battle at Bull Run, to which defeat was in a measure attributed, created great sensation both in the government and elsewhere in the country.

For the means of supplying the Army with Tracts, reliance had been placed on individual contributions, and collections in churches, after preaching on the subject; but as such great demands were made by Christian and Sanitary Commissions and other organizations, it was becoming difficult to raise sufficient, and in September, 1862, I devised a special and independent charity for this object, that of Sabbath Schools. Almost every Sabbath School had sent into the army a superintendent, or chaplain, or teachers, and even members, and would not each one love to follow its own with some memorial gift? A Circular was accordingly issued to numerous Sunday Schools, inviting them to send $2 50; and a thousand tracts should be forwarded by Adams' Express, which volunteered to take them free of expense, to such regiments as they should name, giving its location and Colonel or Chaplain. It was delightful to see the response, and the interest and spirit manifested; and still more to hear of their reception by company after company as from their own Sabbath Schools. "I burst into a flood of tears," wrote a Chaplain from Iowa, "as I received a package from my own dear Sabbath School, and I carried them through the regiment, saying to the soldiers: 'Here is a present for you from home.' All joyfully received them, and in a few moments were reading them." These tracts were multiplied until they reached thirty varieties. Over a thousand schools contributed to their spread; and, before the war closed, I had sent from the office over three millions; many direct to the army, and many through the Christian Commission. Many no doubt were lost; many perhaps never read, or treated with contempt. But they checked drinking and drunkenness, strengthened the hearts of temperance men, and ensured the return of many a soldier to his dear ones in sobriety and valor.

During the war Mr. Delavan made a like effort at Albany; publishing a single tract of a large size for officers and soldiers, and sending it forth by the million under the recommendation and patronage of the high officers of

Government and the Army at Washington. Tracts were published also for soldiers and seamen at Philadelphia and Cincinnati and Chicago, and both the American and Boston Tract Societies made large issues of tracts and papers to counteract the evil influences which were everywhere operating for the ruin of the soldiers. No seed was ever sown with better effect.

At the Twenty-fifth Anniversary of the A T. U., May, 1863, Governor Buckingham presided, and said: "The question of Temperance has a peculiar importance today. Events fraught with the interests of humanity are passing before us with the rapidity of thought. The whole people are engaged in earnest controversy respecting principles which lie at the foundation of the Government, and are contending by argument, and by force of arms, for a new adjustment of civil rights. Engaged in the conflict are armies embracing a million of men. This fact presses upon us the duty of surrounding them with good influences; and, if possible, of saving them from the evils of intemperance." He would not hold up the army as a school of morals, but he would have it so cared for, that our sons and brothers should come home better citizens than when they left. He manifested great interest, therefore, in our temperance operations with the national forces.

Senator Pomroy, from Kansas, gave a lengthy and very able speech, chiefly on the condition and habits of the the army, and the dangers to which they were exposed. He said:

"In ordinary years, it was calculated that 30,000 went down to the grave—the home of the drunkard; but it would not be too much to double that number each year since the war began. For the vice of intemperance has followed the army; has visited the quarters of both officer and private; has taken down some of the bravest and truest of the land, who, before, had always stood erect in their manhood and their pride. It has made disorderly and riotous the loyal camp of the soldier; has made disgraceful the tent of the officer; and, on more than one occasion, defeated and demoralized an army on the field of battle. Of the thirty thousand victims of disease and death attending on the Peninsular campaign, the last year, at least ten thousand may be set down as chargeable to the daily ration of whiskey and quinine. Intemperance and its fruits made such sad havoc in the Mexican war, that it was feared that the dead would more than outnumber the living. General Scott said that, in his Mexican campaign, fifty per cent. of all he lost in his army, who are left in unmonumented graves, are there from this source, rather than from the bullets of the rebels. He therefore plead with us to speak out, and act effectively; for the voices of New York reached over the continent, and awakened an echo from the deep, rich valleys of the West, are reverberated across the prairies of the Northwest; and even over the mountains, to the golden shores of the peaceful Pacific."

The friends of religion, temperance, and humanity, had just been called to follow to the grave all that remained of the venerable Dr. Lyman Beecher. He died in Brooklyn, New York, January 10, 1863, aged 87. At the meeting, the Rev. Dr. Newell, of New York, offered the following resolution:

Resolved, That we lovingly cherish the memory, and earnestly strive to emulate the deeds, of that early Apostle of Temperance, the Rev. Lyman Beecher, D. D., for many years a Vice-President of this Society.

Dr. Newell remarked:

The early heroes of the temperance revolution are fast passing away. Their venerable forms are disappearing from our platforms and our pulpits. They were men of original ideas, large hearts, and great valor. Let us gratefully embalm their deeds, and honor their memory. It is their due. It is our safety. Who like Dr. Beecher could incite men to mighty deeds? He never feared the face of man; yet he was genial, modest, laying all his vigorous powers on the altar of God.

Dr. Beecher's six sermons on the evils and remedy of intemperance, preached at Litchfield, Connecticut, in 1826, have lost none of their freshness and power, to this day.

They form, and ever will form, a standard work among temperance men. He was mighty in argument, and mighty in speech. His word in public assemblies had a ring like that of the hammer upon the smooth and polished anvil. He survived the activity and energy of both bodily and mental powers; but was followed to the grave by multitudes who well knew what he once was, and what he had done for his race.

In the same year, passed away the Rev. Robert Baird, D. D., who, in former years, with almost incredible industry and despatch, spread the principles of temperance over the North of Europe, and obtained favor for it in the courts of kings and the palaces of emperors. He died at his home in Yonkers, New York, March 15, 1863, aged sixty-five.

On the 26th of June, another great champion of the temperance cause went to his rest, Rear-Admiral Alexander H. Foote. He died at the Astor House, New York, of severe illness, at the age of fifty-six. He was the hero of Fort Henry and Fort Donaldson; but preëminently the Christian hero and friend of temperance. He was one of the first to introduce the principle of total abstinence from intoxicating drinks into the navy; and during his cruise in the flag-ship Cumberland, in the Mediterranean, he induced the entire crew to abandon liquor, and personally engaged in their religious instruction. I have already had occasion to speak of his labors, at home and abroad, on the platform, and in abolishing the spirit-ration in the navy. But too high a monument could not be erected to Rear-Admiral Foote. Well was it said:

"Lower ye the flags
Half-mast; boom ye the minute guns; toll ye
The funeral bell, on every spire and ship.
On all our coast, through all our land, drape ye
The yards and ports, the Bethel flag, and churches,

The naval rendezvous, the temperance hall,
The Christian Sabbath-school, the room for prayer;
And let the distant Heathen Mission join,
To bear our signs of mourning round the globe.
Who saw him once but loved to see him more?"—*Denison.*

Other men of influence and zeal in the cause of temperance were removed in 1863: CHIEF JUSTICE SAVAGE, at Utica, a strong pillar in the Temperance Temple. So impressed was he with the evil of wine-drinking, that he refused uniting with the temperance men in their efforts, until they adopted the total abstinence principle. Then he gave them his hearty concurrence. He abstained, while on the bench, from Court-dinners, because his example was a reproof to other judges; this gave him time for a thorough examination of his cases, so that, the next morning, he was better prepared than any with opinions, which soon gave him precedence over others, though themselves distinguished men. This I had from his own lips. He was long of opinion that wine destroyed more of our public men than all their arduous labors. His argument in favor of the constitutionality of the Prohibitory Law which was set aside by the Court of Appeals, was exceedingly able. For one year he was President of the American Temperance Union. I loved him like a father. His house was ever my home when at Utica.

SAMUEL CHIPMAN, the Howard of the age, also passed away, aged 74. He went through all the jails and poorhouses of the State, to ascertain the evils of Intemperance, the pauperism and crime and sufferings of the great community. His reports were exceedingly valuable and very thrilling.

PRESIDENT HITCHCOCK, too, of Amherst College, laid aside his armor. Few men did more for the cause. His example, his conversation and productions, were not surpassed in worth and power.

EDGAR B. DAY, of Catskill, was a gentleman of much intelligence, decision and munificence, in the cause. Prompt in his attendance on public meetings, judicious in counsel, and self-sacrificing beyond most others, he was ever to me very precious. For many years he and his father, Orrin Day, supplied our Foreign Missionaries with the Journal. But he was more especially interested in the young, and often able articles appeared from his pen in the public papers.

Rev. R. S. CRAMPTON, of Rochester, was long an efficient and eloquent Agent of the State and other Societies. He devoted his life very much to the cause. His Tract, "Look at your Taxes," and his discourse, "The Wine of the Bible," had wide circulation.

Temperance in the navy, through the decision of Admiral Foote and others, had become a fixed fact—a wonderful revolution for the nations to contemplate. The spirit-ration removed, flogging abolished, good order and great valor were constantly exhibited. So long on the water, the men knew but little of the temptations of the grog-shop, and were not often its victims.

Numerous letters from chaplains in the army, continually assured me of the receipt of tracts, and their distribution; but the evils of intemperance were great, both among officers and soldiers. So great was the evil flowing from the whiskey-ration in the army of the Potomac, spoken of by Senator Pomroy, that, on the 19th of June, 1862, General McClellan issued an order for its immediate discontinuance; and that hot coffee be served immediately after the reveillé.

Most of the chaplains, and such as acted as temperance and tract agents in the army, were men of high character, who exerted a good influence for the suppression of intemperance and other vices and immoralities among the officers and soldiers. The first who devoted himself fully to the work of addressing the soldiers on temperance, was the Rev. J. B. Merwin, of Chicago, who, at the recommendation of Governor Cass, of Detroit, to General Scott, went to Washington, and was commissioned by the General, with the approbation of the President, and immediately addressed a large number of regiments, making a deep impression of the importance of such an agency in each department. The chaplains often took counsel with each other, and their officers, on the proper discharge of duty. A general council of chaplains of the Army of the Cumberland was at one time held at Murfreesboro', Tenn. About forty were present, and divine wisdom and guidance were sought, that they might faithfully discharge their duties. In many of the places of rendezvous, in camps and hospitals, regular weekly temperance meetings were held, and large numbers of names were attached to the pledge. Often, the most effective speaker was the common soldier himself, who had once experienced the evils of intemperance, and knew what the enticing cup would do to man, in all his physical and moral powers.

At Camp Convalescent, Alexandria, there was a roll of over five thousand soldiers' names to the temperance pledge; stretching round the hall in which the soldiers held their weekly meetings. Among the marked temperance men in the army, was my long-tried friend, Neal Dow. He had long labored for his country in one way; he was now willing to lay down his life for it in another. He had given him a general's commission, and became active in the army. But his known character for temperance was not favorable to him among reckless, wine-drinking officers. His opportunities were not great for military display. His duties lay quite at the South, where he was taken prisoner. His welcome home was very gratifying. Such was the bad influence of drinking and drunken officers, that the Grand Division of Massachusetts Sons of Temperance memorialized Gov. Andrew on the subject, asking him to withhold commissioning officers to the army of intemperate habits. A great evil existing was the distinction made between officers and soldiers —allowing officers to have liquor in their tents, which was forbidden the soldier. Hence, officers were accustomed to treat such as called upon them; brother officers and even chaplains. The New York State Society was so impressed with the evil that, at their annual meeting, at Rome, they appointed a Committee of six, to repair to Washington, and address the President on the subject, and see if they could not induce him to revoke the order allowing it. I was one who repaired to Washington, and presented the petition to PRESIDENT LINCOLN, who most kindly received it, and promised to give it his early attention. Alas! even then, his days were numbered, and almost finished. But who suspected it?

With the defection of officers, bringing great injury upon themselves and the army, there were several of high rank, both in the army and navy, greatly cheering the hearts and strengthening the hands of the friends of temperance.

If laws were enacted by Government relating to the traffic, their basis was prohibition. In the last magnificent display of 200,000 troops at Washington, as the war was closed, no liquor was allowed to be sold. Perfect quiet and order was the result. Not a drunken man was to be seen. No fighting. No contests. No abusive language. A wonderful spectacle of what the suppression of the liquor traffic could accomplish amid vast masses.

As the war was terminating, and the army to be disbanded, and thousands of noble men would be passing through our cities, to be tempted on every corner by the deceptive and destructive glass, I issued the tract, MUSTERED OUT; NOW LOOK OUT! the production of George W. Bungay. Of these I sent forth, chiefly through the

Christian Commission, 250,000. It was in great demand, and was, it was believed, a great check to drinking and drunkenness.

The general appearance of the troops, as they reached their homes, showed a most effective discipline. Many came back to their farms and mechanical employments better men than they were when they enlisted. But few miserable, drunken soldiers were anywhere visible—far less than after the Mexican war. So far as temperance agency had connection with this, we desired to give God the praise.

But the nation was in mourning for its beloved chief. ABRAHAM LINCOLN, the man of the people, the friend of the oppressed, the liberator of four millions in bondage, the pure in heart, and the pure in life, was, on the 15th of April, 1865, awfully assassinated by a pistol shot, in a theatre at Washington, by a wretch, who called for brandy, brandy! as he went to do the deed. All hearts were in agony, as the wires bore the sad tidings.

"But yesterday, the exultant nation's shout
 Swelled on the breeze of victory, through our streets;
But yesterday, our banners flaunted out,
 Like flowers the south wind woos from their retreats—
Flowers of the nation, blue, and white, and red,
 Waving from balcony, and spire, and mast,
Which told us that war's wintry storms had fled,
 And spring was more than spring to us, at last.
To-day, the nation's heart lies crushed and weak.
 Drooping, and drest in black, our banners stand;
Too stunned to cry Revenge! we scarce may speak
 The grief that chokes all utterance through the land.
God is in all. With tears our eyes are dim,
Yet strive in darkness to look up to Him.

Tribune.

CHAPTER XXVI.

Fifth National Convention—Governor Buckingham, President—Prepared dissertations—New National Organization proposed—Termination of American Temperance Union—Results of labors—Helps and Hindrances—Future prospects and expectations.

As the war came to an end and slavery was no more, the friends of temperance throughout the United States felt it incumbent on them to make a new and vigorous effort for the revival of the temperance cause and securing for it another glorious triumph. To meet this desire, I invited a public meeting in New York, on Anniversary week, in which the subject was discussed, and it was resolved to call a FIFTH NATIONAL CONVENTION, to be held at Saratoga Springs, on the first of August, 1865. A large Committee, from various States and Societies, were requested to issue the call, and prepare for the Convention. It excited great attention, and promised an attendance which was not disappointed.

Three hundred and twenty-six delegates from twenty States and the Canadas, all temperance organizations and many churches were present. Governor Buckingham, of Connecticut, was unanimously elected President. Many of the surviving fathers of the reform were present, to give it strength, and supplicate blessings upon its deliberations. Besides being of a highly intellectual and reformatory cast, it was pre-eminently of a moral and religious character. Several papers on important topics, prepared by request, were read as opportunity was given; one by Dr. Chickering, of Boston, on the connection between temperance and religion; one by Dr. Charles Jewett, on the proper place of Alcohol in the Materia Medica; one by James Black, of Pa., on the importance of a National Temperance and Tract Publication Office; one by Dr. W. W. Newell, of New York, on the subject of Prohibition; and one by Mr. Pardee, of New York, on efforts among the young and in Sabbath Schools. Out of each, much discussion was elicited. Other subjects came up for notice and action.

Some were anxious and much was said on the Sacramental question, or the wine to be used in communion services. The sympathy of the Convention with the Government in its late suppression of the rebellion was great; and the resolution determined, that as slavery was now dead, so also should intemperance be put away from the nation. To form a new era and bring all organizations to work together, a large Committee were appointed to organize a New National Temperance Society, which should embrace all orders and associations and give a new impulse to the cause. Several eloquent speeches were made during the sitting of the Convention, and important resolutions were adopted; and on the fourth day, the Convention adjourned with great thankfulness for the spirit, harmony, and bright anticipations for the future.

In the autumn, the Committees on organization of a New National Society and of a Publication House, held several meetings in New York, and established the two under one name and roof, and appointed Wm. E. Dodge, Esq., a distinguished citizen, wealthy and philanthropic, President of the same.

Though nothing was said to the American Temperance Union relating to its surrendering its charter, given by the second National Convention held in 1836, yet the incongruity and difficulty of having two National Temperance Societies laboring at the same point and in the same city, led the Executive Committee to assemble and take the following action on the subject:

"*Whereas*, It was presented that the National Temperance Convention, held at Saratoga Springs, in August, had resolved on a new and enlarged National Organization, uniting all temperance societies of every name, with a National Temperance Publication House, so desirable, and *whereas*, a Committee embracing many of the officers of the Temperance Union, have met in this city and organized such an institution, and have made proposals of assuming our work and liabilities, continuing our periodicals, tracts, and agencies, which are satisfactory to the Committee and promising great results to the cause; therefore, after much deliberation and many expressions of attachment to our now venerable institution, it was

"*Resolved*, That the work of the Union be suspended after the 1st of December, 1865, and that its periodicals, documents, tracts, stereotype plates, and good-will be transferred to the National Temperance Society and Publication House.

"*Resolved*, That the new Society be commended to all the patrons and friends of the Am. Temp. Union, and that a greatly increased amount of donations be solicited, and an enlarged circulation of the periodicals, tracts, &c., be earnestly looked for throughout the nation."

Thus terminated the labors of our venerable Institution and my official connection with it, just at a point where, under a kind Providence, we had been more influential in the four years' war, than in any previous period whatever. I was grateful that I had been permitted to take part in this work, and to leave it at a moment when our country could best dispense with the labor.

To give any correct and satisfactory estimate of the results of the temperance reform during the long period in which it has been my happiness to be employed in it, is impossible, and will not be attempted. A few things are to be borne in mind whenever we consider it; as, first, the difference in the state of society fifty years ago from the present time; in the habits, usages, and opinions on all points touching temperance and intemperance. Had no change been effected in fifty years, beyond what had been effected here in five or ten years past, we might almost say we had labored in vain and spent our strength for naught. To understand what has been done, we must go back to the day when drinking was universal; when no table was properly spread unless it contained a full supply of intoxicating drink; when no man could be respectable who did not furnish it to his guest; when no man had the liberty of refusing it, on its being offered him; when no laborer could be found who, for any price, would work without strong drink; no farm, no manufacturing, no mechanical work could be carried forward unless it was furnished; when no sailor would enlist for a voyage without his spirit-ration, and no soldier enter the army unless this was secured; when on all parties of pleasure it had a prominent place; when ministers of the Gospel, meeting for association or ordination, were abundantly supplied by their people; and when moderate drinkers, and those who sold the drink that destroyed body and soul, were received without hesitancy, if piety was unquestioned, to the Church of Christ; when all the natural results of so much drinking was common and universal; and when enormous sums in every town and city were worse than wasted, keeping the people in poverty and ignorance, and without most of the comforts now enjoyed. Such times I knew. I have seen all the changes; but how few are there on the stage who have?

Another point to be considered is, that the greater part of the subjects of the work have passed away, and the present inhabitants of the country constitute but a small portion of its conquests. Of the first converts to temperance, nearly all are gone. Of the Washingtonians, how few are living! In twenty-four years a generation has almost passed away. The country has more than doubled, almost trebled its population; and who for the last twenty years have, for the most part, contributed to this increase? A mighty host of Germans, and men from the north of Europe, and Irish, but not plentifully of the Father Mathew school.

But to speak positively—a mighty work has been accomplished, and few are the men who will not acknowledge it. If we had only gained the liberty of drinking or not drinking, as we pleased; of having or not having the drink on our tables, as we pleased; of giving workmen drink or not giving, as we pleased; we should have accomplished a great work. But we have gained a vast and most important knowledge of the subject of Intemperance; the nature, cause, and cure of drunkenness; the nature of the alcoholic poisons, and subject of adulteration. We have firmly established the great principles of temperance; we have driven liquor from our farms, our manufactories, our firesides, our sideboards, our shipping, our navy; from our Christian and ministerial families, our pulpits and Christian Churches, and all missionary stations, and from among those who would evangelize and save the world. Here, under God, are the triumphs of temperance.

And in our labors, we have had various encouragements and discouragements, which rush upon our recollection. If, at times, we have felt distressed, and exclaimed, "The power of the adversary is too great for us!" a voice has said to us, "The battle is not yours, but God's, and if God be for us, who can be against us?" We have heard the voice of science saying, "This is the way; walk ye in it." Health, and life, and domestic happiness; public peace and prosperity; sound morality, and great success have cheered us onward. One wave has followed another —to-day, the old Hewitt and Beecher movement; to-morrow, the Irish movement; next day, the Washingtonian;

and then the Maine Law, chaining up the dragon, that he should deceive no more.

And then, we have had hindrances in our work, and discouragements, whose recollection brings bitterness to the soul.

The power of appetite, and the power of habit; the ignorance, the want of faith, and the stupidity and indifference of those we would subject to our principles and practices, very often caused our hands to hang down, and our hearts to fail within us.

A great hindrance to advance in the cause has been the want of funds to sustain meetings, procure tracts and papers, pay lecturers, &c. The cause, to use a common expression, has been in many places starved to death. Regular and good societies were organized; good officers appointed, pledges made, meetings appointed, a lecturer secured, but who should foot the bills? Two or three individuals for a time; but those individuals got weary of their work and were missing; collections were then resorted to, and these were of the smallest possible change, scarce sufficient to pay for lighting the room; and as the result, the meetings ceased to be held, and the cause died out. The Order of the Sons of Temperance had made wise provision against this deadly evil by the regular payment of weekly, monthly, or annual dues, severely exacted, and this kept the Order alive, doing its work through many years; while associations of communities preferring other systems, speedily went to decay and perished. Foreseeing the certain death of the cause through this evil, Dr. Charles Jewett began, as early as 1858, to sound the alarm, and was the instrument, by conversations, lectures and pamphlets, of placing the cause in many places in a much better position than it had been for many years.

Another hindrance to progress has been a want of perseverance in that which has been found to be right and good, and a disposition to go back to old experiments, or try something new. By this, all that has been gained in a course of years has been given up and lost, and the cause has in many places fallen backward. By the greatest effort, and with the approbation of the wisest and best men in the country, prohibition in opposition to license had been obtained in many States, and was doing a great work; suppressing the traffic in a few years, more than the law of license had done in a hundred; and yet because it did not suppress it entirely, which it did not pretend to do any more than the law of God which said: "Thou shalt not kill," would prevent murder; men got weary of it and said it was a failure; even ministers of the Gospel got weary of it, and said, "Let us try something else; go back to moral suasion or a license law;" and so laying all the blame on prohibition, and crying out for something new, put back the cause.

Before the vast Congregational Convention at Boston, in June last, a leading member would no longer commit himself, nor the churches, nor the country, to prohibition. "The temperance cause had been wrecked," he said, "on the Maine Law." By this assertion, endorsed at the time by the Convention, we have been thrown back, and the enemy has raised the voice of triumph. On the bended knee, we have asked him what he will give us in its stead? Will he go back to a license system? He does not answer. He well knows that all the drunkenness for two hundred years has grown up under a license system. Will he give the traffic a clear pass, as in bread and meat? He gives no answer. He knows the land would not endure it a year. But, ultimately, he would substitute for prohibition some distinction between distilled and fermented liquors; some indulgence in the mild alcoholics, though shutting out those which rend and devour; all, discouragements and hindrances, until we saw their fallacy; then we moved on, stronger than before. This controversy with a brother beloved has been painful to me; but I can already see it has been for the good of the cause. It has brought out talented men in support of the truth; so that prohibition, in opposition to license, stands stronger to-day than ever.

Another hindrance, whose recollections press painfully upon me, has been in learned and devout ministers of the Gospel, standing aloof from the cause, and treating it with neglect, if they have not directly opposed it. I have looked with pain upon the vast and intelligent body of ministers in the Episcopal Church, who have stood in the doorway and hindered the entrance of the cause among the communicants of that church. While a Bishop Alonzo Potter, lately fallen asleep, and the faithful Dr. Tyng, have lifted up the standard, and cried to all, "This is the way! walk ye in it," the great mass of that ministry have felt it to be a part of their work to let the temperance cause alone. But how will they and their sons escape the wiles of the adversary?

And so in other denominations; a talented, learned, polished divine, head of some wealthy congregation, proclaiming moderation the true Scripture doctrine, in opposition to total abstinence, has been, in cases not a few, a most serious hindrance to all within the circle of his influence. "Surely," the young have said, "the Doctor knows."

Another hindrance to progress has been an unwillingness in temperance men to stand by the Government. The Governments of many States have made good laws, shutting up the traffic; and made them at the request of temperance men; and yet, the temperance men have stood afar off, and done little or nothing towards the execution of those laws—have virtually said, "It cannot be done. If it is done, it must be done by State officers; it cannot be done by us." And so, withholding their influence and aid, it has not been done at all; and the cause has been hindered and has rolled backward.

Another hindrance to progress has been an indifference in temperance men at the polls in giving their votes for the right law-makers. They have sacrificed temperance for politics; and, for the sake of sustaining a political party, or an anti-slavery party, suffered temperance to perish. Until a higher standard is raised, there can be no great progress. If intemperance is the destruction of all that is good in the State, temperance is the salvation of all; and so it must have control at the polls, or it can never expect anything but defeat. But can the temperance men afford to sacrifice temperance for other objects?

These and other hindrances are fresh in my recollections, as I review the cause. They are not new to-day. They will not pass away to-morrow. But, in despite of all, the cause will roll on. It is destined to prosper, and bless the earth. It is an emanation of the Gospel, and a blessed auxiliary.

In relation to the prospects and expectations of the cause in the future, a variety of thoughts will arise; some, doubtless, of a desponding and despairing character. But, as I believe and know that the cause is God's, and that the power of truth is omnipotent, and that this world is given to Jesus Christ, and that Satan is to be bound a thousand years, I can give way to no such sensations. Dark may be the hour; but darkness never prevents the introduction of light.

As we leave our shores, and go to the Fatherland, and there see what wonders God hath wrought within half the time allotted to us; what progress the permissive bill has made in the hearts of rulers and people; how large and influential is the Church of England Society; what crowds of children and youth are gathered and instructed in

Bands of Hope; what floods of valuable publications the Scottish League and Edinburgh Societies are pouring over the land; as we look into the principality of Wales, and see there 20,000 gathered at a temperance meeting, and addressed by some of the most talented and devoted ministers of Christ; as we look into Ireland, and see plainly the footsteps of Father Mathew, and his spirit still hovering over that warm-hearted but excitable nation; at the British army and navy, where, at one period, a temperance society was unknown, but where it is now frequently welcomed, and rejoiced in; no rational man, understanding the influence of moral causes, can be brought to feel that, while England lives, the cause can be otherwise than prosperous and powerful. Indeed, the life of England is much in the temperance cause; far more than in anything else on which she may place her dependence. Rum and beer are the cause of ignorance, poverty, and crime which may be dragging her down to death. These put away, she has piety and trust in God sufficient to save and prolong her existence to distant ages.

Every missionary station on the globe is a sure guaranty for Africa, Asia, and the Islands of the Sea. As the Gospel goes around the world, so now will temperance. As soon would Christian missions give up the fundamental principles of their faith and practice, as they would yield their attachment to the principles and practices of temperance. But as all success is the result of action, we say, "Be not we weary in well-doing, for in due season we shall reap, if we faint not." Africa, Asia, and the verdant spots in the ocean like the Sandwich Islands, will taste the blessedness of our great enterprise.

Just released from the war at home, we may ask for rest; but when better prepared for battle than when we have our armor on? when better, than on retiring from a fallen foe, whom we once thought unconquerable? Rum and slavery were looked upon as permanent evils, to be continued long as the sun and moon should endure; but He who opened the way for his people out of Egypt, hath now broken the chain of the oppressor, and suffered four millions of his people to go free; and, if we do our duty, no future generation shall see half a million of its number falling into drunkard's graves. A view of 15,000 children and youth, on Boston Common, last June, marching under the temperance flag, confirmed me in the belief that all our children, from the Atlantic to the Pacific, may easily be induced to become total abstainers. While our Temperance Orders have wisely secured to themselves needed pecuniary means, by the payment of weekly dues, the admirable essays of Dr. Charles Jewett on "WHERE WE ARE, AND WHAT WE NEED, have awakened all open organizations to the necessity of a pecuniary basis, and, I trust, secured them from positive distress and peril in the future.

To the Church we may look, in this day of the Redeemer's power, to purify herself from the great abomination, and to lead the nations in the way they should go. Our judiciary has been the hope of the destroyer; pleading for liquor-dealers' rights. But there is a God above, as well as a god below; and judgment and justice will not always go backward. The late decision of the Supreme Court of the United States, blasting the hopes of the venders in Massachusetts, that, on their paying their excise tax to the General Government, no prohibitory law of the State could shut them up, we receive with thankfulness. It inspires us with confidence, as did the old decision, that we are right and shall prosper.

If those who peruse these few reminiscences have half the pleasure I have had in recording them, I shall be satisfied. Another life I should be willing to spend in the cause; insuring, as it does, the relief of thousands from sin and vice, and aiding in the salvation of immortal souls. But it may not be. We do all fade away as a leaf.

Toward my early companions in labor, still among the living, I look with peculiar emotions. If they were once the men who "would turn the world upside down," busy-bodies in other men's matters, intruders upon personal and domestic habits, they have lived to receive the gratitude of the wise and good throughout the world; and have given a beautiful illustration in their own persons of the connection between temperance and longevity, and not only longevity, but activity and vivacity. Some, as Pierpont and Hunt, are doing public service; some, as Hewitt and Hawes, yet making their voices heard from the pulpit; some—Tappan, Sargent, Walworth, Delavan—yet wise in council, rejoicing in hope, ready for a translation at the Master's bidding. May their mantles fall upon many who shall be as bold and vigorous. To the new National Society, State, County, and Local Organizations; to Sons of Temperance, Good Templars, Rechabites, Bands of Hope, a voice comes, "Fear not." "Be of good courage, and play the men for our people, and for the cities of our God." "More are they that are for us than they that are against us." May heaven, friends, strengthen and bless you, and reward you abundantly; and it shall be done, as you make God's glory the great end of all your action.

APPENDIX.

TEMPERANCE PRINCIPLES.

The following principles were unanimously agreed upon by the Convention at London, as forming the basis of the temperance reformation in all countries, and throughout the world:—

Resolved, "That, in the opinion of this Convention, as a means of extending the temperance reformation, the following truths should be spread throughout the world, and the temperance men and temperance organizations be exhorted to give them the widest possible extension.

"That Alcohol, the intoxicating principle, is a subtle poison, at war with the physical, intellectual, social, and religious interests of men.

"That it is generated by the process of fermentation, and is the same, as existing in different degrees, in cider, wine, and malt liquors, as in distilled spirits.

"That it is a perpetual fountain of disease, poverty, crime, temporal and spiritual death, never needful or useful to men in health, in any clime or any employment.

"That total abstinence from it, as a beverage, is the only true principle of the temperance reformation; the only hope for the drunkard, and security for others.

"That the whole manufacture and sale of intoxicating drinks as a beverage, though a source of revenue to thousands, is a manufacture of human misery, and highly injurious to the souls and bodies of men; and should not be licensed more than other moral evils, by human governments.

"That the Word of God often prescribes total abstinence to avoid existing evils; and that the spirit of Christian love directs us to shun wine, or anything whereby our brother stumbleth, or is offended, or is made weak.

"That a voice comes up from every part of the globe, calling upon kings, and all that are in authority, upon reflecting and influential men of all classes, upon parents, teachers of youth, medical men, ministers of religion, and all true lovers of their race, to put forth the hand and stay the plague which is filling our world with woe, and which, unless checked, will continue to sweep thousands of succeeding generations prematurely and wretchedly to eternity."

SPEECH AT COVENT GARDEN THEATRE, AUGUST 9, 1846.

Mr. Chairman: There is not a more beautiful figure in the sacred Scriptures than that handed down to us from one of the old prophets which represents the Gospel as a little stream reaching first to the ankles, then to the knees, and as it flows onward becoming broad and deep, a mighty river diffusing joy and blessedness among all nations. Almost every favor which has been bestowed upon our world, has been small in its beginning. The first morning ray; the little sapling; the beautiful infant, all how small and yet how expansive and glorious. The Church of Christ was once in an upper chamber. The glorious Reformation of the sixteenth century was at one period all in the heart of a single monk. For twenty-six years your Wilberforce, that man beloved in America, and whose memorial rushes upon us as we come in sight of your shores—the land, we said, of Wilberforce; yes, for twenty-six years he pleaded the cause of bleeding Africa before humanity and truth could begin to prevail over the horrors of the slave-trade. In no work of mercy under the Gospel, it is believed, have the waters risen so rapidly and spread so widely, and diffused so great joy and blessedness as in that which is now delivering our world from the curse of Intemperance. But yesterday it was a little rivulet, though of the purest water; now millions have quenched their thirst and bathed their limbs, and are healed of their wounds, and with thanksgiving to God will it increase and roll onward to the ocean of eternity.

Sir, I know not what to say in so short a time as you have given me. Intemperance! Why, Sir, if this curse had come upon us in any way but through the delusive gratification of appetite or pecuniary gain, the earth would have been clothed with sackcloth. A blast or mildew which should, year by year, cost this nation thirty millions sterling, would raise an universal cry of ruin, and yet intemperance costs you sixty millions a year. A Nero or Caligula, who should strip six hundred thousand of the population of food and clothing, and habitations and lands, and turn them out to be a moth and a curse to the community, would be a tyranny which not even Rome in her most degenerate days would have borne; and yet it is the tyranny of Intemperance. Or had some dreadful spirit been let loose from the bottomless pit, with power to cripple the moral and physical energies of men, waste their affections, and excite to the commission of every abomination and crime; you would plead for wings that you might fly to some distant planet for safety to yourselves and your children. And yet such a spirit infests every gin-shop in London. Look at its victim! What a wreck of man! Look at his family! Look at him on his bed of straw, dying amid delirium tremens in all the agonies and despair of hell. See that burning ship on the ocean in the darkness of midnight; see the flames rolling up on high, the rigging, the sails all on fire, and behold those human beings rushing to and fro on the deck in all the agony of wild despair plunging into the yawning deep—only a faint image of 30,000, drunken men and drunken women in America, and 60,000 in Britain hurried frightfully year by year, all on fire, to the bar of God. And yet for this tremendous evil, whose magnitude no mind can grasp, there is a cure; a cure so easy, so simple, that like the proud Syrian we despise it; costing us nothing but the sacrifice of pride and fashion and momentary gratification of appetite; saving us everything, money, health, morals, domestic quiet, and public prosperity, and preparing the way of the Lord among all people. And I say (excuse me, Sir) I say it is our duty to adopt it, it is the duty of England, it is the duty of America; it is the duty of the church. It is the duty of the world; and if we cannot fasten this on the conscience, we cannot do anything.

Sir, there was a beautiful anecdote related in our papers of your youthful Queen, I think in the first year of her reign, which gave us in America a high opinion of her Majesty, which I can assure you has in no degree diminished (Loud and long applause, and waving of handkerchiefs.) It was this: As one of her ministers was urging upon her Majesty the expediency of a measure, her Majesty turned to him and said: "My lord, talk not to me of expediency; is it right?" Now, Sir, I should like to put to her Majesty and her Majesty's Government the question: Whether, when so much drunkenness and pauperism and crime prevail in this realm, it is right for the manufacturing of it to go on, and for the government to derive a revenue from it? Whether it is right for all, from the throne to the children in the Sunday-school, to keep up those drinking usages which result in this misery? I should like to put it to every minister of the Gospel, whether when these intoxicating liquors do more than anything else to harden the heart, sear the conscience, hinder the spread of the Gospel, and send souls unnumbered to eternal death, it is right for ministers of the Gospel to use them? I should like to put it and must put it to every philanthropist and patriot, to every father and mother, whether it is right to continue in the use of that which may give thousands of children and their own children the inheritance of a drunkard's life, and a drunkard's eternity?

Sir, many tell us moderation is temperance. Moderation is temperance until the steam is up; and then the locomotive dashes on with such fury that you cannot overtake it; and wife and children, and fortune and happiness are all dragged onward and dashed in pieces. Sir, it is not moderate drink, but it is total abstinence from all that intoxicates that is the only true principle of temperance. And we have to fasten this truth upon the consciences of men and women in America, that as good men and women, having the fear of God before our eyes, we dare not drink, for we feel "that to him that knoweth to do good by abstinence from such evil, and doeth it not, to him it is sin." And we adopt the same principle in relation to the traffic. For a beverage, it is all wrong. The supply creates the demand. When the intoxicating cup was on all our tables and sideboards we were ever craving it, and ever using it; now that it is removed we seldom think of it. So it will be in England. So it will be round the globe. Renounce the traffic, that scourge of the world, and men will return with delight to the pure beverage which God hath given them. Sir, great things are to be accomplished. Through the help of the Lord God Omnipotent, we will deliver our world from this scourge, intemperance. Then the kingdoms of the world will speedily become the kingdoms of our Lord and Saviour, Jesus Christ. My God, hasten the day. (Loud cheers.)—*London Patriot.*

TESTIMONIALS.

At the closing up of the affairs of the American Temperance Union, the undersigned were appointed by the Executive Committee to express their appreciation of the services of the Secretary of the Society, Rev. John Marsh, D. D.

For nearly thirty years, Dr. Marsh has toiled in this glorious cause, with a devotion and persistence that is truly commendable. We cannot here review his labors. But we believe that his periodicals have been, decidedly, the most able temperance papers in the United States. The millions of tracts that have been provided by him for our army have been vastly beneficial.

His fidelity and ability have won for him the respect of some of the best and ablest men in this country, and in Europe. Thousands now living are grateful for his benign influence, and generations yet unborn will call him blessed.

W. W. Newell,
Thomas Denny,
Committee of Exec. Board of the A. T. U.

New York, *December* 1, 1865.

A LIFE WELL SPENT.

BY REV. DR. TYNG.

The present paper will announce the action of the Executive Committee of the American Temperance Union, in transferring their influence and their labor to a new central association, formed by the National Convention, which assembled in Saratoga on the 1st of August last. The wisdom or necessity of this important step we will not now question or discuss. But we cannot allow the sun to go down on the labors of our valued and venerated friend, the Rev. Dr. Marsh, without recording our solemn and faithful testimony to the value of his services to the great cause which this Union has sustained, and to the fidelity with which he has labored for the best welfare of his fellow-men. For thirty years have we worked with him, and continued by his side. His earnestness in the cause has been an unceasing encouragement, and his wise fidelity an inestimable example. No man, in any country, since Dr. Justin Edwards left the field, has written or spoken with greater effect in the cause of temperance. No man has more thoroughly understood the whole field of warfare, or more boldly maintained the contest. His pen, in argument, has been sharp and mighty; his speech, in advocacy, has been unflinching and clear. The fire and energy of youth have remarkably endured with him, even to old age. Nor have we ever seen his force abated in the great warfare in which he was engaged. Such a man is a true hero in the great contest for human happiness and freedom. No one in his generation more truly deserves to be honored by his companions, or commemorated by those who come after him. At the close of a long life, and of a faithful career of labor, Dr. Marsh retires from the field, honored, trusted, and beloved by all who have been united with him. The *Journal*, in his hands, has been a fitting continuation of the Permanent Documents of Dr. Edwards. His tracts, prepared for various classes, especially for the soldiers and sailors of the nation, have been unsurpassed by any in point and power. The army and the navy have acknowledged the great blessing and favor of his efforts. The children of two nations will lament his separation from the work which has so much interested and excited them; and the multitudes of the wise and good of the land, of every class, will remember his fidelity with honor, and think of his usefulness with delight. They who have been most intimately associated with him value him the most highly; and the writer, one of his oldest and long-tried friends, feels it to be a privilege, as they both draw near to the close of earth, to give his cordial, spontaneous testimony to his excellence as a man, and his usefulness as an agent.

S. H. T.

December 9, 1865.

LETTER FROM L. M. SARGENT, ESQ.,

BOSTON, *December* 10, 1865.

I thank you, my dear sir, for your note of the 8th, and the

kind wishes it contains. I regret to learn that the Journal is to be stopped. What are the reasons? Of one thing you may be very well assured, that your long-continued and valuable labors of humanity cannot be over-estimated. Some of the seed you have scattered, may have fallen on stony places; but God's blessing has, doubtless, caused much of it to spring up and bear fruit abundantly. When you look back, in a dying hour, upon the devotion of your time and talents to this glorious enterprise, you will count all your toils and trials, in this holy cause, among the things *reminisse juvabit.*

How much would it be worth, in gold or currency, to get a glimpse for five minutes, and unobserved, of the group gathered in some humble cottage, around the reformed inebriate, with his first meeting with his wife, and children, after years of sloth and abandonment! If you have never witnessed such a scene, you cannot reasonably doubt that similar results have been produced by your efforts in the cause of temperance for thirty years.

Excuse this long letter, and believe me, dear sir, very sincerely your friend.

L. M. Sargent.

Rev. Dr. Marsh.

LETTER FROM MR. DELAVAN.

South Ballston, *April* 2, 1866.

Rev. Dr. Marsh:

Dear Sir,—I intended to have called on you before I left New York. I wanted to say to you that I fully estimate your long and faithful labors in the temperance cause. And as to your forthcoming history, no living man, that I know of, is better qualified than yourself to do the work. I pray God that you may be preserved to complete the work to your own satisfaction.

Yours truly,

Edward C. Delavan.

CHANGES IN THE COUNTRY.

To those who are confirmed unbelievers in any good effected by temperance labor, I present the following extract from a discourse delivered at North Coventry, Ct., March 10th, 1859, by George A. Calhoun, D. D., on the fortieth anniversary of his settlement among the people of that parish. No man has sustained a higher character for correctness and veracity than Dr. Calhoun:

"Forty years ago, there was but little property in this parish, or in the county of Tolland, compared with what is now possessed. This was apparent, not only from the aspect of buildings, orchards, fences, the cultivation of farms, and the appearance of domestic animals, but from the furniture of dwellings, and the equipages then in use. There were, in this parish, but four houses painted white; but four floors covered with a carpet, and less than half a score of four-wheeled vehicles. Even the expense of whitewash, as an application to the walls of houses, was incurred by few of the inhabitants. And these were not the only indications of poverty, compared with the present. There were few persons who had money at interest, or were the possessors of stocks, compared with the number who were in debt, and whose farms were mortgaged. Even our larger and smaller farmers were obliged to resort to banks to save their property from foreclosures or attachments, to what would now be considered a fearful extent.

"And what was the reason of this depression in worldly circumstances? The people were industrious, and, in all respects but one, frugal. The expense of living was small, compared with that at the present time. *Their gains were consumed, and they were oppressed by the use of intoxicating drinks.* Think of the annual expense of manufacturing and storing in cellars, fifteen hundred or two thousand barrels of cider, and then drawing it out and bringing it forth, a quart at a time. Think of the expense of making, transporting to distilleries, and converting into cider-brandy, an equal amount to be consumed here and elsewhere. Think of the expense of hogshead after hogshead of rum retailed to this little community during the season of haying and harvesting. Think of the expense of supplying various kinds of intoxicating drinks with which to express their respect and hospitality to friends who called to see them. Think of the expense of providing these drinks abundantly, for all gatherings—civil, military, social, ecclesiastical, and clerical. Think of the expense incurred at stores and taverns for liquors dealt out in small measures. Examine the ledgers of our old merchants, and learn what proportion of their trade was in intoxicating drinks. Learn how much idleness, litigation, and crime, were then occasioned by their use.

"Could any community secure a livelihood and gain wealth from a rugged soil, under such a pressure? This community was then composed almost exclusively of small farmers, without investments or business abroad. If there were a few individuals who engaged in manufacturing, the enterprise to them was a failure. And is it a matter of surprise that farms were mortgaged, and that what would be considered marks of poverty were seen over the place and the region? Is it a matter of surprise that at least one man in every score became a drunkard, and that not a few women were addicted to habits of intemperance? Is it strange that the church had far more cases of discipline from the use of intoxicating liquors, than from all other sources?

"I here present my solemn protest against the conclusion from what has been said, that this people were more addicted to the use of intoxicating drinks than other communities. They were, compared with people of other towns, temperate, sober, and religious. And, as long as I live, I shall cherish them in respectful, affectionate, and grateful remembrance. They did not sin in the use of intoxicating drinks, as persons are now sinning, who in health use them as a beverage. They, in common with all other persons in the country over, were strangely and dreadfully deluded. Forty years ago, there was probably not one in five hundred who did not believe that the use of intoxicating drinks as a beverage was absolutely needful, and that hence it was a duty to make use of them. Since that time, a flood of light has been cast on the subject of temperance, and no community were more prompt than this in *coming to the light, that their deeds might be reproved.* And, just in proportion as they were delivered from the oppression of intoxicating drinks, their worldly circumstances were improved, and their moral condition became more and more eligible. Within the last forty years, property in this parish and in this county has increased fourfold, if I do not misjudge. And the county, in appearance and enterprise, is forty years younger than it was in 1819.

"The times of that ignorance God winked at; but now He commandeth all men everywhere, who use intoxicating drinks, to repent. If there is a person who is ignorant of the evil consequences of their use as a beverage, it is his own fault.

PRESIDENT LINCOLN'S ANSWER TO THE SONS OF TEMPERANCE.

As to the suggestions for the purpose of the advancement of the cause of temperance in the army, he could not now respond to them. To prevent intemperance in the army is a great part of the rules and articles of war. It is a part of the law of the land, and was so long ago, to dismiss officers for drunkenness. He was not sure that, in consistency with the public service, more can be done than has been done. All, therefore, he could promise was, to have a copy of the address submitted to the principal departments, and have it considered whether it contains any suggestions which will improve the cause of temperance, and repress drunkenness in the army, better than it is already done.

October, 1863.

LETTER FROM COLONEL NEAL DOW.

HEADQUARTERS OF THE 13TH MAINE REGIMENT,
Camp Beaufort, *February* 1, 1862.

DEAR DR. MARSH.—You cannot possibly do so much good for our country's cause, in any other way, as in circulating among the soldiers of our army your admirable Temperance Tracts. If our men of wealth could only see the eagerness with which they are read, and the salutary influence that they exert in our camps, they would furnish means to place them, in any desired quantity, in the hands of all our men.

Intemperance is a terrible enemy to the soldier, and kills far more of them than fall on the battle field; and it is a great interest to the country to preserve them from its foul contamination. My regiment suffers very little in that way, as it consists of a select body of men, and all my officers sustain me fully in the policy I enforce in relation to it.

Truly yours,

NEAL DOW,
Col. 13th Maine Volunteers.

TEMPERANCE TRACTS FOR THE ARMY AND NAVY,

Of which over three millions were issued.

Ellsworth and his Zouaves,
War and Intemperance,
The Temperance Soldier,
Beware of the Bottle,
Havelock and His Crotchet,
The Soldier's Sacrifice,
The Soldier's Crown,
The Wounded Soldier,
The Soldier's Soliloquy,
The Best Drink,
Do Thyself No Harm,
The Sick Soldier (Thoughts of Home).—*A Lady.*
Tract for the Navy,
The Temperance Admiral,
The Polished Arrow,
Temperate Drinking,
Our Stumbling Brother—*Cuyler.*
Address of a Soldier to His Comrades,
License or No License,
The Town Meeting,
The Sentinel and the Spy,
The Pocket Tales,
The End of the War.—*Gibson.*
Medical Use,
Adulteration in Liquors,
Blood-guiltiness of Rumselling.—*Gibson.*
Wine Drinking and its Effects.—*Cleveland.*
The Pledged Regiment,
Appeal to Army Officers,
Lager Beer,
Constitutional Question,
Why Legislate on Temperance?
The Lobster Bite,
The Rum Maniac.—*Alison,*
Getting the Worst of It.—*T. P. Hunt.*

PICTORIAL CHILDREN'S TRACTS,

WIDELY CIRCULATED IN SUNDAY-SCHOOLS.

1 The Upas Tree,
2 Benjamin Franklin,
3 Bible *vs.* Intemperance,
4 The Monkey Imitators,
5 The Dragoon and His Horse,
6 Settling the Question,
7 The Rum-seller's Grave,
8 Out of Doors,
9 The Jug Turned Out.

RECENT PUBLICATIONS.

"Nephalia," "Dr. Mairs' Letter to E. C. Delavan," "The Temperance Cause;" "Past and Present, or Where we Are," *Dr. Charles Jewett;* "Considerations of the Temperance Argument and History," *E. C. Delavan, John Vine Hall,* "True Temperance Platform," *Trall, M. D.;* "Drunkard's Heart the Devil's Palace," *J. Marsh.*

OPINIONS OF THE U.S. SUPREME COURT, ON THE LICENSE QUESTION, 1847.

Chief-Justice Taney: "Every State may regulate its own internal traffic, according to its own judgment, and upon its own views of the interest and well-being of its citizens. I am not aware that these principles have ever been questioned. If any State deems the retail and internal traffic in ardent spirits injurious to its citizens, and calculated to produce idleness, vice, or debauchery, I see nothing in the Constitution of the United States to prevent it from regulating and restraining the traffic, or from prohibiting it altogether if it thinks proper."

Mr. Justice McLean: "The acknowledged police power of a State extends often to the destruction of property. A nuisance may be abated. It is the settled construction of every regulation of commerce, that no person can introduce into a community malignant diseases, or anything which contaminates its morals, or endangers its safety. Individuals in the enjoyment of their own rights must be careful not to injure the rights of others."

Mr. Justice Catron: "I admit as inevitable that if the State has the power of restraint by licenses to any extent, she has the discretionary power to judge of its limit, and may go to the length of prohibiting sales altogether, if such be her policy; and that if this Court cannot interfere in the case before us, neither could we interfere in the extreme case of entire exclusion."

Mr. Justice Daniel said of imports, that are "cleared of all control of the government," "They are like all other property of the citizen, whether owned by the importer or his vendee, or may have been purchased by cargo, package, bale, piece or yard, or by hogsheads, casks or bottles. If then there was any integrity in the objection urged, it should abolish all regulations of retail trade, all taxes on whatever may have been imported." In answering the argument that the importer purchases the right to sell when he pays duties to government, Mr. Justice Daniel continued to say, "No such right is purchased by the importer; he cannot purchase from the government that which it could not insure him, a sale independent of the laws and polity of the State."

And Mr. Justice Grier said: "It is not necessary to array the appalling statistics of misery, pauperism, and crime, which have their origin in the use or abuse of ardent spirits. The police power which is exclusively in the States, is alone competent to the correction of these great evils, and all measures of restraint or prohibition necessary to effect the purpose, are within the scope of that authority. All laws for the restraint or punishment of crime, for the preservation of the public peace, health, and morals, are, from their very nature, of primary importance, and lie at the foundation of social existence. They are for the protection of life and liberty, and necessarily compel all laws on subjects of secondary importance, which relate only to property, convenience, or luxury, to recede, when they come in contact or collision. *Salus populi suprema lex.* The exigencies of the social compact require that such laws be executed before and above all others. It is for this reason that quarantine laws, which protect public health, compel mere commercial regulations to submit to their control. They restrain the liberty of the passengers; they operate on the ship, which is the instrument of commerce, and its officers and crew, the agents of navigation. They seize the infected cargo and cast it overboard. All these things are done, not from any power which the State assumes to regulate commerce, or to interfere with the regulations of Congress, but because police laws for the preservation of health, prevention of crime, and protection of the public welfare, must of necessity have full and free operation, according to the exigency that requires their interference. If a loss of revenue should accrue to the United States from a diminished consumption of ardent spirits, she will be the gainer a thousand fold in the health, wealth, and happiness of the people."

Thus all the judges of the United States Supreme Court reaffirmed and corroborated the decisions of each subordinate State Court, that the entire control of the sale of intoxicating drinks is within the legitimate province of the State Legislature. And this control is not limited to any mere regulations or partial restrictions, but extends to the entire prohibition, whenever the Legislature of any State think such legislation essential to the public welfare.

DECISION OF THE U. S. SUPREME COURT, MARCH 26, 1866.

Case of Massachusetts vs. *John Maguire.*

Maguire plead that he had a right to keep and sell intoxicating liquors, though the State law forbade him, on the ground that he had paid his license-tax levied by the General Government. The State Court decided he had no right to sell. The case was referred to the Supreme Court. Great expectations were raised by the liquor-dealers. But the decision was affirmed. The Court said: "The sixty-seventh section of the act of Congress enacts, that no license hereinbefore provided for, if granted, shall be construed to authorize the commencement or continuation of any trade, business, occupation, or employment therein mentioned, within any State or Territory of the United States, in which it is or shall be specially prohibited by the laws thereof, or in violation of any State or Territory."

The decision, it was estimated, would carry dismay to a vast number of convicted liquor-sellers whose sentences had been suspended during the pendency of this appeal.

DEPARTED LABORERS.

The names of good men who have founded and urged on this moral temple shall live in the hallowed recollections of millions of men, of high and spotless honor, when the blackness of darkness has extinguished the hosts of its opponents in everlasting oblivion.

DR. S. H. TYNG.

Armstrong Rev. Lebbeus, Essays on Temperance Reformation, Fulfilment of Prophecy, ob. 1860.

Archer Hon. Stephenson, Chief-Justice of Maryland, President State Temperance Society, ob. July, 1848.

Baird Rev. Robert, D. D., ob. March 15, 1863. 61.

Bartlett Charles, Poughkeepsie, May, 1857.

Beecher Lyman, D. D., Litchfield, Ct., author of six sermons on the nature, evils, and remedies of intemperance, ob. at Brooklyn, N. Y., January 10, 1863. 87.

Brantley Rev. T. W., Philadelphia.

Briggs Hon. George N., N. Y., Governor of Massachusetts, President Congressional Temperance Society, ob. at Pittsfield, September 13, 1861. 65.

Caldwell Prof., Dickinson College, attended World's Convention, ob. June, 1848.

Chapin Calvin, D. D., Rockyhill, Ct., author of "Total Abstinence the only Infallible Antidote," ob. March 17, 1851. 88.

Chipman Samuel, Rochester, N. Y., visited all the jails and poorhouses, ob. March 5, 1814. 76.

Clarke Rev. Daniel A., Bennington, Vt., a powerful temperance preacher, wrote "Reminiscences of a Ruined Generation."

Clarke Billy, formed the first temperance society at Moreau, N. Y., 1808.

Christmas Rev. Joseph, Montreal, a poet, died young.

Collins Deacon A. M., merchant, Hartford, Ct.,

Coffin J. P., a powerful pleader, ob. February 17, 1863. Reclaimed ten thousand inebriates.

Dickinson Rev. Austin, "Appeal to Youth," ob. August 15, 1849. 53.

Dickinson Rev. Baxter, "Alarm to Distillers and their Allies."

Doolittle Hon. Mark, Belchertown, Mass., statesman.

Downer Rev. D. R., New York, wrote, "Intemperance the Destroyer," ob. 1840.

Day Orrin, Catskill, N. Y., refused carrying liquor for freight; gave one hundred dollars a year to supply foreign missionaries with temperance journals.

Day Edgar B., as a firm and munificent promoter of the temperance cause, gave same for missionaries, and was much devoted to the young. Ob. 22d November, 1863. 60.

Edwards Justin, D. D., Andover, Mass., Corresponding Secretary American Temperance Society, ob. July 26, 1863. 66.

Fisk Rev. Wilbur, President Wesleyan University, Middletown, Ct, ob. March, 1839.

Foote Andrew H., Rear-Admiral U. S. Navy, first introduced total abstinence in the Navy, and induced his whole crew in the flag-ship Cumberland to dispense with their grog. He fought many naval battles. Ob. in New York, June 26, 1863. 57.

Frelinghuysen Hon. Theodore, President Rutgers College, N. J., ob. 12th April, 1862. 75.

Grimke T. S., Charleston, S. C., ob. 1838. Great writer.

Grant Moses, deacon, Boston, Mass., the Children's Friend, ob. July 23, 1861. 75.

Griswold Charles, Lyme, Ct., ob. 1840. Early Advocate.

Hawkins John H. W., Baltimore, the great reformer, ob. July 26, 1854. 60.

Hitchcock Edward, President Amherst College, great writer. Ob. February 27, 1864. 71.

Hudson Commodore, U. S. Navy, of great influence for temperance in the service.

Humphrey Heman, D. D., President Amherst College, author of "Intemperance and the Slave Trade Compared," and many other works. Ob. at Pittsfield, Mass., April 20, 1861. 80.

Ives Ansel, M. D., New York, an active promoter in the early stages.

Keener Christian, Baltimore, editor Maryland Herald.

Leavitt John W., merchant, active and bountiful.

Mitchell Prof. O. M., astronomer, general in the army, an eloquent abstainer. Ob. at Hilton Head, October 31, 1862.

Mason Anthony, Union Springs, N. Y., ob. April 6, 1863. 59.

Merrill Rev. David, author of Ox Discourse, lived in Ohio. Ob. at Peacham, Vt. 1850. 62.

Nott Eliphalet, President Union College, author of "Temperance Lectures." Ob. 1866. 93.

Nott Samuel R., Galway, N. Y., "Temperance and Religion," one of the most influential books.

Noyes W. C., eminent lawyer, one of Ex. Com. A. T. U. Ob. December 23, 1864.

Phelps Anson G., merchant, N. Y., converted under Dr. Hewitt's first sermon, Chairman Ex. Com. A. T. U. Ob. May, 1858. 82.

Pond Hon. Judge S. M., devoted to the cause. House a home for lecturers. Had more temperance works and statistics than any other man. Ob. August, 1850.

Potter Alonzo, D. D., Bishop of Pennsylvania, author of tract, "Drinking Usages." Ob. at San Francisco, Cal., August 4, 1865. 65.

Reese D. M., M. D., New York, ob. 1861. 60. Great speaker.

Savage Hon. John, Chief-Justice, Utica, N. Y. Ob. October, 1863. 84.

Sewall Dr. Thomas, M. D., author of "Drunkard's Stomach Plates." Ob. April 10, 1859.

Silliman Benjamin, Prof. Chem. Yale College. Ob. November 24, 1864. 85.

Stewart Alvan, Utica, N. Y., great political writer.

Stuart Prof. Moses, ob. at Andover, January 4, 1852. 71.

Sigourney Mrs. Lydia H., Hartford, Ct., "Only this Once," "The Upas Tree," "The Intemperate, a Tale." Ob. July 10, 1865. 74.

Tappan Arthur, merchant, N. Y., ob. at New Haven, July, 1865. 80.

Tappan W. B., a sweet temperance poet, ob. at Boston, of cholera, 1859.

Thurston Rev. David, Maine, Father of Temperance, ob. July, 1865. 96.

Tabor Azor, State Senator, eloquent defender of the cause in Albany, N. Y. Ob. June, 1858.

Taylor Elisha, long Corresponding Secretary New York State Temperance Society. Ob. at Cleveland, O.

Teal Oliver, Syracuse, N. Y.

Terry Seth, lawyer, Hartford, Ct., Vice-President Am. Temperance Union. Ob. 1865.

Tew Thomas, Providence, R. I., long a successful State agent. Ob. August, 1850.

Van Loon Charles, an extraordinary young advocate, Poughkeepsie, N. Y. Ob. November, 1849.

Warren John C., M. D., Boston, an eminent surgeon, and thirty years President of the Massachusetts Temperance Society. Ob. May 14, 1856.

Wayland Francis, D. D., President of Brown University, Providence, R. I., an eminent writer. Ob. 1865. 65.

Wilder S. V. S., Bolton, Mass., owner of the well-conducted farm. Ob. in N. J., March 3, 1865. 85.

Williams Hon. Thomas Scott, Hartford, Chief-Justice of Connecticut, President State Temperance Society. Ob. December, 1861. 84.

Woods Leonard, D. D., Prof. Theological Seminary, Andover, Mass., Chairman of Ex. Com. of American Temperance Society. Ob. 80.

Wilkinson Robert, eminent lawyer, in Poughkeepsie—once reformed—active member of first National Convention. Ob. 1863.

Woodward, Samuel B., Insane Hospital, Worcester, Mass., "Treatise on Asylums for Inebriates."

ENGLISH.

Buckingham James Silk, first brought Temperance before Parliament, and procured the great Temperance Report; travelled round the world, and lectured on Temperance. Ob. 1861.

Miller Professor, Edinburgh, author of "Alcohol, its Place and Power." Ob. 1864.

Parsons Rev. Benjamin, author of Anti-Bacchus. Ob. 1855.

Sturge Joseph, Esq., Birmingham, a great supporter of the cause. Ob. 1859.

Jeffreys Arch-deacon, Bombay, ob. in England, of cholera, September 9, 1849.

Alexander Richard Dykes, Ipswich, England, printer and distributor of tracts. Ob. January 16, 1866. 77.

Eaton Joseph, (a Friend), gave liberally to the cause at his death. Ob. May 26, 1858.

Mathew Father, Ireland, ob. 1856.

Cassell John, London, much in America. Ob. April 2, 1865. 44. A great publisher.

Swindlehurst Thomas, Preston, ob. 1861.

Spenser Rev. Thomas, ob. 1853.

A TESTIMONIAL FOR LONG AND USEFUL SERVICE.

We, the undersigned, impressed with the value of the long and self-denying labors in the cause of Temperance which have been performed by the Rev. John Marsh, D. D., deem it just and due to him, to offer some fitting and appropriate Testimonial of our appreciation of his services in that cause, and of his character as a minister and a man.

The undersigned deem this expression needful and called for—

Because, Dr. Marsh has labored faithfully and usefully in the Temperance cause, through a period of more than thirty years, in doing good to others, for a very inadequate compensation; and

Because, the organization of the National Temperance Convention, held last summer at Saratoga Springs, has superseded the American Temperance Union, whereby Dr. Marsh, who has been the faithful Secretary of the Union, from its formation by the National Temperance Convention held at Saratoga Springs in 1836, has been compelled to close his long and useful labors, of which the country has reaped the benefit, and for which he has received merely a scanty support.

The undersigned cordially and heartily commend the object of this testimonial to the friends of Dr. Marsh, with the respectful request that any sums they may be willing to contribute, may be transmitted by mail, or otherwise, to the address of Thomas Denny & Co., Wall street, New York, who have kindly consented to receive them for the purpose designed, and for which the proper acknowledgments will be duly returned.

Thomas De Witt, D. D., William A. Booth,
Stephen H. Tyng, D. D., Hon. R. H. McCurdy,
Bishop E. S. Janes, Thomas Denny,
Joshua Leavitt, D. D., W. H. Bidwell.

New York, *January* 1, 1866.

The following sums have been received up to April 1.

William A. Buckingham, Norwich, Ct.. .... $100

Gen. William Williams, Norwich, Ct.	$100
James Lenox, New York	100
Samuel F. B. Morse, New York	100
Joseph Battell, "	100
Thomas Denny, "	100
William E. Dodge, "	100
S. B. Chittenden, "	100
S. Marsh, "	100
H. B. Claflin, "	100
John Tappan, Boston	100
Hon. Thomas W. Williams, New London	50
Samuel Williston, East Hampton, Mass	50
H. C. Marquand, New York	50
R. H. McCurdy, "	50
Stewart Brown, "	50
H. K. Corning, "	50
C. C. North, "	50
The Church, Orange, N. J.	50
Rev. P. H. Fowler, Utica, New York	10

www.ingramcontent.com/pod-product-compliance
Lightning Source LLC
LaVergne TN
LVHW020124110826
845151LV00001B/261